Routledge Revivals

Trading in West Africa, 1840–1920

Trading in West Africa (1976) provides a vivid portrait of conditions in the West African trade – trade that was at the heart of the economic development of nineteenth century shipping. The trade also made a significant contribution to the growth of Liverpool and the prosperity of Merseyside.

Trading in West Africa, 1840–1920

Edited by
P.N. Davies

Routledge
Taylor & Francis Group

First published in 1976
by Croom Helm Ltd

This edition first published in 2026 by Routledge
4 Park Square, Milton Park, Abingdon, Oxon, OX14 4RN

and by Routledge
605 Third Avenue, New York, NY 10017

Routledge is an imprint of the Taylor & Francis Group, an informa business

Publisher's Note

The publisher has gone to great lengths to ensure the quality of this reprint but points out that some imperfections in the original copies may be apparent.

Disclaimer

The publisher has made every effort to trace copyright holders and welcomes correspondence from those they have been unable to contact.

A Library of Congress record exists under LCCN: 76364634

ISBN: 978-1-041-29580-8 (hbk)
ISBN: 978-1-003-77022-0 (ebk)
ISBN: 978-1-041-29583-9 (pbk)

Book DOI 10.4324/9781003770220

Trading in West Africa 1840-1920

P.N. DAVIES

CROOM HELM LONDON

Croom Helm Ltd, 2–10 St. John's Road, London, SW11

ISBN 0–85664–129–4

Printed in Great Britain by Biddles Ltd., Guildford, Surrey

CONTENTS

ACKNOWLEDGEMENTS

It gives me great satisfaction to be able to place on record my appreciation for the assistance and encouragement I have received in the preparation of this work.

A number of eminent scholars have shown a sympathetic interest in the project and I would particularly like to express my sincere thanks to Christopher Fyfe, Tony Hopkins, Frederick Pedler and Bill Reader.

My gratitude is also due to Wilfred M. Cotterell (H.D. Cotterell and Company of Amsterdam), Mrs. C.P. Bodenham Cowley (niece of James Deemin), Mr. G.J. Ellerton and Mr. M.B. Glasier (Ocean Transport and Trading Limited), Mr. D.U. Gregg (Unilever Limited), Mr. F.D.H. Mather (John Holt and Company, Liverpool, Limited), Mrs. F.N. Mocatta (great-niece of Sir Alfred Jones) and Mr. D.M. Williams (Editor of *WEST AFRICA*).

Lastly I would wish to acknowledge my permanent debt to Francis E. Hyde, formerly Professor of Economic History at the University of Liverpool, for his unfailing kindness and advice.

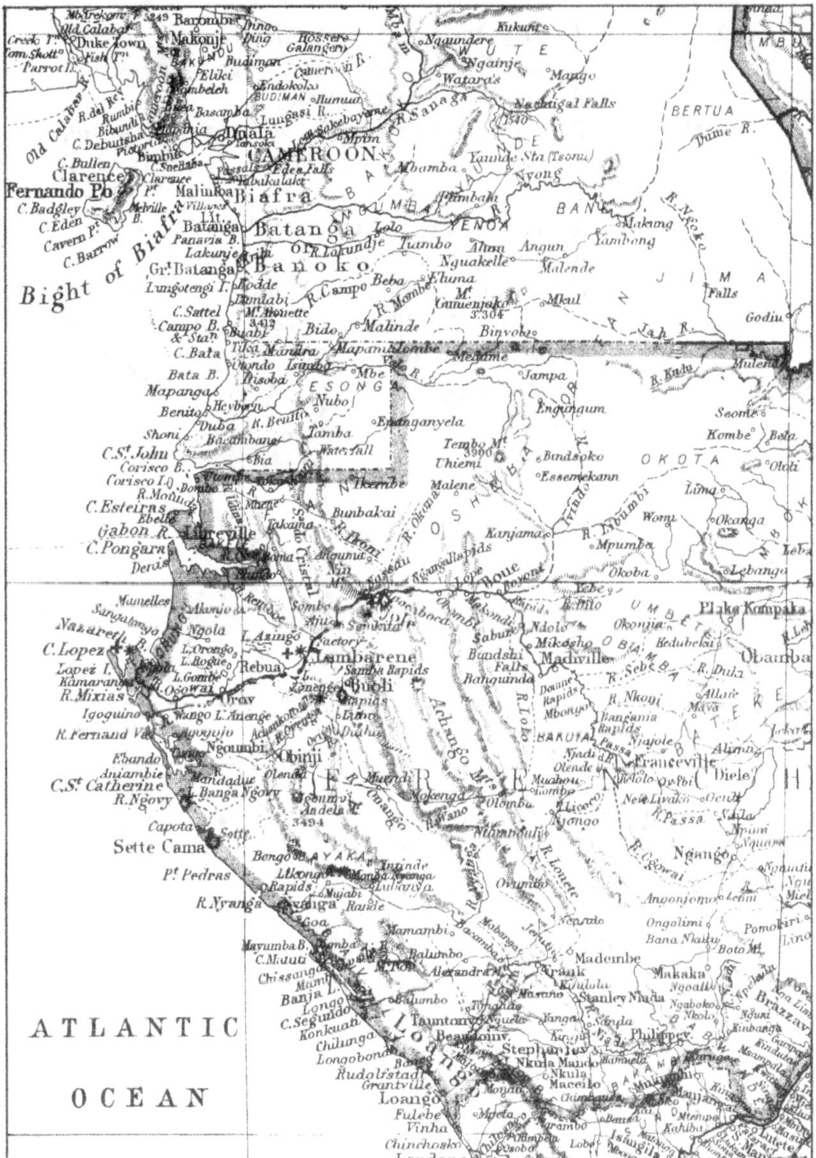
ATLANTIC
OCEAN
Bight of Biafra
Fernando Po
Clarence
CAMEROON
Duala
Batanga
Batanga or Banoko
Biafra
Gr.t Batanga
Duke Town
Old Calabar
Barombi
Makonje
Ngaundere
WUTE
BERTUA
Nachtigal Falls
Sanaga
Yaunde Sta (Tsonu)
Kukuna
Ngainje
Watara's
Mango
Nyong
Lolo
YENOA
Angun
Yambong
Makung
Malende
Nguakelle
J I M A
Falls
Godiu
Mt. Genuenjako 3.304
Binvolo
R. Campo
R. Mombe
Malinde
Bido
C. Sattel
Campo B.
C. Bata
Bata B.
Mapanga
Benito
Shoni
C. St. John
Corisco B.
Corisco I.
ESONGA
Nubo
Tamba
Waterfall
Mbe
Enanganyela
Tembo Mt. 3900
Uhiemi
Malene
Bndsoko
Essemekann
OKOTA
Jampa
Engungum
R. Kudu
Mulenda
Seome
Kombe
Bela
Otoli
Lima
Okanga
Lebango
Wom
Mpumba
Okoba
Kanjama
R. Ivindo
Bunbakai
Ikembe
C. Esteiras
Gabon R.
Libreville
C. Pongara
Manelles
Nazareth B.
C. Lopez
Lopez I.
R. Mixias
Ngola
L. Azingo
L. Orongo
L. Rogue
L. Gombe
Rebua
Ogowai
Orav
Lambarene
Factory
Samba Rapids
Buoli
Achango Mts.
Igoguino
R. Fernand Vaz
Ngoumbi
Obinji
Ebando
Aniambie
C. St. Catherine
R. Ngovy
Capota
Sette Cama
Pt. Pedras
R. Nyanga
Mayumba B.
C. Matuti
Banja
Longo
C. Segundo
Konkuati
Chilunga
Longobonda
Rudolfstadt
Grantville
Loango
Fulebe
Vinha
Chinchosko
Landana
Lope
Boue
Ndolo
Mikosho
Madiville
Bandshi Falls
Banguinda
Okonjia
Hedubekui
R. Dula
Obamba
Alima
Franceville
Diele
Ngango
Angonjomo
Ongolimi
Bana Nkalu
Pomoliri
Boto Mt.
Madembe
Makaka
Frank
Stanley Niada
Philippev
Taumton
Beaudoinv
Stephanlev
Nkula Mando
Nkula
Maceilo
Manjanga
Brazzav
Isangila
Lubanya
Balumbo
Alexandra Mt.
Mamambi
Plake Kompaka

ABBREVIATIONS USED IN THE FOOTNOTES

U.A.C. Hist.	*The History of the United Africa Company to 1938.* Compiled by J.J. Rankin and circulated privately by the Company, London, 1938.
Trade Makers	P.N. Davies, *The Trade Makers, Elder Dempster in West Africa, 1852–1972,* Allen & Unwin, London, 1973.
Wharton MSS.	Mr. F.R. Wharton spent his whole business career with Henry Tyrer & Company of Liverpool. His major historic interest was in the hulks of West Africa and when he died in 1973 his collection of manuscripts was sent to the author of the present work by his estate.

INTRODUCTION

During the past thirteen years my academic research has been largely concerned with the economic history of British West Africa during the nineteenth and twentieth centuries. The results of this work are mainly to be found in my M.A. thesis, *Sir Alfred Jones and the Development of West African Trade* (University of Liverpool, 1963) and in my Ph. D. dissertation, *British Shipping and the Growth of the West African Economy* (University of Liverpool, 1967).

A major part of these studies, together with substantial additional material, has been published in *The Trade Makers. Elder Dempster in West Africa, 1852–1972* (Allen and Unwin, London, 1973), in 'The African Steam Ship Company' (J.R. Harris (ed.), *Liverpool and Merseyside*, Frank Cass, London, 1969) and in 'Lord Kylsant and the Royal Mail' (with A.M. Bourn in *Business History*, July 1972). Two further items will be printed in the near future. *The West African Trade* is in preparation for A. and C. Black's 'Merchant Adventurers' series and 'Group Enterprise: Strengths and Hazards', originally given as a paper at Cranfield School of Management's symposium on Business History in March, 1973, will appear as a contribution to a *festschrift* in honour of Professor F.E. Hyde, Emeritus Professor of Economic History at the University of Liverpool, during 1976.

In none of these publications has it been found possible to include more than the briefest extracts from the original source material. The limitations of space make this inevitable in most cases and it is right that it should be so for part of the task of the discerning author is to present the distilled essence of his subject to the busy reader. Nevertheless there are cases where particular manuscripts seem to demand verbatim reproduction. For some reason or another these have a specific contribution to make which cannot be summarised in a satisfactory manner.

My first association with a paper of this type was Harry Cotterell's *Reminiscences of one connected with the West African Trade from 1863 to 1910.* Cotterell, born in 1841, went out to the Coast in 1863 and worked there for various merchants or on his own account until 1881. Thereafter, although based in Liverpool, he continued with his West African interests being at various times a partner of John Holt, a manager for Alfred Jones and a founder member of the African Association Limited.

Harry Cotterell died in September 1923, leaving behind a small number of typewritten scripts which he had produced for circulation within his family. One of his sons was Captain George A. Cotterell, who subsequently became Marine Superintendent for Elder Dempster and it was probably from him that the Company obtained their copy. This was brought to my attention in 1968 and once I appreciated its importance I got in touch with the present Cotterell family.

Wilfred M. Cotterell, the son of H.D. Cotterell and grandson of Harry Cotterell, not only knew of the manuscript but was aware of its value and had already arranged for his firm, H.D. Cotterell of Amsterdam, to reprint a number of copies. In spite of this, however, he gladly gave me his permission to reproduce it again. My first inclination was to publish it as a monograph but it was not possible to do this at once because of a number of prior obligations. Further reflection then decided me to wait until I had completed my research and then to publish a number of complementary papers if these could be found.

This decision was encouraged by a meeting which had taken place in 1965 with Mr. W.K. Findlay for a transcript of his conversation with Unilever undoubtedly needed a wider circulation. Confirmation that the right choice had been made came shortly afterwards for my cataloguing of the letters and documents left by James Deemin in John Holt's office led to a further important find. Yet another additional discovery came as a result of contacting Deemin's family for they had carefully preserved Coker's letter as it contained such generous praise of their uncle.

The extract in respect of Peter Stuart is included as an example of the type of writing which is frequently used to describe the life and times of a West African merchant. Publications of this sort can be extremely irritating for they merely whet the appetite but this particular one is valuable in that it provides a useful insight into profitability.

The extracts regarding Alfred Jones are provided to supply a brief outline of the man and his career. At best they can only give a faint indication of the most important single influence on the development of West African shipping and trade but as a comprehensive biography of Jones has yet to be written they are included without apology.

It is not suggested that these items are necessarily the most informative or best written accounts of conditions in West Africa during the latter part of the nineteenth century – they just happen to be the ones revealed by my research. Nevertheless they may go a little way towards providing personal evidence for or against some of the generalisations produced by such authorities as Dike,[1] Hopkins,[2] Lathom[3] and McPhee.[4] Some accounts of a similar nature have already been published by

Whitford[5] and by Clough[6] while the recent work of Frederick Pedler[7] has enabled part of the research of J.J. Rankin[8] to reach a wider public.

Unfortunately numerous other sources such as the *Reminiscences of Harry Martin*[9] are still virtually unknown and are only available in their original manuscript form. Furthermore there is no doubt that much valuable material remains uncatalogued in private archives and collections. It is to be hoped, therefore, that other workers in this field will produce new and even better contemporary eye-witness accounts of the period – an item which remains unpublished can contribute nothing to our understanding or scholarship.

University of Liverpool P.N. DAVIES
August 1975

References

1. K.O. Dike, *Trade and Politics in the Niger Delta, 1830 – 1885,* Oxford University Press, London, 1956.
2. A.G. Hopkins, *Economic History of West Africa,* Longmans, London, 1973.
3. A.J.H. Lathom, *Old Calabar, 1600 – 1891,* Oxford Studies in African Affairs, 1973.
4. Allan McPhee, *The Economic Revolution in British West Africa,* George Routledge, London, 1926. (Reprinted by F. Cass with an introduction by A.G. Hopkins in 1971.)
5. John Whitford, *Trading Life in Western and Central Africa, 1877.* (Reprinted by F. Cass with an introduction by A.G. Hopkins in 1967.)
6. R.G. Clough, *Oil River Trader* (with a Foreword by J.D. Fage), C. Hurst, London, 1972.
7. Frederick Pedler, *The Lion and the Unicorn in Africa,* Heinemann, London, 1974.
8. J.J. Rankin, *The History of the United Africa Company to 1938,* circulated privately by the Company, London, 1938.
9. Harry Martin (formerly Rosenthal) joined Swanzy's in the Gold Coast in 1902. (Unpublished MS. in Rhodes House Library, Oxford.)

1. REMINISCENCES of one connected with the WEST AFRICAN TRADE from 1863 to 1910

Some of my friends to whom I have repeated incidents in my life connected with West Africa have suggested to me that I should place them on record, as being of interest to them and also to others who may have the opportunity of reading them. Hitherto, I have considered them only as ordinary incidents in my life which would have been common to most of my contemporaries who were in that part of Africa at the same time as myself. Unfortunately, through the effects of climate, many of these have been removed, and as my connection with the active life of West Africa is now fast becoming a thing of the past, there may perhaps be more reason or excuse for my placing my experience on record for another generation than there was when actively employed in going to and from, or residing in that part of the Coast of Africa.

For the benefit of my children I think it would be better for me to give an account of myself from my birth and earliest recollections, as no authenticated account has been given to them of my early life and struggles in the commercial world of Liverpool, to which I was introduced at a very early age, and under circumstances that did not promise any great amount of success in its initiatory stages. I do not know that anything has been withheld from them of my life or antecedents; at the same time, it was not a general subject of conversation between us, as it might have been if I had been continuously at home with them in the early years of their lives.

I was born in Newbury, Berks., on the 30th December, 1841, my father being a Publican, or Brewer, in that Market Town. My earliest recollection was of this place, when I could not have been more than two to three years of age: I understood my father was unsuccessful in business in this town, and removed to Reading, some 15/20 miles from Newbury, where he took an Inn and Brewery attached called the 'Castle Brewery', in Castle Street; this, however, was only for a very short time, as my next recollection was of a small house in Somerstown on the outskirts of Reading, where my father had removed to, being at that time out of business and in very poor circumstances, so much so that it was a hard struggle to keep the wolf from the door, and success only attained in this respect through the assistance of his relatives, and a small income which came through my grandmother, who was bedridden, and lived in the same house with us at this time.

My father was born in Ruscombe, in Berks., being one of a large family who were all born in the same homestead or farm which had been in the family for several generations. Early in life my father had migrated to London, and had become a commercial traveller for a large Firm of Oil and Colour Merchants established in London. During one of his journeys he told me he had been put into a damp bed, and in consequence had contracted rheumatic gout, from which very early in life he suffered dreadfully, and ultimately became a permanent cripple therefrom.

My recollection of him has always been with a crutch and stick, without which it was impossible for him to walk. He was, therefore, very seriously handicapped in his efforts to make a living for his children. He was, however, a very sanguine man, and as repeated opportunities came to him in the shape of small legacies from his own or my Mother's side, he persisted in entering into business, which as often failed. About the time of our living in Somerstown, where I went to a Church School, one of these legacies came in, and I with two of my brothers was sent to a Boarding School at Steventon, near Abingdon. I was then about six years of age, and having been there for a short time, on very poor fare, educationally and otherwise, I with my two younger brothers was removed to a better-class school, of the Grammar School type, in Hungerford, where I remained for some three years, my father in the meantime having established himself in another brewery and Public House in the Market Place, Newbury. We used to go home every six months for our holidays, and this was to my recollection the happiest term of my life up to that time. Circumstances, however, rendered another change necessary, and this venture had to be given up, as had been the case with its predecessors. The change from Newbury to Liverpool was made during the time myself and brothers were at school, and it was not until some time after the holidays were long over for other scholars that we were taken away to join our parents in Liverpool.

We were brought to Liverpool in the Autumn of 1851, at which time I was less than 10 years of age, and had practically completed my school life, except that for a few months I attended a school in Burlington Street, off Scotland Road, and for a shorter time at St. Peter's School, Everton, which was held in Upper Bean Street. My father had invested the remainder of his money in the purchase of a Public House in Great Homer Street, and it was to this home I returned from my school in Hungerford. Here the same unfortunate result attended the business in which my father was engaged, and our next change was to a private house in Duke Street, Everton, where my parents had to make the best of life under circumstances of hardship and poverty, their only income being an allowance made to my father by a sister in Twyford, who had married a man of means named Poulton. My father by this time was a constant martyr to gout, and was quite unable to do anything outside the house. It, therefore, became necessary for each and all of us, able to do so, to contribute in some way to the family wants.

There were at this time living nine of us out of sixteen, four of whom were girls, and five boys. My eldest brother Charles, being married and having a family, could not do anything for his parents, or to assist the home. My sisters, three of whom were older than myself, went into service. The youngest, Nelly, being then not old enough to give any assistance, while the two younger boys remained at school until old enough to take their share in providing for themselves, or others unable to work. It was at this time that I first made my start in life as an errand boy for a Baby Linen Shop kept by a Mrs. Cheers, situated at the top of Ranelagh Street, where the palatial emporium of Messrs Jacob & Company now stands. How long I remained here I cannot say, possibly only a few weeks, when I occupied a similar position with a Firm of Booksellers, Publishers, and Librarians in Church Street, and had to take out a weekly paper published by them to their customers in Birkenhead, Tranmere, and Rock Ferry, and I well remember traversing the neighbourhood (which afterwards became more familiar to me) footsore and hungry, ill-clad and weary; very often using the pence received for the papers to satisfy the craving of nature, and having the amount regularly stopped from my week's wages afterwards. After this I was for a short time in the service of a gentleman named Millichaps, who then took photographs by the Daguerreotype process, my duty being to polish on a velvet buffer the plates used for this process. With these various changes I had arrived at the mature age of twelve years, when I was apprenticed to a Mr. Daniel Baugh, Cigar and Snuff Manufacturer, in Wolstenholme Square. Here I remained for three years, and occupied many varied positions in the Packing and Sorting Rooms, working from seven o'clock in the morning until seven to nine o'clock at night. My brother Fred was also employed by this gentleman for a short time, and often he and I would have to trudge a handcart with packages of snuff or cigars to the Clarence or other Docks for shipment to Ireland after six o'clock at night, and return to the Warehouse before going home. Notwithstanding hard work and little leisure, I was making some good use of my time, and acquiring knowledge, there being a free library within a short distance of the Warehouse, where I used to go during my dinner hour, and on such evenings as I could find the time; I have always been a most omnivorous reader, and was delighted to get books and learn from them anything they had to teach. In this way I read all the novels of the day, including Scott, Dickens, Thackeray, James Fenimore Cooper, besides books of travel and adventure such as boys usually indulge in at such an age. I also studied arithmetic, and such other subjects as were possible within the limits of my small brain. After three years with this Firm I obtained a situation as Junior Clerk with the Great Western Railway at Duke's Dock, receiving goods, making out Invoices, and generally making myself as useful as possible to those who had a right to direct my work. I remained here for three years, which brings me up to eighteen years of age, when I became infected with a desire to go abroad. It was while I was in this situation that my attention first became directed to Africa. The ships from West Africa used regularly to be brought to the Wapping Basin to discharge their cargoes of Palm Oil, and it was here that I first became acquainted with ships in that trade that afterwards became familiar as household words to me. My time for Africa had not yet come, as on applying to Messrs. Hatton & Cookson[1] to send me out to the Coast in one of their small ships then lying in Wapping Dock, I was told I was too young and inexperienced for their service. I subsequently obtained a situation with the London & North Western Railway Co. at Waterloo Goods Station as Assistant Correspondence Clerk, where I remained for about six months, until the spring of 1860, when my desire to go abroad was at last gratified. Before, however, referring to this I would like to say that the preceding seven years of my life had been attended with considerable hardship, and but little pleasure. To eke out my small wages, not dignified in those days as 'salary', I used to deliver letters to their addresses in town (saving the postage, which we were entitled to) after leaving the Office at night, and in this way saved up for occasional treats to the theatre or across the water, of which I used on every possible occasion to avail myself. Out of my wages I was allowed so much per day for dinner money, and often my brother and I would spend a part of this only in the direction it should have gone, and satisfied ourselves with bread and treacle or butter, instead of more substantial meals. During these seven years I was brought into contact with people whom I came to know more intimately in the later years of my life, and it is some satisfaction to know that notwithstanding the humble positions I occupied under them, they evinced the greatest amount of pleasure in hearing of my subsequent success in life. Among these I can number Mr. Hunt, whom I served under with Mr. Daniel Baugh; also, Miss Baugh, a lady who now resides in Waterloo and whom I used to accompany to St. John's

Market on Saturdays to carry the market basket with her purchases: Mr. Daniel Parsons, who was the Manager of the Great Western Railway, and Mr. David Proctor, of the same Company at Duke's Dock. The former is now dead but the latter I have seen very recently, having just retired on a pension from the Dock Board, while with Mr. Edward Cookson[2] I have long been on intimate terms, as Co-Director of the African Association.

During this epoch of my life I made the acquaintance of some families who resided within an area of half a mile from my own home, and became intimately acquainted with them socially, deriving such pleasure from this connection as could be desired, and being interested in each other's welfare as friends, the first of these being the Bowers, comprising a son and two daughters, to the former of whom I became much attached; she, however, was not reciprocative, except spasmodically, when the other fellow was away: she ultimately married a cousin who commanded one of Edward Bate's ships, had a very numerous family, became a very portly person of about sixteen stone in weight, and died a comparatively young woman. The second family was named Hogg, and comprised two daughters and two sons, with the latter of whom I was on most familiar terms, and continued so for a later date, until our separate occupations took us away to different parts of the World, the third names being the Lloyds. This family resided in Scotland Road, where they had a business as Dyers, living over the shop: the whole of us were very closely associated together during the six or eight years over which this epoch extended, having our pleasures and amusements in each other's company, besides being generally interested in each other's welfare. This family consisted of one son and several daughters, the former of whom died very early in life, while the latter, after giving up the business, became dispersed in various directions, without knowledge of their whereabouts, so far as I was concerned.

This, as above related, was as things were when I made a change in my occupation, which brought me into contact with new scenes and new companions, and made a very marked difference in my life.

In the early part of 1860 I obtained an appointment, through Mr. Donald Curris, as 'Cook's Mate' on board the s.s. 'Palestine',[3] belonging to the Cunard Line, and then loading for Montreal. I had a very vague idea of the duties and work of a 'Cook's Mate' when I accepted the situation; all that I knew of it was that I was going to sea, and in this way could visit strange lands, and gain experience of something different to what I had become accustomed to in my ordinary routine life at home. I cannot say, however, that there was any glamour of romance in my mind as to what I was going to be, or what I should have to do. I had been brought up to make myself useful, even in domestic matters at home, and it therefore came lightly to me when finding the duties of a Cook's Mate did not necessarily mean a knowledge of cooking so much as an aptitude to clean pots and pans, peel potatoes, light fires, and other drudgery of this kind in the Cook's Department. We sailed from Liverpool late in March or early in April, being about six weeks going to and returning from Montreal, during which time I had gained a thorough knowledge from experience of the elementary life in a ship's galley, as they were then called. I had to get up at 5 o'clock in the morning to light the galley fires, and otherwise prepare material for cooking breakfasts for passengers and crew. After breakfast came the washing up of utensils, and preparing for luncheon, dinner, and ultimately to bed about 9.30 p.m., to rest for the same routine the day following, and so on until the voyage was completed. I was dreadfully sick for several days, during which time I had no respite from the 'glory hole' over the screw as a resting-place, and the 'fore peak' as it was called, where I had to go some three or four times a day for vegetables and potatoes, with which by this time I had become very familiar. My opportunities of observation under such circumstances of the surroundings of scenes and doings were somewhat limited. I have, therefore, only a very indistinct remembrance of my first impression of the beauties of the St. Lawrence as we passed up this River from Quebec to our destination, besides which, having been there on more recent occasions, it is natural that these will be more vividly impressed on my mind than those first seen under less favourable circumstances. I arrived in Liverpool on my return journey early in May, and having served my apprenticeship to a seafaring life in the steward's department of an ocean-going steamer, I did not find any difficulty in obtaining employment in a similar capacity from time to time by presenting myself at the Shipping Office, where the crews were engaged as required. In this way, I was appointed as attendant on the Ladies' Cabin in the s.s. 'City of Baltimore'[4] going to and from New York. I remained in this Company, then known as the 'Inman' Line, serving in various capacities in the Stewards' Department, and generally running to and from New York, and occasionally to Montreal during the summer time in some of the outside steamers, or in the steamers of the Allan Line. I continued at this work until the close of 1862, when an opportunity arose for me to gratify my desire to see something more of the World by a longer voyage to West Africa. I, therefore, joined a sailing ship called the 'Iphigenia', belonging to Messrs Tyson Richmond & Jones[5] of Liverpool, and sailed in her on the 1st January 1863 as a Steward. In this capacity I had charge of all the Provisions and Stores, and my duties were to cater and arrange for the Cabin Messes, make bread and pastry, and generally to actually do the work of a steward instead of a waiter, as I had been doing during my services and voyages on board the ocean-going steamers. As my joining the 'Iphigenia' brings me to the commencement of my West African life I will reserve any further reference to it until I have dealt with the second epoch thereof, as experienced from the commencement of 1860 up to the date of leaving for Africa.

During this time many changes had occurred in my own family, among whom the struggle for life still continued. My father became even more afflicted with gout than before, and had more frequent attacks, while means provided by his relatives became more precarious. It was, therefore, necessary for each and all of us to assist so far as possible the necessitous requirements of our family. As I was kept in constant employment without cost for board and lodging my wages were generally contributed to my parents for the home requirements, the only part kept to myself being the 'tips' I received from those whom I attended on during their voyages across the Atlantic, and as the 'City of Baltimore' was at that time one of the crack Atlantic steamers, in charge of a popular man as Captain, the best class of passengers travelled by her, and consequently our tips were sometimes liberal and numerous.

On one of my return voyages in 1862 I found my Mother had died during my absence. I can well remember her; a dear, kind, thoughtful woman, who was always working and striving to make us and keep us respectable, a hard task indeed under such very trying circumstances, and one which might well have tried the patience and temper of a better woman than she. Her death had been brought about by that fearful scourge Cancer, and when the end came, it was most rapid, as there was no apprehension in my mind of such an end when I had left home six weeks before it happened. During the time of which I am now writing, my eldest sister was married to a Mr. Roberts, my second sister to a Mr. Hall, while my sisters Louisa and Nelly had gone to Crewe and Stafford as attendants at these Railway Stations. My brothers Fred and Jem had taken to the sea as a means of earning a living, while my youngest brother Tom became a ship's Carpenter, apprenticed under a man named Sutherberry. On my visits to New York I became acquainted with my cousin Belle, who had married a Mr. Conklin, a well-to-do Merchant in New York City. I often used to stop with them, and was a connecting link between my cousin and England, of which she was delighted to talk: as her recollections of this country were fresh in her mind of her country life over here, she was always most anxious to know anything which was in any way connected with her native home. Her father was born in Ruscombe, on the Cotterell's Farm, but after having lived for some time in Henley-on-Thames, he emigrated with his wife and family to New York. My cousin Belle was the only surviving member of that family, and had become an American citizen in everything but birth, yet at the same time keeping up her associations by visit and correspondence with the Old Country, to which she was passionately attached. At the time of my first meeting her she was residing in Brooklyn, where her husband had a very fine residence, and lived in very good style. There were two girls and a boy, members of the family, the eldest being Minnie, then about 5 or 6 years of age, the second girl Annie, about 4, and a baby boy about 12 months old. Her husband, John S. Conklin, was a very sterling man, in a good way of business, holding a good position in New York Society, an excellent husband and father, and a most delightful man to know personally, as a friend. We were very much attracted to each other, and I found in America a warm welcome from my Brooklyn friends whenever my duties admitted of my taking advantage of the open invitation given to me. My cousin Belle has from that time to the present kept up a periodical correspondence with me, in which each of us has given an account to the other of our families, progress in life, & matters of all kinds in which we have been interested in each other; on her side I am sorry to say it has been full of trials, troubles, and disappointments, her husband having died at an early age, leaving her a widow with three young children, with the eldest daughter of whom in later years she had become estranged, the second daughter being mentally afflicted, while her only son died just as he was entering manhood, and when she had hoped to have him as the support and comfort of her declining years. On my side the circumstances have been reversed, as from my last seeing her the change came to me which has placed me in a position to return to her in some small measure some of the kindnesses and help given to me in my younger days. So many incidents of this kind have occurred during my life that I am, and have been, a firm believer in the promise that to cast your bread on the waters is to have it returned to you after many days, as I do not remember any single instance in my life where sooner or later I have not been able to return a kindness received by an equal kindness, or been able to return slight for slight, if not actually blow for blow.

I had always been very fond of singing, and think I must have had a good voice, as nothing ever came amiss to me. I had never known a single note of music, yet I found no difficulty in repeating songs of every description I heard from time to time in my journeyings, and as I used frequently to treat myself to the gallery of the Theatre Royal in Williamson Square, when the Pryne & Harrison Opera Company acted there, I heard some of the best musical talent of the day in Opera and other music. I was a welcome visitor among my friends when there was any singing going on, and my repertoire became of the most varied description from the low penny gaff comic songs of Billy Barlow type to the gems in the Opera of Balfe, Wallace, and other composers: this talent was especially welcomed among my fellow-workers at Baughs, where the Cigar sorters could sing while doing their work, and as I became one of them in time, I used to lead the solos to their choruses, and thus acquired some knowledge of how to render the songs I sang with some feeling. At the time I am speaking of there was no question of accompaniments of any kind. It was, therefore, a matter of each person starting a song as a precentor in his own particular key note, and the others chiming in in harmony or otherwise. I sometimes sang songs at free-and-easy Concerts where there was a piano and an accompanist who would vamp and follow the singers in this way while quite ignorant of the time and music. My visits to America gave me especial opportunities of acquiring knowledge of American songs which at that time were very numerous, and mostly all of the patriotic type, as the struggle between North and South commenced, if I remember rightly, early in 1860, and continued until 1863, or after I had left the American route for West Africa. It was during one of my voyages across the Atlantic that a passenger tried to persuade me to have my voice cultivated, with a view to becoming a singing professional. I had not sufficient belief in my own talent, however, to take up this view; otherwise, who can say where my voice may have led me, or what a change in my life may have been effected. I only know that on all and every occasion I continued to sing, sometimes as a soloist at a Staff Dinner, or as a leader in our hours of idleness, or perhaps as one of a number of others in part songs. When I was in Africa there was ample opportunity of indulging in this amusement, as our evenings were very quiet, except for occasional exchange of visits among us, and those of us who did not indulge in card-playing used to pass our time in this way, so much so that we had special invitations for this purpose. Under these circumstances I achieved a reputation for singing which lasted all my life, and was frequently called upon on extraordinary occasions; one in particular I remember was when Captain Hart, one of the principal Chiefs of Bonny, succeeded to the Head of his House; a large number of Traders were invited to dine with him in state; all the Under-chiefs with their many wives were present in most gorgeous and varied costumes; after dinner I was asked to sing for them, which I did, and the audience were most enthusiastic, although I hardly think the greater number of them would understand a single word of what I sang; the place and its immediate surroundings were thronged with black people of both sexes, and I was encored most vociferously, and consequently had to sing for them again, which I did, and earned for myself the sobriquet of the 'singing white man'. On festive occasions when we were entertaining visitors, such as the Officers commanding the ships on the Stations, I was requisitioned for this service repeatedly, always of course without accompaniment, as there were no pianos during my sojourn in Africa. We were, however, more fortunate on one occasion, when a Concert was given on one of the new steamers provided with such an instrument, but as I could not sing any of the songs from the selection on board, I was asked to sing, and on consenting to do so, the Chairman announced that Mr. Cotterell would sing a song 'without music'; it was certainly without accompaniment, but scarcely without music, seeing that I was invited to repeat it. I am dwelling somewhat lengthily on this episode in my life and character, with a desire to include all its features in the remarks I am now making, rather than refer to it again, and as a final reminiscence I may mention that when returning from Africa on my first voyage, after being some 33 months away from home, I took passage in a steamer at Bonny with about 30 other passengers, a good many of whom I had come to know intimately during this time. We had an Open-air Concert almost every night during a voyage which lasted for some 35 days, and I sang one particular song nearly every night during that voyage to an audience that appeared never to have enough of it: I gave copies of it to most of them, and certainly became well tired of my own pet song before I got to my destination. I sang entirely from ear, and when compared with the actual music I found it so difficult to eradicate my own errors, or to assimilate them with the musical score when accompanied by a piano that I had so much of the conceit taken out of me, and became so conscious of my inaccuracies, that I never sang with the same confidence as I had done before finding out my mistakes and ignorance.

I have now come to the point of my life dealing more particularly with Africa and my experience there. As I have formerly written, my desire was to go to Africa, and the only way I could get there was by 'working my passage' as it is called. I, therefore, joined the 'Iphigenia', and left Liverpool on the 1st January, 1863, for Bonny. The 'Iphigenia' was a fast-sailing full-rigged ship of about 950 tons net register, carrying about 30 hands, including three Mates and a Master named Chinn.[6] The evening before sailing, a Mr. Stanley Arnold came on board to see the ship away, and to give the Captain his final instructions; I spoke to this gentleman, Mr. Stanley Arnold, who represented the owners, about my remaining in Africa on arriving there, and he kindly promised, after asking me a lot of questions, to write out to the Agent in charge of their business in Bonny, recommending my engagement as a clerk, or assistant as they were then called, and I think it may have been due to his influence that I ultimately attained my wish.

We had a very quick passage out to Bonny, as I think the voyage only took some 39 days, but during this time I had ample opportunities of observing the life a sailor leads under a tyrannical and bullying Captain, as the man in charge of this vessel turned out to be a regular 'Palm Oil ruffian' of the most pronounced type; his Officers were bullied and sworn at on all and every occasion; in fact, two or three times during the passage out there was every prospect of a free fight between the Captain and his Officers. The first Mate was a soft easy-going man who took his gruelling very resignedly; the second Mate was a man of a different type, who had been several voyages to Africa before, knew the ropes pretty well, and could give in return cursing or blow as much as he received. To see the Mate with a ballast shovel standing up to protect himself against the Master, with some other weapon in his hand, was a new experience for me, and one which soon worked on my nerves in a way which lasted for a long time. I very soon learned that my life under such a man would be a burden to me, and as my deficiencies as a steward became more evident every day, I soon came under the lash of this man's fury, and the weight of his foot. Fortunately for me, the Cook was an experienced one, black as the ace of spades, but a good-hearted fellow notwithstanding, and he willingly made up for my shortcomings, so that under his tuition and guidance before we had arrived at Bonny I. could make bread, pastry, arrange the meals, wash and iron the Captain's shirts and clothes, to satisfy the brute for whom I had these duties to perform. There was little of interest during the voyage beyond what I have here related, one day being a repetition of another so far as the vagaries of the Master were concerned, until we reached our destination. We had one passenger on board who sailed with us from Liverpool, a son of King Pepple of Bonny, who had been in England for some years to be educated. He was now returning to his country, and looked forward to succeeding to the throne of Bonny at some future time with an amount of self-assurance and gratulation, born of the fact that among his schoolmates in England he had been addressed and looked up to as 'Prince George' of Bonny, the son of the reigning King of that place. He was at this time a quiet inoffensive kind of youth, and used to resent with indignation the disparaging remarks of the second Mate, who, having been in Bonny before, knew the social position of his father, and was not disposed to pay much homage or attention to his son, even though he claimed and used the title of 'Prince'. On our arrival in the Bonny Bay we were boarded by a native pilot, Jack Brown, of Ju Ju Town, who took us up the River, where we anchored some time during the afternoon of the same day. The payment this man had to receive in part for his services were so many pieces of beef, so many pounds of bread, & so many gallons of Rum, all of which I had to give him from the ship's stores. The remainder of his pay he received from the supercargo in cloth and other goods, as per scale, according to the tonnage of the ship. On coming on board he certainly recognised Prince George, but not in such a way as to impress anyone with his importance. I afterwards came to know each of these distinguished personages very well, and will have to refer to the former pretty frequently, as my duties brought me into contact with each of them, and the one holding the less distinguished position proved in my estimation the better man, so far as honesty and integrity were concerned.

Immediately on our arrival in Bonny the ship was dismantled and housed-in for a long stay. All the upper masts and spars were sent down, the topmasts 'housed' and covered, the sails dried and stowed away, while the yards were used to form skeleton rafters and became to support the thatched roof with which the ship was to be covered. I was set the work of receiving and counting the sticks and mats brought by the natives for this purpose, and had to give receipts for them. This was my first experience of natives in Africa, and I soon learnt that they were a lot of unmitigated scoundrels, whose sole object and aim in life was to see how much they could gain from you by cheating. I was not long, however, kept at this work, as Mr. Stanley Arnold had been as good as his promise and had written to the Agent, a Captain Macintosh,[7] about me. I was, therefore, summoned by this gentleman to an audience, and carried from the ship to a hulk then lying on the beach in a native canoe, and got on board with difficulty up the side by wooden cleats nailed across, the deck being about 30 ft. from the water. During my interview with the supercargo, I had to undergo a very rigorous examination on my past experience, and it was ultimately decided that I should be sent over to New Calabar the following day to take the place of a clerk who had recently died there. I, therefore, returned to the 'Iphigenia', packed up my traps, which did not take long, made over the stores, keys, and duties to the cook, and prepared myself for the morrow's journey, a distance of about 20 miles to be covered in a schooner long boat worked and sailed by three Kroomen,[8] to become a clerk or assistant trader in a factory established for the purpose of purchasing Palm Oil by barter.

With this change in my occupation the period of flunkyism was left behind, and I entered into a sphere which was to give me opportunities little dreamt of when the step was first taken. I must not, however, anticipate. In leaving my sea-going life behind, I did so with few regrets or conscientious qualms. I had come to regard it as offering very poor prospects of advancement or remuneration, and with little scope for personal ability or ambition, while at the same time I could not but recognise that it had been so far as I was concerned a most beneficial change, as during the three years I am now referring to I had grown stronger, healthier, and more fit to cope with the difficulties of life, being better equipped in experience and physique, thanks to good abundant food, regular hours, strict discipline, fresh air, outdoor life, and exercise, besides which I had succeeded in acquiring knowledge and in developing characteristic traits which have stood me in good stead under the varying circumstances which I subsequently had to deal with. I had certainly made some progress, and obtained promotion from time to time, which gave me confidence in myself, and I therefore became as a consequence self-reliant, independent, and able to take care of and decide for myself any question which required such treatment. My many voyages across the Atlantic were made without any exciting incidents; they were, however, interesting from many points of view, as in the summer-time we had plenty of amusement and diversity from the number of passengers we carried – some hundred in the steerage, with from 60 to 120 or 150 in the cabin. There was certainly always something going on, the greatest fun being among the Irish emigrants, who were seeking new life and scenes in America. In the winter, circumstances were different, as although the ships of 40 years ago were good substantial steamers, well-found and seaworthy, they could not be compared to the leviathans of to-day, equipped as they are with the most modern improvements and scientific accessories; consequently, travelling in 1862 was quite different to what it is now, and many hardships had to be endured from weather in the Atlantic during winter: I have been thirty days from Queenstown to New York and never expected to arrive at all, the cabins being flooded, skylights battened down, and only sailors allowed on deck. In some of these passages the rigours of an arctic winter had to be endured. On more than one occasion the ship arrived in New York a perfect iceberg from truck to water's edge, everything and everybody frozen, and even frostbitten. The stewards had to keep watch in the saloon during the night, and it was a weird kind of occupation to realise that you were keeping solitary watch below without prospect of escape, if you had to, everything being fastened down to keep you in. It requires people to experience these kinds of things to realise what is meant by the dangers of the sea, and the risks that are run by those who go down to the sea in ships and do their business in great waters.

My first introduction to my new sphere of life and duties was gained in New Calabar, to which place I was taken in a sailing long boat laden with shooks[9] and hoop iron. We left Bonny early in the morning, after being furnished with Provisions for the journey, consisting of crew biscuits and salt beef, with a bottle of water thrown in. We sailed under a blazing sun at the rate of about three miles an hour, mostly with the tide in fact, and arrived at our destination about nine or ten o'clock the same night. Here I presented my letter of introduction to a Mr. John Carney, the sub-agent in charge of the hulk 'Osprey',[10] which was to be my home for some months. I retired to bed, and was up early in the morning to view my surroundings, and found that I was on board a vessel of good size, fitted up as a floating warehouse, covered in with a corrugated iron roof, the poop portion being fitted up as a dining or living room, with a portion set apart for sleeping accommodation, while the cabin was arranged as a shop or sample room, in which were displayed the goods for trade, the hold of the ship being filled with goods as in a warehouse, while the deck was kept clear for the purpose of receiving and stowing the casks of Palm Oil brought for us by our native customers. I found Mr. John Carney a rough uneducated coarse Irishman, with a brogue which I have since recognised as belonging to County Cork. He had been some time in charge of the Factory, and I had been sent round to acquire a knowledge of the trade before he left for home; with him was a younger brother about 17 to 18 years of age, who had come out in the same ship with him, and each of them had been out in Africa from three to three and a half years. The Senior Agent by whom I had been appointed was a typical Scotchman, named Andrew Macintosh,[11] an old sea-captain, shrewd, careful, economical to the point of parsimoniousness, and suspicious of everyone about him. He was, however, a strict disciplinarian, and as such exercised a potent influence on everyone under his control, with beneficial results to those who were desirous of doing their duty or obtaining advancement.

I was initiated into my duties immediately after my arrival, and found they were most varied and numerous. I had to get up at 5.30 in the the morning, by which time the natives were alongside the hulk with their canoes of Oil. It was my duty to see this hove on deck, tried, to ascertain its quality, measured, to ascertain its contents, upon which a receipt was made out, when everything had been satisfactorily arranged, and ultimately to prepare it for shipment by 'starting' or packing it into other casks than those in which it was brought, and finally send it over to Bonny by the sailing schooners which passed to and fro each day. Receiving the Oil from Natives took up the time at one's disposal before breakfast, after which the goods paid in exchange had to be delivered to the natives: this was done by the Agent issuing Delivery Orders on the ship or hold to the person (myself) in charge of them, and I was made responsible for carrying out this part of the business. After I became more experienced in the ways of the trade, I had to attend the shop with the Agent in charge and 'jam', or contract, with the natives for the goods to be paid for Oil to be brought after the contract was completed. In this way my time was actively employed from early morning until it became dark (as it was in the tropics about 6.15 each night), after which I had to make up the accounts and enter up everything in the books for transmission to Bonny, as each opportunity offered. This was my daily routine of duties, varied in some measure by the order in which they came, rather than in any other sense. Our evening's recreation, after completing books and accounts, would be in reading, writing, or occasionally playing cards with other Agents, or supercargoes, as they were sometimes called, who came on board to visit us: the Carneys were evidently habitual gamblers, and played for pretty large amounts, and having referred to cards and gambling, I may appropriately here give my experience of it, and how I managed to get in and out of it without much harm to myself. A party had been arranged to play a game called 'Loo', at which, withstanding I was a perfect novice, I had been induced to join, and the result of the evening's play was that I found myself the loser to the extent of some £7/-/-, for which I had to give an I.O.U. On retiring to my room I turned this over in my mind, and began to see all kinds of disaster following a course so unfortunately begun. My wages were six pounds per month at this time, and I looked upon the loss as irreparable, and to imagine dire consequences as the result of my foolishness in doing something opposed to common sense, and of which I had no knowledge or ability to win success; this, however, did not prevent my playing again a few nights later, when the cards were more in my favour, and I consequently won a larger sum than I had previously lost, with which I paid my debts, and from that time would not play again, except for such small stakes as I could afford to pay if I lost, and as this was not a sufficient inducement to others I was consequently left out of their card parties for the future. I afterwards realised that it was a wise and fortunate resolve on my part not to play for money, as I found this form of recreation or amusement was largely indulged in by Agents whose means enabled them to play for high stakes, and large amounts changed hands from time to time, the game being kept alive until the small hours of the morning, after hundreds of pounds had been lost or won. On one occasion some years later than the incidents above referred to, I was present when most of the Agents in Bonny were playing 'unlimited Loo', and hundreds of pounds were changing hands with each deal, when I was again invited to take a hand, with the remark that it was a more rapid road to fortune than buying Palm Oil; I, however, resisted, and was thankful I did so – the losses on that night amounted to £3,000, for which I.O.U.s were given. One of the heaviest losers, who was just on the eve of returning home after a successful voyage, realising that his earnings for the voyage would be jeopardised if he honoured his bills, repudiated them, which created a great sensation and almost led to blows, if not something worse, when more reasonable counsels prevailed, and all gambling obligations were cancelled; play was brought to within smaller limits, and the person who had brought about this change by repudiating his obligations was blackballed from the parties for the future. This was known as the 'Wheeler Movement', and became a tradition on the Coast so long as I remained there.

I have wandered a little bit from the chronological order to give an account of this incident, in order to dispose of it as a corollary to my own experience as a novice in New Calabar.

The Native Chiefs in New Calabar were a fine wellmade type of negro, clever traders, smart and ready to avail themselves of every turn in their own favour. They used to come down the River from their town, about 8 miles distant, in gaudily painted canoes, pulled by about 24 to 30 men, with flags flying, Tom-Toms beating, to which the paddlers would keep time with their paddles, getting through the water at the rate of six to eight miles an hour, or even more than this with the tide. The tom-tom was an instrument made of pieces of wood, in form like a dulcimer, the high or low notes being made by striking the larger or smaller pieces of wood as the cadence required. Each canoe would have its Ju Ju or fetish emblem on the bow, dragging in the water, and covered by a piece of white calico, which had been consecrated to 'Ju Ju'. The Chief would be dressed in a long flowing robe, made from brightcoloured Madras Handkerchiefs, in the form of a large shirt, with open collar; around his neck would be a string of coral beads of considerable value; on his arms ivory bracelets two to three inches broad, cut from the thick part of the elephant's tusk, and of great weight, sometimes with his own name inscribed thereon, and the more dandy Chief would have red parrot tail feathers as an adornment in the hair Each Chief would be accompanied by his own special bodyguard of one or more young men in similar but less conspicuous attire, to carry snuff box, chop stick, or papers referring to trade. After taking a morning drink of Gin, Rum, or Ginger Wine from a small glass, he would begin to talk business, which meant 'jamming' for Oil. This was done by going into the shop, or sample room, and bargaining for such goods as he required in exchange for the Palm Oil he had to sell; this being satisfactorily arranged, it was then left for him to deliver his Produce, which was generally left over to the following day, when it would come alongside early in the morning, be tried, gauged, and filled-up by the time the Chief came down to see the transaction completed, and to take away his goods. It required a great deal of rigorous supervision to see these details were carried out, as the Natives were fully alive to every move by which they could gain an advantage either in giving you less Produce or obtaining a larger tale (or) quantity of goods than they were entitled to. It was also necessary to have your eyes open to guard against theft, as all kinds of schemes were resorted to to distract your attention, during which time some of their accomplices would be ready to pounce on something they could easily appropriate and conceal in their dress.

Every 8th day was known as the Calabar Sunday, upon which day no visits were made to the hulks at all by the Natives, nor any trade done by them: this was not a religious observance, but simply an old time custom brought about by the canoes with Produce returning from the markets, when a holiday was made of it, and a general day of rejoicing among those who had returned to their families after weeks or months of absence in the interior markets, buying Oil to fill their canoes before completing their voyages. On these days the white men would go up to the Native Town to see their traders, and to induce them to sell them their Oil on the morrow, which was the market day. Large quantities would be brought down during the night, and kept waiting at the mouth of the creek close to the shipping, to be taken to the hulk if sold, or to wait until jams or contracts had been made for its disposal. Each of these canoes would have their Tom-Toms going, and night was made hideous by the incessant noise from these instruments, or the shoutings and quarrelling of rival canoe men who belonged to different Chiefs or Houses. King Amachree reigned in New Calabar when I first went there, but died soon after, leaving his son Prince Will to reign in his stead.

I continued this life for some time in New Calabar, when I again had to make a change and return to Bonny, where I became an assistant under the Chief Agent, Captain Macintosh, and had to acquire a knowledge of Bonnymen, as I had done with the New Calabarmen in the latter place. My duties and daily work in Bonny continued to be of the same character as in my previous place, except that they became of a more responsible and exacting nature. Having gained some knowledge and experience of Native ways I was now entrusted with the work of 'jamming' with the minor chiefs for their Produce, kept entirely in the shop, which it was my duty to keep properly stocked, paying out everything from thence and from the bale room, which was under my personal charge, keep an account of the serving out Provisions, Stores, etc. for cabin, crew, and Kroomen. The deck work of receiving Produce devolved in a 'mate' who had charge of it, and also of the goods in the main hold or portion of the ship used for this purpose. The person occupying this position had been one of the mates on board the 'Iphigenia', an old Coast hand who was gifted with a vivid imagination, and could spin yarns by the hour relating to his experiences, embroidered more or less by fancy, and depending only on the credulity of his listeners to absorb them. We got on very well together during the time I remained on board the 'Celma',[12] and our friendship continued for many years after, under different circumstances.

The Hulk I was now on board of was lying on the Beach; there were in all about seventy to eighty men on board, consisting of the Agent, a Doctor, two white Assistants, two Mates, about five or six Coopers and Carpenters, fifty to sixty Kroomen labourers, with the usual complement of cooks and stewards, all of whom were black. The assistants, coopers, and mates were treated as seamen, having their provisions served out according to Board of Trade regulations, and notwithstanding there were plenty of provisions on board, these were kept by the Agent entirely for his own use, our daily diet being varied by an occasional joint of goat's meat on Sunday, with our allowance of flour made into pancakes with water in lieu of milk, and without eggs. As I now had charge of the provisions, I frequently regaled myself surreptitiously when working in the bale room with delicacies restricted by the Captain to his use only.

I got on exceedingly well with the native Chiefs in Bonny, and found them much the same in character as those of New Calabar. A vacancy having occurred in New Calabar, owing to Mr. Carney's leaving for home, I was again transferred to the 'Osprey',[13] this time, however, being in charge of the Agency myself, and having to conduct the business alone. I was, however, only a short time in this position when an incident occurred which made a great change in my life, and led to results far exceeding any of our expectations.

In the early part of January 1864 one of the Kroomen came running to me to say that a ship lying ahead of us was on fire; this I found to be the case, and immediately everything was in a state of commotion and consternation, as the ship in question was known to have a large quantity of Gunpowder on board, and it was rightly assumed that she would not be long in burning herself out, and in blowing up. There were some ten or twelve ships and hulks lying in a line directly to leeward of the burning one, and as there was a strong Harmattan, or North Eastern wind blowing, the smoke and sparks were drifting across them, and the gravest fears were entertained that some of the others would be ignited by the burning debris which floated over them. Most of the hulks were only covered in by palm mat roofs, used as thatch, and the Harmattan wind having been blowing for several days previously, everything had become as dry as tinder, so that a spark might at any time create a conflagration. I was the only white man on board the 'Osprey' when the fire broke out on the 'Merlin',[14] and it was with some difficulty that I got the Kroomen to slip the moorings to enable us to get away from the burning ship by the aid of the tide, which was then ebbing: this succeeded very well for a time, and would have carried us quite out of danger if the tide had continued to ebb, but before we got very far down the River we were met by the incoming tide, and brought back to our former position, when another hulk swinging round on a loose cable collided with the 'Osprey', and we were both lying together when the 'Merlin' exploded, and in doing so set fire to seven or eight other ships lying close to her, and as every one of them had large quantities of Gunpowder on board, confusion reigned supreme. I found the 'Osprey' was on fire also, and burning fiercely; there were some 60 tons of Gunpowder on board her, and as the Kroomen knew this, I was not surprised that they should want to get out of danger. I was not, however, prepared to find myself the only soul left on board, as on going on deck I found the Kroomen had all deserted, taking with them the only boat there was, leaving me to my fate. I had been busy cleaning a rifle when the fire was first reported, and I fortunately was able with its assistance to bring my deserting Kroomen back under its cover to the bow of the hulk, and getting into the boat saved my life. We pulled on shore, and were not there long when one after another of the hulks and ships blew up with terrific explosions, leaving nothing behind but floating wreckage of the fleet that previously existed there. The fire broke out about nine o'clock in the morning, and at three in the afternoon nothing remained but the old hulk, which was fortunately to windward of the fire, was lying on the Beach, and consequently could not get away. There were some nine or ten ships and hulks destroyed, with many thousands of pounds' worth of property, and a busy community rendered homeless and non-effective in a few hours. I escaped from the hulk with a very meagre wardrobe, consisting of what I had on, and as clothing is not a strong point in the tropics, and being a very hot day, my entire outfit consisted of a pair of pants, boots, socks, and shirt, while of course everyone else was in the same impoverished condition. It was customary in these days of which I am writing for the Agents in Bonny to give themselves a holiday on Saturday, so as to be out of the way of the necessary cleaning up that was to be done on that day, and to form parties to go down to Breaker Island. This was a small sand island lying at the junction of the Bonny and New Calabar Rivers, and was formed by the washing of the sand from these two Rivers into the estuary. The Agents had gone down in their boats as usual when the report of the first explosion was heard by them, and realising something must be wrong, they came up to New Calabar just in time to see the last of the ships disappear, and to ascertain what had been the cause of it. My Senior, Captain Macintosh, took me on board his boat, and we all made the best of our way to Bonny, where I again had to resume my ordinary duties, and remain until other arrangements could be made to take our position again, and to resume trade in New Calabar.

The conflagration took place on the 15th January 1864, and by a strange coincidence a similar one took place in Liverpool on the same date, when a ship called the 'Lottie Sleigh'[15] took fire in the Mersey, and was destroyed, having on board a large quantity of Powder. A terrific explosion occurred, which did immense damage in Liverpool and Cheshire. The ship was loading for West Africa, and belonged to Messrs Hatton & Cookson, to whom one of the hulks belonged which was destroyed in New Calabar. The cause of the fire on the 'Lottie Sleigh' was the spilling of a paraffin lamp, while in that of the 'Merlin' it was caused by a cooper putting a lighted pipe which he had been smoking into the palm thatched roof, thus causing its ignition, and the consequences which followed.

Some two months after this a small schooner which had been lying in Old Calabar was brought round from there to New Calabar, to be fitted up as a temporary hulk for trading, and I was placed in charge of her; she was a leaky old craft of about 150 tons register, and only fit for burning, except for the exigency of the occasion. I was on board her when she was towed round from Bonny, and after sticking on several sandbanks, we eventually arrived there, and my work of fitting her up began, with the assistance of old Myers, whom I have referred to before in these memoirs. She did not last very long, as I awoke one night to find her partly full of water, which the pumps could not keep under, and in consequence she had to be beached, this being done in a position opposite the shipping, but as she was a very small craft and beached on a muddy bottom at the top of the tide, she was consequently almost up in the bush, and was only surrounded by water for a few hours during the twelve of high and low tide. I was not long here before my health began to suffer from my surroundings, and I ultimately had to be removed from my charge, if my life was to be considered. I was, therefore, invalided home by a Doctor's orders, and left New Calabar with this intention to go round to Old Calabar, where a ship was completing her loading, and was expected to sail soon after my getting there. Fortunately, the ship was much longer in getting her cargo than was expected, and under the different circumstances of my surroundings in Old Calabar I was not long in recovering health, and being useful to the supercargo, or Senior Agent, I was kept there as Senior Assistant, thus acquiring a knowledge of the Old Calabar trade, besides further experience generally, which was helpful to me in many ways. My life in Old Calabar was much more congenial than it had been under my previous Agent, as I was fortunate enough to be with an old sea captain, who took a different view of his responsibilities and duties to Captain Macintosh, as we were allowed to take our meals at the cabin table, had much more liberty in going about among our fellow-men, and, generally, had more pleasure in our lives, apart from business, than had been accorded before. Captain Mullen was a man who had broader views than the other named; consequently, what with better food, more liberties, and freer intercourse with other men, it was less like penal service than my 18 months in Bonny and New Calabar, with the result that my health became fully re-established before the 'Golden Age' was ready for sea, and I was kept back to serve the remainder of my term and to assist Captain Mullen, expecting to remain with him until my three years' engagement had expired. I was certainly very comfortable and happy in my new sphere of duties, and managed to get on well with my senior, with the native chiefs, and everyone with whom I was brought into contact in Old Calabar. I remained here about six months, when I was called upon to make another change, which brought me back to Bonny and greatly influenced all my future life. Captain Macintosh had been succeeded in his Agency in Bonny and New Calabar by a man named Green, who had been appointed by Messrs Tyson, Richmond & Jones as their Agent. This gentleman had been previously on the Coast as a 'Palm Oil' Doctor; (this term was used to define the class of Doctors then sent out to the Coast, who were medically in charge of the crew and staff of the Firms who engaged them. They were mostly unqualified men, with some elementary knowledge of surgery and drugs, which was considered all that was necessary in those days for the class of men sent out to West Africa). He had not previously traded in Africa at all, and it was, therefore, a matter of surprise that he should have been sent out in this capacity. I was supposed to be in Bonny at the time, and it was expected I should be able to initiate him or assist him in the trading until he acquired a knowledge of it himself. Being in Old Calabar I had not this duty to perform; it, however, fell to the lot of another Assistant who had been junior to me to take him in hand, a Mr. De Cardi, who, on realising the man's ignorance, left him to himself, while he returned home to apply to the Firm personally for the appointment, which, from the conduct of Mr. Green, he saw would be soon again vacant. Mr. Green soon showed his incapacity, and this being allied to intemperance, report was made to Captain Mullen, as Senior Agent of the Firm, to protect their interests by sending someone to supersede Mr. Green, who was misconducting himself, and the Firm's interests were suffering in consequence. I was the only person available, and was started off by the same steamer which brought the news. I arrived in Bonny to find that Captain Chinn (who had again come out in charge of the 'Iphigenia') was in possession of the keys, and carrying on the trade, having superseded Mr. Green on his own initiative during the time taken up by representations to Captain Mullen. Having regard to my instructions, and finding Captain Chinn had taken steps to protect the Firm's interests, I had an interview with this man on my arrival, and having explained to him that I had been sent round to do the trade, I left it to him to decide if he would continue to do so, or hand over the responsibility to me. His desire was that I should work under him, but my previous knowledge of the man and his brutal methods prevented me from falling into this error. I, therefore, placed on him the responsibility of acting on Captain Mullen's instructions or of taking the consequences of refusal, in which case I should return again to Old Calabar. Seeing I was firm on this point, he handed me over the keys and returned to his own ship, and I was careful not to permit any interference on his part in anything I had to do thereafter. I had to assert myself more than once to prevent him doing so, as only in this way could I hope to have freedom to do as I thought in the interests of the Firm. Poor Green was a weak silly creature, without any self-control – and it was not long before I found it necessary to get rid of him, which I did by sending him on board the 'Iphigenia' to return home as a passenger.

I was now in full charge of Tyson, Richmond & Jones' business in Bonny and New Calabar at 23 years of age, a position of great responsibility for one so young, and my anxiety was great to do justice to the opportunity. I, therefore, commenced trading, and for about two months had the thing to myself; the Firm, having heard of Mr. Green's shortcomings had notified Captain Macintosh to return to Bonny until they could make more permanent arrangements to send someone in whom they could place greater reliance than the person previously appointed. Captain Macintosh, therefore, arrived out in Bonny early in February, 1865, to find me in charge of the business, Mr. Green in durance, and everything going on satisfactorily, except that a stoppage of trade had been proclaimed by the British Government against the Bonny Chiefs, until they had purged their offence of disregarding their Treaty obligations, and had paid a fine of some 500 puncheons of Oil, which had been imposed on them by Consul Burton some months previously, and up to which time they had not paid or shown any disposition to do so. The stoppage was to be for three months, unless they paid the fine earlier, in which case trade would be resumed.

This was the condition of things as Captain Macintosh found them on his arrival, when, after looking into everything, he finally decided to return to England by the same steamer in which he had come out, and to leave me in charge of the business subject to its confirmation by the Firm, to whom he would report when he got home. It was, therefore, a matter of great gratification to me that my actions had passed the careful scrutiny and investigation of such a strict man as Captain Macintosh, by whom I was now appointed as Agent of one of the largest and most successful Firms in the African trade at that time.

Captain Macintosh arrived home, made his report, and the Firm at once wrote me appointing me their Agent, with a salary of £300 a year, and a promise of participation in profits to the extent that my predecessor would have received if he had behaved himself, and made them.

The stoppage of trade continued in Bonny until early in May, when Commodore Wilmot arrived with a fleet of warships, for the purpose of collecting the fine imposed on the Bonny-men, and was able to use such effective arguments with them, aided by his warships moored opposite the town ready for action, that King Pepple's objections were overruled, and the fine was paid, after which trade was resumed, and as the Oil bought in the interior markets had been accumulating for three to four months, a lively trade followed, which enabled me to complete the loading of the 'Iphigenia' in an incredibly short time, and she sailed early in June for home with a full cargo, and a new Captain, whom I had appointed in place of Captain Chinn, who had died during the February previous.

In New Calabar I had Mr. de Cardi as my Junior Agent, with whom, however, I did not get on well, and consequently had to dispense with his services, leaving it to me to go over there very frequently, which the stoppage in trade enabled me to do without injury to our Bonny business. My Principals at home had now decided to withdraw from the African trade, and I was instructed to dispose of the stock, plant, and everything belonging to them as best as I could. Fortunately, the circumstances favoured me greatly in following out my Employers' instructions, as the long stoppage of trade had created such a demand for goods that I was able to realise everything to the last penny, and eventually to sell the hulks, beach property, and all the appurtenances of trade to other Agents who were in want of them. I, therefore, cleared up everything, and embarked for home on the 6th August, 1865, where I arrived on the 10th September, having been two years and nine months away, and risen during that time to the highest point attainable as an African Agent.

I had a very gratifying reception by my Employers, who treated me liberally for my services, but not to such an extent as I should have been entitled if I had been paid a proportion of profits as promised; they were, however, anxious to retain my services, and to send me out again as Agent for a new Firm they proposed to establish as successors to Messrs. Tyson, Richmond & Jones, which was not carried through, owing to the objection of Mr. Stanley Arnold (the gentleman whom I first met on the eve of my leaving for Africa) not caring to enter into the African trade.

I found on my return to England that my brothers and sisters were all scattered, one in one place and one in another; my father had died in the previous January. I had, therefore, to make my home with my eldest sister, married at this time to a Captain Binnie, her first husband having died soon after my leaving for Africa.

During my voyage home in the 'Athenian'[16] I had met a young lady who joined us in Sierra Leone with her parents and two brothers, as fellow passengers. They had been resident in that Colony about the same time as I had been in the Delta of the Niger, and were returning home, the father being on furlough: he had been Band Master of the 3rd West India Regiment, taking his wife and children with him to England.

The young lady and myself had frequent opportunities of meeting, and were thrown into each other's company very much during the voyage. There were many subjects we had in sympathy, and under these circumstances we were drawn affectionately towards each other, until an understanding was arrived at between us that we should consider the matter from another point of view after our arrival in England. The parents were no obstacle to a closer intimacy, and as I found on my arrival home there was none existing from any other direction, I formally proposed marriage to the lady who is now my wife, and we were married in London on the 13th November, 1865, within three months of our first meeting each other. It is not my intention here to refer more particularly to this episode in my life at this stage, except to say that it has been my dearest recollection, and brought with it all the happiness I had hoped for, with abundant blessings in its train to each of us.

I had now become settled down, and having taken upon myself the responsibilities of a married man, I had to turn my attention to fulfilling them, and I fortunately was successful in receiving offers of employment from several different directions to represent Firms in Africa; one of these came from a Firm who were desirous of commencing business in Bonny, and having just closed up there for Messrs. Tyson, Richmond & Jones, the prospects of success there were greatly enhanced by this circumstance. I, therefore, entered into an Agreement with Messrs. Irvine & Woodward[17] to go out for them to Bonny. My time was now fully occupied in making preparations for this voyage. Mr. Irvine had been in Africa himself for some years, and had been successful in a small way when I joined him in this more important venture. A ship was bought named the 'Calcutta'[18] which was to be converted into a trading hulk on her arrival in Bonny, and she left early in 1866 for that Port. I followed on the 24th February, and arrived there a month later, to find the 'Calcutta' had not arrived. I, therefore, waited until she came in, when I commenced at once, and soon had her ready to begin trading. Messrs. I. & W. had conscientious objections to trade in spirits with Natives; I was thus to some extent handicapped in not having this commodity, as compared with other Merchants. I did not, however, fully realise this until some time after making a start. The method of carrying on our trade was to be in some respects different from that of our competitors, as, in order to economise capital, it was our intention to make use of the steamers to keep up our supplies of cargo, which were to be sent out from time to time as opportunity offered, or trade required.[19] We commenced in this way, but owing to want of capital, and also the want of spirits, I was very seriously hindered in the business; the steamer at this time only ran once a month, and for some months I found myself for one or two weeks at least without goods to carry on the trade. My supplies were sold immediately after they arrived, and as the Season's trade was over in August, I determined to return home to discuss matters with my Principals, with a view to obtaining more capital, or perhaps to overcome their prejudice against the sale of spirits.[20] I, therefore, arrived home in August without having advised my Employers or my wife of my intentions, each of whom were greatly surprised for different reasons at the course I had taken. I found my Employers obdurate so far as spirits were concerned, but my visit home resulted in their getting additional capital into the business, and having made other arrangements with them with regard to my personal remuneration, I left England again on the 24th September, after being six weeks at home, to resume my duties in West Africa. From this time, everything worked out successfully and satisfactorily, until November of the following year, when I again returned home, having established the business on a firm basis, and made an excellent profit while doing so.

I remained in the employ of this Firm for sixteen years, going to Bonny to take up their Agency as they required me. I was well treated, well paid, had complete control of the business in Africa, and always succeeded in making good profits for them, of which a proportion came to myself. If they had been satisfied to limit their operations to the business and its extension under my control, they would certainly have become and remained wealthy men. We found that our system of working the trade by steamers answered well, as compared with the old-fashioned way followed by other Merchants of sending sailing ships out with full cargoes, and keeping them waiting for months in the River until they were loaded, as in addition to our advantage of getting out fresh goods by each steamer, we also had the advantage of sending our Produce home by them, thus getting it to market, and the proceeds converted into the goods two or three times, while the other Merchants had theirs waiting until their ships arrived home, when the same process was again repeated. By this means the trade became revolutionised, and all of the Merchants in turn had to dispose of their sailing ships, and adopt the system inaugurated by us. As they were all large shipowners, making a profit out of their own carrying, this change was not effected without strenuous opposition from them, which culminated in a determined effort on the part of some of the leading Merchants to drive us out of the trade by making prices unprofitable. This policy utterly failed, as we were satisfied to do a moderate share of business on profitable terms, and having a very different class of goods to those which were held by our competitors, we were able to hold our own, and even make money, while they were playing into the hands of the Natives and losing it in thousands. In the latter part of 1868, when at home, I superintended the fitting out of a new hulk for Bonny called the 'Onward',[21] which subsequently became my home in Africa from that time until leaving it in 1881. I fitted her out in Africa for my own convenience, and to my own taste. She was a large roomy ship, and consequently I had everything most comfortable for myself and other white assistants, and as I was always most punctilious about discipline and cleanliness, my hulk, boats, and schooners, were always in apple-pie order, as well as being the 'pink of perfection'; in fact, I was considered a faddist as regards sanitation, and other matters of this kind, but as I realised the benefits to myself and staff by this expenditure of trouble, I was not much concerned about what my neighbours thought of me. For some years after commencing, Messrs. Irvine & Woodward were very prosperous, and extended their business from Bonny to New Calabar and Brass, the former being directly under my charge, and became a part of my agency, while over the Brass extension I exercised supervision and authority by Power of Attorney, without being responsible or interested in its working. As it was essentially a place which depended on the spirit trade, it was unsuccessful, and ultimately had to be given up. They (I. & W.) continued to extend their business into other parts of Africa, with the result that they made some very heavy losses, which necessitated them in 1875 compounding with their creditors, and with the assistance of my Native friends in Bonny, I was instrumental in enabling them to meet their liabilities and putting them so far as their African business was concerned, on a good footing again. Mr. Woodward at this juncture withdrew from the Firm, leaving Mr. Irvine to carry it on; he, however, turned his attention to more speculative ventures in Produce at home, through which he became involved, and in 1877 had to retire, his confidential clerk having the business and its contracts transferred to him, and at this time I was offered a partnership with Mr. Capper, who succeeded Mr. Irvine; there was, however, too much risk in this venture to suit me, and particularly that I should have but little control over the home business. I, therefore, entered into an Agreement with John Capper & Co. to serve them until 1880, when another change became necessary in consequence of the failure of Messrs. John Capper & Co. to meet their engagements through the losses made in the speculation above referred to. From 1877 and 1880 the African business under my charge had yielded duly large profits, all of which were required to make up the losses incurred at home, and which necessitated the sale of the business. In 1877 I had become associated in business, with the consent of my Employers, with Mr. John Holt,[22] and in conjunction with him we bought the business of Capper & Co., and in 1881 I became a Principal where I had so long worked as a servant. I went out again to Bonny early in that year, returning home towards the end of it, having made a most successful voyage, reorganised, and re-established the business on such a footing that it became unnecessary for me to go again. I entered fully into partnership with Mr. Holt, taking up my share of the work on this side, having attained the object I had been so long and steadily working for. Our partnership continued for nine years, and was successful, when an amalgamation of the principal Firms in the African trade took place, and became incorporated under the Act as a public Limited Company called the African Association, with whom I became a Manager, and remained with them for five years.[23] These five years were about the most anxious and unremunerative I had spent for a long time. There were so many different interests to assimilate, so many different characters to understand, besides such diversities of opinion to reconcile that from day to day and month to month there was perpetual dissension, not only between the Managers, but the Board themselves, that life was a continual worry, so much so indeed that I determined to disassociate myself from it, and ultimately did so.[24] I recognise now that in doing this I had not acted with the prudence I might have done, and in leaving the business under such circumstances I was jeopardising my interests and capital to people less capable of protecting them than I could be myself. The first few years of the African Association's existence were anything but successful, by pursuing a policy of open hostility to everyone in the trade not incorporated with them, and to such an extent was this carried on that everyone became dissatisfied, discontented, and desirous to find a scapegoat for their shortcomings and mistakes. Finding how difficult it was to work pleasantly in my surroundings I resigned my position as Manager, while retaining my seat on the Board, and as my wife was in poor health, I went with her to Egypt, and remained away six months. During this time the fatuous policy of the Association was continued. I had embarked the whole of my capital in this undertaking, and as things went from bad to worse I realised that some determined effort must be made if I was to be spared from having my savings lost, and perhaps having to make a new start in life. This was the position of things as I found them on my return from Egypt in 1895, when I immediately set up a strenuous opposition to the policy which was bringing our business in Africa to such a pass, and notwithstanding that this opposition was directed against my former partner, I ultimately succeeded in convincing my Co-Directors that our interest consisted in having it reserved with the result that in doing so we also removed the cause of it, as in 1896 Mr. Holt resigned his Chairmanship and seat on the Board, to the satisfaction of all concerned.[25]

The events just narrated took some two years to bring about, and fortunately during that time I had been successful in finding occupation for my spare time in managing the business of the Sierra Leone Coaling Co.[26] for my friend Sir Alfred Jones, to whom I have many reasons for being grateful, but particularly so in giving me this work to do at a time when it was most necessary for my health and peace of mind that I should have active employment.

With Mr. Holt's influence removed from the African Association, I found my services to that Company were more appreciated, and being Vice-Chairman, with Mr. Tunnicliffe holding the senior position, I was able to bring about a different condition of things for the Company and those of us who were so largely interested in it. With Mr. Holt's withdrawal from the Board we have enjoyed fourteen years of unexampled prosperity, with harmony at the Board, happiness and contentment among the Staff at home and abroad, together with good substantial dividends to the Shareholders, bonuses to the Staff, and commissions to our African Agents.

On the death of Mr. Tunnicliffe in 1900, I was invited by my colleagues to take his place; I could, however, only do justice to this by relinquishing my connection with the Sierra Leone Coaling Co., which I most reluctantly did, in order to become once again the servant of the African Association, under different circumstances to those which pre-existed, and had caused me so much trouble, annoyance, and anxiety. I was very sorry to give up my appointment with the Coaling Co., I was, however, reconciled to this by the knowledge that during the time it was under my direction I had re-organised that business, set it on a sound basis by converting losses into profits, and with the knowledge that Sir. Alfred Jones'[27] interests in the African Association as a shareholder were as important as those in the Coaling Co., besides which, our business relations being of the most cordial character, my taking the Chairmanship of the Association would enable me to work amicably with the Steamship Company, for our mutual benefit: it is satisfactory to know that these expectations have been fully realised, while at the same time increasing the kindly regard and good feeling which has so long existed between Sir Alfred and myself. I, therefore, became duly appointed as Chairman and consulting-Director of the African Association, which position I still hold at the time of my writing these memoirs.

In the foregoing pages I have thus traced out my business career from its commencement to date, and I may be pardoned in expressing myself proud of what I have attained to as the result of patient industry, hard work, persistency, combined with honesty, integrity of purpose, and an honourable life. I am not a wealthy man as compared with some of my contemporaries, but I can glory in the fact that I do not possess a single sovereign that should by right belong to someone else rather than to myself.

I now propose to place on record some of the incidents which have occurred during the time to which I have referred that may prove of greater interest as reading than the matter-of-fact record of my business life as given above.

Health is one of the matters that causes the greatest anxiety to anyone connected with West Africa, and I have no hesitation in saying, as the result of my own personal experience and reading, that it is one of the worst climates in the World, aggravated as it is by oft-recurring epidemics of a malignant type of a fever bad enough to be characterised and placed in the same category as plague, yellow fever, or such other scourges known to exist in tropical climates. I refer here to Yellow Fever, which I have been told by medical experts does not occur in West Africa; I think, however, there must be some mistake in this, as the cases that came under my own personal observation resembled in every detail the symptoms described in medical books as common to Yellow Fever.

When I was preparing to go out to Africa first, I remember seeing in the obituary columns of the daily paper published towards the end of 1862 a long list of deaths which had occurred in the delta of the Niger during an epidemic of this nature which had visited the district in the preceding months, and on discussing this with some of my friends who knew more of such climates than myself, I was given to understand that this was more or less the normal condition of things to be expected. Having consoled myself with the thought that I should have as good a chance as anyone else of getting through, if I exercised ordinary care, I was not deterred from going through with what I had begun. During my voyage out, and after I arrived in Bonny, I had ample opportunities of realising that even the worst reports were no exaggeration of the actual facts. During the previous Autumn there had been a most virulent epidemic, the consequences of which were given in the newspaper to which I have just referred, and as these epidemics often became recurrent on the change of Season after, it was expected to return in the early part of 1863, which I found to be the case, as on my arriving in New Calabar in March of that year there was scarcely a day that some poor fellow was not carried down to Snake Island Point for interment in his last home. There were several ships lying in the River with their crews on board, and the circumstances under which these men lived made them an easy prey to such a devastating scourge as was then prevalent. Consequently, it was not long before there were several ships without crews at all, with the incessant anxiety ever present with us as to who would be next. At this time I was stricken down with my first fever, which came on me like a flash of lightning, as without the least warning I was carried off to bed, where I lay for many days. I have no recollection of anything that occurred in the early stages of my sickness; I do, however, remember when returning health began to assert itself, finding myself lying on a wooden couch in the Cabin, or Dining Room as it was called, with a Krooman sitting on his haunches watching me by the light of a palm oil lamp, and with some kind of refreshment for my use. I also remember someone coming on board and, with the callousness that often influences people's minds on such occasions, asking if I was not dead yet! Fortunately, I recovered from this attack, and had to take my turn in nursing the two Carneys, who became stricken in the same way as I had been: they also recovered, and with returning rains, the epidemic passed away, leaving me with better prospects. In Bonny there had been the same influence at work, and many of the sailors who came out in the 'Iphigenia' paid the penalty, and added to the list of mortality during that time.

In the early part of 1865 there was another visitation, but of a less virulent type, as it occurred about the time Captain Macintosh came out to make his inspection. I was given to understand that this fact materially influenced his decision to return home and enjoy the wealth he had acquired by a long and industrious life, leaving me in charge of the business, to follow his example if I could. It was about this time that the Captain of the 'Iphigenia' died, besides several others of his crew. The next visitation of the kind was in 1873, when I was in Bonny, and brought more directly into contact with it, inasmuch as I felt the effect of it through having two of my Assistants carried off within a week of each other, after only a few hours illness. They were to me most valuable Assistants and able men, each of them only 28 years of age, with every prospect before them of long and useful lives. The term over which the epidemic lasted was only about six weeks, during which time some 17 out of 23 Europeans in responsible positions were called away: it was a most distressing time for everyone, indeed, it became questionable whether those of us in charge of responsibilities were called upon to take such risks as were confronting us for the mere sake of looking after money and protecting our employers' interests. There were some of my contemporaries, who, in face of such danger, deserted their posts, leaving subordinates to undertake the anxiety and duties occasioned by the loss of so many of my friends. I kept in good health, and notwithstanding that trade had been practically brought to a standstill, leaving us but little to do, I kept myself and others employed by finding work to distract our attention from our immediate surroundings. For six weeks or more the wind blew directly off the land, bringing with it a heavy yellow haze, opaque in its character, while the water was filled with phosphorescent light, quite unusual, and more abundant than I had ever seen before. With a returning sea breeze, these abnormal conditions of atmosphere passed away, and the ordinary conditions of life were resumed. There were no recurring circumstances of this nature the remainder of my residence in Africa, for which I had much reason to be thankful.

The Coast has a reputation among its residents for excesses, and while in many cases this may have been well merited, it was a strange circumstance, which impressed me greatly, that those who suffered most during these times were those who were most careful, moderate, and even abstemious men, with respect to the use of intoxicants. I never think of the foregoing circumstances without realising with thankfulness my own good fortune in being preserved where so many of my friends were taken. It is with some satisfaction, however, that I also recall to mind that these two young men of whom I have written were the only two persons who lost their lives from the effects of climate from the time of my having charge of them and exercising any influence on their actions or habits. Thus, during twenty-four years, from 1865 to 1889, only three deaths occurred in the Firms with which I was associated, two as related above, and one from the effects of intemperance.

I attribute this in a great measure, in the first place to the class of men selected, and in the second place to the regime and discipline to which they were subjected when coming under my control. I was always careful to give them the best advice, how to avoid the risks of climate, never unnecessarily exposing them to sun or other baneful climatic influences, where such could be avoided, giving them liberty to live their own lives, under certain restricted conditions, being methodical, systematic, temperate and regular in my own life as an example which they could follow. I never prohibited or attempted to control their use of intoxicants, as long as they knew how to make a proper use of them, and to this, together with inspiring in them a feeling of good-fellowship and confidence in and with myself, I attribute the result so satisfactory to them and myself, as regards health in Nigeria.

My recent remarks on the subject of health have been confined to the more serious results which followed epidemics rather than to ordinary sickness in Africa; the latter is, however, of such a nature that the greatest care should be given to everything which may in any way prevent disease, or cure it when affected.

After my first attack of fever referred to in my recent note I kept in good health, until I became so infected with Malaria while living on the Beach in New Calabar that I had to be removed, and was invalided home. My whole system must have been impregnated with poison from the stench arising from decaying vegetation in the bush and deposit on the beach that nothing but removal therefrom would remedy the disease.[28]

Mosquitoes, Sandflies, together with Mangrove Flies were a pestilence in themselves sufficient to produce fever or other sickness, even if other conditions had been more favourable. Some of the worst forms of sickness Europeans suffer from arise from skin diseases, which are contagious, and as Natives are seldom without such, it follows that unless segregation is observed in every relation of life, white men become infected with these distressing diseases, which are not so fatal as loathsome and distressing. A skin disease called 'Kraw Kraw' is one of the worst, being a form of ringworm that extends over the body in ever increasing circles, and which it is difficult to cure. Then, various forms of Eczema, arising from prickly heat, ulcers and sores from bites of insects while not actually fatal, produce sickness and fever that may become so. Bad water, lack of vegetables, and poor food, create dysentery, scrofula, and anaemic troubles, while fever and ague and other mild forms of fever are prevalent, and particularly so at the changes of the Seasons, which come on about March and September, the former month being the commencement of the rainy season, while the latter month is the closing of it. Having now referred to the question of health, generally, I can complete my own record of it by stating that during the remainder of my residence in Africa I suffered but little from the effects of the climate, with the exception of some of the minor troubles that affect residents of long standing. I was certainly most careful in my habits, and being abstemious and regular in my life, I escaped many troubles which others became subject to.

During the later portion of my time I made much shorter voyages, while from 1877 to 1881 I only remained six months on the Coast from March to September, being home or voyaging for the other six. I was, therefore, very favourably circumstanced under these exceptional conditions.

During the epidemic in 1873 I carefully avoided making any reference to the state of things then existing when writing to my wife, thinking it unnecessary to add to the anxieties she always experienced when I was in Africa, and as a reward for this consideration, I found one of my personal friends, who gloried in such details, had gone purposely to acquaint her with the particulars, which lost nothing at his hands through repetition. This was most unfortunate, and resulted in her anxieties being increased to a point of exaggeration which almost created the disaster it dreaded: there was no cable communication in those days to resort to for accelerating information, so that things occurring with us were only known at home after the effects of them had passed away.[29] I returned home soon after this, and remained for some months, when I again went to Bonny, to find that things had resumed their normal conditions, with the places of the absent ones filled up by others, who were taking the same risks, living the same lives, and going through the same daily routine.

One of the most painful and distressing of the circumstances in connection with my career in West Africa is the recollection that of the many persons whom I became acquainted with in my business there, so few of them now remain. I can count only about three who were contemporary with me in the early years of my life, and these are persons who were especially favoured by fortune in being successful in their early years, and able to become their own masters, and to regulate their own lives, while those who were less fortunate or less provident, looking upon their African connection as a means of livelihood only, have long since passed away, and joined the great majority. Where this applies to persons of mature years, who had performed their life's mission, there can be little cause for regret; I am now, however, referring more particularly to men who were even younger than myself as personal contemporaries who have long since paid the penalty of nature, notwithstanding that at the time I am referring to everything appeared in their favour, as compared with myself, and who under other conditions than those existing in West Africa might have been still enjoying the pleasures of life, under happy circumstances and surroundings.

I consider myself to have been singularly fortunate with those who were appointed to serve under me, as with only one or two exceptions each of them became persons of position and responsibility in the trade, while several of them commenced business for themselves, and succeeded in making a good living, with the advantage of doing so under more favourable circumstances than they could have done in England. The one or two exceptions were persons who were either unfit constitutionally for the climate, or realised early in their lives that their special vocation was not in connection with West Africa, or that their lack of enthusiasm in the palm oil trade would be a hindrance to their success in this particular direction. As compared with my more recent experience of Assistants going out to West Africa I had reason to congratulate myself on not having to send anyone home as incompetent or unable to perform their duties through intemperance, one of the most fruitful sources of failure with people who embarked in the West African trade.

While on the subject of intemperance, it may be well to recall some of my experiences connected with this, and while doing so I would desire to treat it very leniently, not from a wish to condone the vice, so much as to explain the many temptations that influence people living under the circumstances before related in West Africa. It may be all very well for those of us who are and have been more fortunately circumstanced to deal censoriously with those less favoured, for giving way to temptation, but when one knows the daily life and surroundings of young people, especially who go to Africa, it may well be a matter of surprise and gratification to know that even more do not succumb to the pernicious habits of which I am writing. From the detailed account given in the earlier pages of my memoirs of the duties and routine the young men were called upon to go through, can it be wondered at that they fall an easy prey to vices and temptations which surround them on every side? Agents as a rule in my time took little or no interest in their Assistants or their welfare, giving them but little comfort, and less recreation, while too often exhibiting towards them a harsh, arbitrary, and autocratic manner that often rendered them callous and indifferent to their own character and self-respect. In a community such as existed in Africa in my time, and, I presume, does so still, there was no moral restraint or refining influences existing of any kind to prevent a man going wrong; if he once got on the slippery path which led to this degradation, and it only too often happened that where a person, either as Agent or Assistant, shewed a tendency in this direction, he was encouraged to indulge rather than restrain it.

Some of the most promising careers and capable men have been wrecked through this unfortunate habit of personal indulgence, while many of those whom I regret as having passed away owed their premature death and commercial failure to their weakness in not being able to overcome temptation in this form. It is not my purpose here to recount the many instances of this nature that came under my own personal observation. I am only desirous of recording here the facts as I found them, and to give such excuses as may be advanced for palliating the excesses indulged in by those who paid the penalty with their lives, or impaired mental and physical health.

It fell to my lot early in my African career to become closely associated with men and women who were imbued with Missionary zeal, and who were making personal sacrifices for the spiritual welfare of the African race, and being the representative of a Firm whose

Senior Partner was closely identified with missionary labours in Africa, I was always in sympathy with them, and was able to render them valuable assistance in their work; this I did most gratefully, in recognition of the many kindnesses received from them under such circumstances as made a lasting impression on my mind. When I went to Old Calabar in 1864, it was customary for Agents and Assistants to attend worship at the Presbyterian Church each Sunday afternoon at Duke Town, where the Rev. Mr. Anderson officiated as resident minister. After service we were entertained to tea by the reverend gentleman and his wife, and in this way we enjoyed the comforts of home for a brief time, with the advantage of civilized life, not experienced during the week. We were also welcomed on similar occasions by a lady, who rejoiced in the sobriquet of 'Mammie' Sutherland, who lived in a house by herself on the Mission Hill close to the Church; a quiet homely spot, with all the refinements of such, in marked contrast to the noise and clamour that environed us during the week. This lady endeared herself to all of us by her willing aid and ready sympathy, and many a fever-stricken man had cause to be grateful to the tender nursing and loving care of a woman who had sacrificed so much to be of help to her fellow creatures requiring such treatment, while devoting her life and energies to converting heathens to Christianity. Some distance from Duke Town was another Mission Station, situated at Old Town, where a Mr. & Mrs. Edgerley resided, and on many occasions our walks led us in this direction, where we were hospitably entertained, and enjoyed the company of the Missionaries whose duties kept them there. Again, another Mission Station existed at Creektown, some seven or eight miles up the River, where a Mr. Goldie lived, and as I had frequently to visit this place on business, I never did so without calling at the Mission House, and holding converse with its occupants. I continued my acquaintance with these friends by correspondence during the whole of my residence in Africa, and have remained in touch with them, either personally or through friends, with whom I have been in closer association since remaining permanently in England.

When Bishop Crowther was appointed to his See on the Niger, I had the advantage of his early acquaintance, and therefore followed his work and progress with great interest, so much so that when he came to Bonny in 1869 to open up a School and Mission Station there, I was able to be of great help to him in the initial stages of his work. He became my guest on board the 'Onward', and it was on board this craft that the first Services were held for public worship in Bonny, as during the Bishop's stay with me, Divine Service was held each Sunday morning, to which many of my co-agents and native friends came. From this small beginning has grown the extension of mission work in Bonny, and the building of schools and churches which have been established there, and also extended to many other places in the Niger Delta, under Bishop Crowther's fostering care, which are now in a great measure self-supporting, and have been of great benefit to the Natives in teaching them the advantages of Christianity. How much this was necessary may be the more freely realised when I explain the condition of things as they were when I first arrived in Africa in 1863; before doing so, however, I would complete my recollections of Bishop Crowther, and my long associations with him and his family, who worked with him.

Bishop Crowther was born in the Niger Delta, and was rescued from slavery in the early years of his life by a British cruiser, who had captured the slave ship in which he, with some hundreds of others, was being deported to Cuba; she was taken into Sierra Leone, where they were released. Adji Crowther, as his name was, was put to school and prepared for the ministry, being ultimately appointed as Missionary Bishop to his own brethren in the Niger, among whom he worked for the remaining years of his life. He was a quiet, unassuming man, with good natural business abilities, common sense, enthusiasm in his work, and a most interesting convincing personality, which stood him in good stead when discussing and explaining the problems of Christianity to his heathen brethren; while showing due regard for their susceptibilities, he could always rely on his own experiences and knowledge of Native ways to exercise influence to guide them right, or to prevent them from going wrong.[30]

His son, Dandeson, became the head of the Mission at Bonny, who, together with his wife, has worked long in this field, identifying themselves with everything of advantage to the welfare of the Bonny people, while teaching their children to become useful members of the Church, as well as better traders and men, or women.

During Bishop Crowther's frequent stays with me he would amuse us greatly with recounting his experiences among the many different tribes he was brought into communication with in his travels up and down the Niger over which his authority extended. He was a typical negro, and would illustrate his tales by quaint comparisons and most inimitable gestures, which were most amusing, and to Natives thoroughly comprehensible. On his several visits to England he used frequently to stay with me, and was as interesting to my family and friends as to his native converts. With my children he was a special favourite; they were, however, somewhat shy, and found some difficulty in overcoming their prejudice and aversion to his black face and woolly hair. He was as simple as a child in everything connected with our home life, and would never go to bed without someone to put out the gas for him, and see him safely disposed for the night. He preached several times in churches with which we were connected, and always did so in a most interesting and effective way, which resulted in good collections for the work for which he was pleading.

I acted as his Agent in Bonny, while my firm did so at home, becoming in this way identified with his mission work in a practical way, and at the same time being of some assistance in enabling him to get his work and materials on the best terms, for which he was always grateful.

The Europeans in Bonny identified themselves particularly in building a church there for the use of themselves and employees, which was well attended by both Europeans and Natives, and still stands as a memorial to those who assisted to build it; many of them I regret to say have only this left to remember them by.

In the foregoing remarks with reference to Missions, I have avoided making any distinction between one denomination and another, as they were all equally zealous in their work, and solicitous for the spiritual welfare of the people, and while disappointment is expressed by some persons of anti-missionary tendencies, I can bear testimony to the beneficial changes brought about through these influences in persons with whom I was brought into immediate contact. Very few, if any, of the Missionaries I have named in the preceding pages are now alive; indeed, some of them were old men and women when I first knew them, having laboured in the mission field for many years before I became acquainted with them. They have, however, left pleasing recollections in my mind of their devotion to duty under circumstances which called for great personal sacrifices, and I am sure they will be remembered gratefully among those with whom they laboured for so long. They were certainly instrumental in saving many lives from the heathen practices prevalent in my day, and if this were their only record of usefulness, it would be more than sufficient to cover any deficiency that may be felt in their want of success to convert their pupils to permanent Christianity, and to excuse the numerous instances of backsliding on the part of some of their own followers, which resulted from living under such conditions as they had to do among heathen and barbarous people. With an organised system of administration as now exists, progress has been much more rapid since I left the Coast, as their efforts are now supplemented by the assistance of the Government in establishing schools for elementary, technical, and advanced education, to whom grants are made out of revenue for this purpose.

In the early years of St. Clement's Church, Native converts became members of the congregation, and as sterling currency was not then established, the offertory was of a varied description, consisting of all kinds of trade goods, obtained by the Natives in exchange by barter for their Produce. The collecting boxes were necessarily large, to contain these gifts, which comprised native currency (Manillas),[31] cotton cloths, heads of tobacco, articles of enamelware, and other things too numerous to mention. These were of course again exchanged for things required by the Mission, and were equally as valuable as money.

When I first arrived in Bonny, 'Ju Juism', or fetish worship, was the only form of religion, if it may be so called, which existed; the sacred emblem in this place was a huge reptile of the lizard species, known as an 'Iguana', which was under the special care of the Ju Ju priests, and was held free from molestation under the most severely enacted penalties; in the case of a Native, the punishment was death, while if a white man injured or destroyed one of them, a fine of £500 was inflicted on him; even this payment did not absolve him from the consequences of such an act, as Natives would not trade with anyone who had so transgressed their law, and in the case of a trader he would be blackballed, and no-one would have dealings with him. One instance of this was on record; it, however, did not occur in my time, as traders knowing the penalty took care to avoid it. These Iguanas were most repulsive-looking reptiles, but perfectly harmless, and on the several occasions I saw them crawling about the roads and pathways leading to the town, I gave them a wide berth; they were, however, fed by the natives, who in doing so supposed they were propitiating a god, who could do them injury or good, as it desired.

In Brass, their fetish god was a boa constrictor, which was held sacred in the same degree by them in Brass as the Iguana in Bonny, and, notwithstanding that a boa was more harmful than the Iguana, no-one was allowed to touch or remove it, even for self-protection, without incurring similar penalties to those imposed in Bonny. As many of the traders in Brass lived in houses on shore, it was not an uncommon thing to have a visit from one of these predatory reptiles, who would find its way into the house, while the Kroomen and everyone else rushed out. The services of the Ju Ju men were then called in, who would after a time succeed in getting the premises clear of their unwelcome visitor.

In all the Rivers of the Delta it was customary to make human sacrifices for all kinds of purposes, all of which were regulated and carried out by the 'Ju Ju' men, and it was a matter of frequent occurrence for us to hear that such sacrifices had been made on what was known as 'Execution Point', a jutting promontory just at the junction of the Bonny Creek with the Bonny River. The power of life and death was in the hands of the Native Chiefs, as the people belonging to their houses were slaves brought from the interior of the Eboe country and belonged to them absolutely.[32] Persons were, therefore, adjudged by him, while his Ju Ju men would carry out the penalty. Witchcraft and trial by ordeal were resorted to for offences committed against each other, the Ju Ju men being the arbiters on such occasions, and as they held this power over the people, they were dreaded, and used their power for personal benefit or revenge, as their feelings dictated. There is no question that, at the time I am writing of, cannibalism was a common practice, as the Native Chiefs would speak openly of it, and make the slaves take part in these orgies with prisoners of war.

The Bonny Ju Ju House was one of the sights of the place, filled as it was with skulls and bones of the human body. I saw this place frequently, and was also living in Bonny when it was demolished through the influences of Bishop Crowther and his ministers, the Natives having become ashamed of it as evidence of their rude, barbarous days. About this time also the Iguana was degraded, and lost sight of. Sacrifices were made in both Bonny and New Calabar to the god of the Bar. This was in this form: an albino negress, that is, a woman with pink eyes, light red hair, and in fact all the peculiarities of an albino as we know them, the progeny of black parents, was bought for the purpose; she would be brought down to the town, where everyone knew she was to be sacrificed, allowed to go into any house for rest or food until the time came for her execution, when she would be taken in a canoe to the mouth of the River, tied hands and feet, then broken across the beams of the canoe and thrown into the water, to become food for sharks, which infested the place. In this way, the Natives believed they propitiated the god of the Bar, which would allow ships a safe passage into the River, and a good trade result therefrom. These and other practices were of frequent occurrence, and notwithstanding that strong remonstrances were made against them by the Europeans, they were continued for many years, either openly or in secret, until through missionary influences they were ultimately abandoned.

The custom of sacrificing twins was also practised in both Bonny and Old Calabar, for many years. It has now become a thing of the past so far as an open acknowledgment of anything of this kind is concerned; at the same time it is a very remarkable fact that there are very few instances of double births recorded, so that it may be a merciful interposition of Providence in preventing such occurrences, or we are forced to the belief that when they occur, the children are disposed of at birth, without going through the ordinary custom such as was known to us. Their reason for disposing of twin children was not to reduce the population, but because it was abhorrent to them that a woman should bear more than one child at a time: they would speak of such an occurrence with the greatest contempt, and compare women who were so unfortunate to lower classed animals, such as pigs, dogs, or cats, and to be treated accordingly, with their progeny also.

Polygamy was a duly recognised institution amongst them, some of the Chiefs having a great many wives; in fact, this was one way of investing their surplus capital, as they were bought when young as slaves, and always remained so; marriage in the sense of which I am writing gave the wives no status, and on the death of a Chief some of them were sacrificed, while others were apportioned as ordinary goods and chattels amongst his successors, who were persons occupying a prominent position in his household, and not necessarily his own children or in any way related to him. In Bonny and New Calabar a woman having borne a child was set aside for 7 years, the idea being that she should devote her attention exclusively to it until grown up, and able to look after itself. I would not like to say that this was rigorously adhered to, and particularly with those wives who were considered favourites, but I am only referring to what was admittedly a general custom, but no doubt disregarded where desire would lead them in a different direction and no restraining influence or law to prevent it.

In connection with Ju Juism and Ju Ju practices, it was customary to have certain days set apart for these rites, and when these occurred, the Ju Ju Chiefs held full power and perpetrated outrages of a demoniacal character upon people whom they found at large in the pathways and roads of the town. These men were invested with power, which they exercised as a means of keeping slaves in subjection to their masters, under the superstitious fear that everything they did became known to their masters, who took summary measures to control or subjugate anyone of a rebellious nature. In Old Calabar they had a secret society called 'Egbo', which was a most potent factor in the same direction as Ju Juism, in addition to which it invested its members with special powers in respect to property, and was a kind of secret tribunal for the punishment of offences, for exacting payments of debts, and other purposes. Some of the white traders purchased these rights for large sums of money, and found them useful in collecting debts, in Bonny. Native law would allow a white man to seize the property of A for B's debts; this was known as 'chopping Oil', the process being to send a boat in charge of a white man to seize a canoe of Oil passing up or down the River, and to forcibly take possession, irrespective of to whom it belonged, the owner of the Produce being given an order on the actual debtor for what had been seized, and which he could exact or claim to have returned to him by Native law. This was, however, such a fruitful source of trouble as between one Chief and another that the British Government declared it to be illegal, and it was consequently discontinued about the time of my leaving Africa. Personally, it was never necessary for me to have recourse to this practice, as I did not give large credits to those except upon whose honesty and integrity I could rely for payment. I had, however, on one occasion to avail myself of this law to obtain payment from a man who could not be influenced by reason or argument to pay his debts. I, therefore, had recourse to strategy, combined with this right of Native Law. I had been too confiding in allowing George Pepple (who was then King of Bonny, and the same young man who had been a passenger in the 'Iphigenia') to remain in my debt for a considerable amount, and having given him the customary notice that I desired a settlement of all outstandings before leaving for home, I waited for some time with considerable patience, expecting payment; finding, however, that he took no notice of my repeated importunities, I gave him a final warning some few days before I had arranged to leave, that if he did not pay I would make an example of him. He disregarded this warning, as he had done all previous ones, and I was left to carry out my plan, or go away without being paid, which I had no intention of doing. It came to the final day for my departure, and having settled with most of my Native friends, I had held over the payment of some of my debts to Natives to an amount in excess of what was due to me from George Rex of Bonny; when my friends came I explained the position to them, and said I would hold their goods as security for their King's debt to me. I had purposely arranged to have a dozen creditors to cover the one debtor, and offered to give them orders or bills on George Rex in favour of themselves. They immediately jumped into their canoes, and in less than two hours my hesitating debtor was pleading for me to exercise clemency and he would pay me. I was equally obdurate as he had been, and my debt being guaranteed to me by a more substantial man, I was satisfied with this, and the humiliation I had caused him in having to appeal to one of his own Chiefs to release him from his prosecutor. It speaks well for the integrity of the people with whom I had traded that I am able to say I did not make a bad debt during the whole of my trading in Bonny and New Calabar that could not be covered by a £10/-/- note, and this among people and in a country where lawyers and legal processes were unknown. I was careful to whom I gave credit, and very often found myself in debt to Native Chiefs for very large amounts for Produce received in anticipation of goods to arrive, and notwithstanding that the Natives had no system of book-keeping themselves, depending wholly on the correctness of the white man's account, which included many items to debit and credit, I never had any items disputed by them, or entry disclaimed. While speaking of book-keeping, it is almost unnecessary to say that among such a varied class as African Agents came from, there were many systems of keeping books and accounts not generally recognised among auditors. One illiterate man had a system of his own for keeping a record of his transactions with Natives by placing a token in one box when he received a puncheon of Oil from a Native, and another in a second box when he paid for it; the two being equal balanced the account. To ascertain his disbursements he counted what he commenced trading with, and added anything received afterwards, while deducting what remained gave the cost of the Produce received, without worrying to account for intromissions, or give details of each transaction; a system which produced the same result as more accurate book-keeping, but scarcely with the same satisfaction. This was the process by which the man I was first under in New Calabar used to render his accounts, being incapable of doing them on any more systemised plan, but as it led to a violent dispute between himself and his Senior Agent when going home, I have no doubt he then realised it would have been more to his personal interest to have taken more trouble over them.

During my trading life in Africa, many incidents occurred of a more or less exciting character, in which I took part, and which have made a lasting impression on my memory. These arose in a great measure from accidents or from the semi-civilized life we led, together with the consequences of a too free indulgence in the use of intoxicants on the part of the men who were employed in the business, and as these form part of my experiences, they may be interesting to those for whom these reminiscences are being written, and in this belief I am placing them on record in the order in which they occurred.

The earliest incident I have recollection of was that an expedition had been arranged to go to the mouth of the Bonny River, to replace some of the buoys that had drifted away from position, and had to be re-moored, to mark the intricate channel for navigation. Each master of the sailing ships in harbour took down a boat with seamen's tackle and other things required for the purpose. The master of the 'Iphigenia', being in charge of a boat from this ship, had taken with him the second mate (Myers), with whom, unfortunately, some dispute arose as to the manner in which the work should be done; Captain Chinn, being a most violent-tempered man, supplemented his arguments by the use of a boathook, the pointed end of which he drove into his mate's hand, who had held it up to protect his head from the blow aimed at it. The man arrived on board exhausted from loss of blood, and was a long time before recovering therefrom. There were no Courts to appeal to; otherwise, Captain Chinn would have found himself in prison for attempted manslaughter; as it was, he was not punished, otherwise than by the fear impressed on him that the man might die, and himself be hanged as his murderer.

My next experience was in having to go down to the mouth of the River to give some instructions to a party who had been sent to give assistance to a ship in distress. One of our ships called the 'Clan Macgregor'[33] while entering the River had been wrecked on the Bar, and driven ashore at Breaker Island. Myers and a boat's crew had been sent down to render assistance, and to salve the cargo if possible. They had left during the afternoon, and I was sent to give them other information, having to start about eight o'clock at night, pitch dark, and raining in torrents, without much knowledge of where I had to go, or how to get there. The distance was about seven miles from the shipping, and after pulling or drifting, I ultimately arrived there at daybreak, to find them all helplessly drunk and unable to do anything at all in consequence. I, however, delivered my message to the most sober of them, and returned as fast as I could to the Hulk. By this time, knowledge of the wreck had come to the Natives, who were getting there as fast as their canoes could take them, with the prospect of loot lending wings to their efforts. The ship was a large one, laden with a general trading cargo, from which they obtained very valuable booty. A part of her cargo consisted of Rum, which had been washed on shore, and proved too great a temptation for the boat's crew I was sent down to find, as some of the barrels of spirits had drifted up to them, and they had regaled themselves, with the results recorded. It is a most unfortunate circumstance that many of the scenes arose from the same cause, as it was not an unusual sight to see the coopers and carpenters rampaging about the decks of the hulk in a state of maddened intoxication, armed with weapons of some kind, and intent on wreaking vengeance for some imaginary wrong on someone, or fighting among themselves like madmen. A carpenter was under such influence on one occasion, and rushing about with a broad axe, seeking the Agent, who was safe from such molestation in a locked room; the mate and I had to deal with him under these conditions, and it required a good deal of moral suasion or physical courage to control men afflicted with this kind of mania.

As Chairman of the Court of Equity (which position I came to occupy very frequently in consequence of my being a more permanent resident than other Agents) I was repeatedly called on to settle disputes which arose between employer and employees, and had to try persons for minor offences such as thefts, insubordination, as also to take primary evidence in matters of a more serious nature, for submission to the Consular Court, from whom the authority to act as quasi-judge was obtained. While acting in this capacity I had to investigate many such cases, which invariably originated from the abuse of intoxicants. On one occasion I was called on to assist in quelling a mutiny which occurred on a ship lying in the River, the crew having become unmanageable. On going on board, I found most of the men under the influence of drink, but not sufficiently turbulent to call for any drastic measures to bring them to reason. The Captain, with an 'Americanised' doctor, was evidently apprehensive that some mischief would result from the violence of the crew; the doctor, being armed with a revolver, was walking about with it in his hand: when I got on board to enquire into the matter, and on asking for explanations of the cause of the tumult, this gentleman waxed valiant, and appeared to be spoiling for a fight, threatening what he would do, at the same time flourishing his revolver to show that he had the means of doing what he threatened, when one of the men walked up to him, and with the remark that there was no need for such things as pistols, took it out of his hand and threw it overboard, the doctor looked very simple as he did so: the matter was soon settled after this, without much trouble, and certainly without any such dire consequences as might have resulted had he been foolish enough to use his pistol as he intended, if his courage had not failed him in support of his boastfulness.

Early in 1867 I had another experience of fire, as one of the large hulks lying up towards the top of the River took fire, and was soon a mass of flames. She had a large cargo of inflammable materials on board, including Rum and Powder; it was, therefore, not long before she blew up with a terrific explosion, but as there was a strong sea breeze blowing, there was fortunately no loss beyond the ship herself, and another one belonging to the same Firm, which was lying as a wreck on the beach.

At this date there used to be sometimes as many as twenty to thirty ships and hulks lying in the Bonny River at one time, as it was then the principal loading port for both Bonny and New Calabar. There was consequently plenty of activity and business life going on from morning to night. There was only one mail per month, which arrived about the 24th of the month, and remained in the River for about ten days, the other ports in the Delta being served by a branch steamer from Bonny called the 'Retriever',[34] then in charge of my old friend Captain Davis, who ultimately became the commodore of the African fleet, and was a most intimate friend of mine during the whole of my African life, and long after my return home from Africa. I remember being on board this branch boat on one occasion, having been in charge of some goods being shipped to Old Calabar: on going for my receipt I found one of the terrors of the River, named Fred Grant, in the saloon, drunk and quarrelsome to a degree; he invited me to drink with him, which I was about to do, taking as much liquor as I required; this, however, did not satisfy him, and he was on the point of forcing me to take more by threatening me with the bottle when old Davis arrived on the scene and stopped him. He was a madman, and ultimately ended his life in an asylum, after commiting such depredations in England as necessitated his being placed under control. This is only another instance of the lawless life lived in the Rivers at that time.

In 1869 an event occurred which has had such far-reaching effects that Bonny is now one of the least important Rivers in West Africa, whereas formerly it was the first. Without going too deeply into the history of the Bonny people, it may be well to give a brief sketch of them as they existed in the early years of the seventies, when I first came to have some knowledge of them.

King Pepple was then the acknowledged King of the whole of Bonny, and was at the same time head of what was known as the Manilla Pepple House, consisting of some of the most powerful and influential chiefs resident in Bonny. There was a rival House called Annie Pepple, equally powerful and influential as that of Manilla, some of whose ancestors had formerly filled the throne, but who had been deposed therefrom by the reigning power. There was always rivalry of a most intense kind between these Houses, and frequent quarrels, resulting in bloodshed and loss of life, became consequent on the antagonism which existed between the two people. In addition to these, there were several other minor Houses, who were considered to occupy independent neutral positions, and were consequently expected to act as intermediaries or arbitors in all matters of public interest or dispute between the rival Houses. During the life of old King Pepple this position was maintained, as he was powerful-minded, as well as an autocrat, making but short work of anyone opposed to his policy or rule. When his son George (of whom I have previously written) 'ascended the throne of his fathers', as he would grandiloquently describe the article of furniture used for this purpose, he became a mere puppet in the hands of his elder subjects, such as Oko Jumbo, Captain Hart, Manilla Pepple, and others, who used their power over him to foment discord against the house of

Annie Pepple. The head of this house was a most clever and astute man named 'Ja Ja', who was formerly a slave, but became the principal Chief by the election of the people belonging to his own master. Ja Ja was a most successful man as a trader, increasing the importance and wealth of the house which he governed to such a degree that he had become a standing menace to the monarch then occupying the throne. His wealth and influence had been long used in absorbing the independent houses, who were relied on as being neutral, by lending them money, acquiring their slaves, as well as by hypothecation of their trading goods and properties. Things were brought to a climax in 1869 by the Manilla Pepple people presenting an ultimatum to Ja Ja and his house, the refusal of which meant civil war. Each of them had long been preparing themselves for this event, and the Europeans were not surprised to receive notice that War had been declared between the two houses, and a notification that all the hulks and ships lying opposite the town and in a direct line of fire of the guns trained against the Ja Ja houses should be removed lest injury should result to them and their crews. Meetings of the white men were held to try and stop such action, but without avail, and as there was no prospect of getting assistance or protection from the Commodore of the Station, things had to take their course. The ships were removed out of the way, and a fair field given to the belligerents for a whole day in September. The guns were firing, houses burning, and the horrors of war were indulged in to their hearts' content. Ja Ja and his supporters were defeated; he and the whole of his house were driven to bay, and ultimately retreated to a place some miles up the creek, which he had prepared and fortified as a harbour of refuge. The victory, so far, rested with the Manilla Pepple people, who remained satisfied for a time with having driven the rebel out of their town and sight. Hundreds of lives were lost, and for some days after bodies were seen floating up or down the River with the tide, some of them disembowelled or otherwise mutilated. The usual custom was observed of eating the prisoners taken in war, and for some days these cannibalistic orgies were indulged in, until the victors became satiated, and returned to reason, to consider the consequences of their outbreak. Urgent messages had been sent to the Consul at Fernando Po, asking him to come to the protection of the lives and properties of the Europeans, as it was feared that the victors would not satisfy themselves by driving Ja Ja away, but might possibly be led to loot the factories, and perhaps destroy life in so doing. The Consul came with a Man of War, prepared to act as mediator between the two Houses, but Ja Ja had in the meantime withdrawn from Minima, his retreat, and made his escape to a neighbouring River called Opobo, where he established himself at the point of a creek commanding the exit and entrance to all the markets to which the Bonny men traded. Having secured this coign of vantage, or Thermopylae, he was complete master of the situation, and in a position to control the traffic between Bonny and the stations above him. Having command of the markets, he confiscated all the property belonging to them, and having established himself at Opobo, some of his European friends who had assisted him in his flight from Bonny now still further assisted him by opening up trading stations in Opobo,[35] in which place he finally became permanently established and was made King. From this time, Bonny gradually derogated to a place of minor importance, the younger generation of the Manilla Pepple House being less enterprising than their fathers, and being satisfied to continue trading in such places as were allotted to them by the British Government, when terms of peace were finally arranged between them. Ja Ja governed Opobo with a strong hand: he came into conflict with the British Government some years later, and was exiled to one of the West India Islands, where he died; he was, however, held in such high esteem by his subjects that they petitioned the British Government to allow his remains to be returned to Opobo, which they did, and a monument has now been erected to his memory as a wise and beneficent ruler.

In the same year, 1869, while we were in the throes of these troubles between the Bonnymen, I went on board one of the steamers lying alongside a hulk ready to leave for home, to post my letters, and while talking with the Captain in the cabin, a loud report was heard in the forward part of the vessel, where they were working with gunpowder, and it was feared that something had occurred there, and in a few moments all was confusion. Native sailors jumped overboard, while men ran about in all directions, and I with the rest got into my boat; some time elapsed before we were assured that everything was right. I had finished my business, and was getting away, when another explosion was heard, and the same consequences followed, everybody stampeding and going for safety. I was some distance away when I saw my friend George Watts[36] yelling frantically for me to come back to take him from his hulk, and save him. I then had two of his assistants in the boat with me, and while hesitating what to do I saw him make as though he would throw himself into the water, which fortunately I prevented him doing by making haste to his rescue; on getting alongside, he was again reassured, as they had found the cause of the explosions to be due to one of the crew going down into a close room where paraffin was stored, and the heat having generated gas, an explosion occurred each time a lamp was taken into the room: the cause having been ascertained, the remedy was soon applied, and anxieties removed. For about two hours we were in such a state of tension that we did not know what might happen. I took Mr. Watts, Gilbertson, and Gillies away with me, and so far as the two former are concerned, the friendship beginning with this incident and those arising out of the Bonny War has lasted from then to the present day, without the slightest intermission to this relationship. I have but few other personal incidents to refer to as having occurred during my life in Africa which would be of much interest, except to recount an adventure on board a steamer in which I had taken passage to St. Paul de Loanda in 1873. I had as a fellow-passenger on this occasion an American who was sent out to represent a New York Firm, and as we both occupied the same cabin, I saw a great deal of him for some days; he appeared all right and companionable, but after this began to show signs of intemperance, and on going into my room, I found him seated on the edge of the settee nursing a pistol, and I then found he was in a most dangerous state of mind, bordering on D.T.'s, and, like men in such a state, he was filled with illusions. How I managed to get the pistol away from him I can scarcely think, seeing it was such a palpable device to get possession of it. I merely said that it was not properly cocked, and volunteered to show him where it was wrong, when, with the simplicity of a child, he handed it to me, and the positions were reversed. He was placed under restraint, and I was no longer troubled with his hallucinations and threatenings. Yet another instance of this kind was where I was called on by a brother trader to investigate a charge of theft which he preferred against his Kroomen of a systematic theft of Palm Oil from the casks on his deck. Not knowing there was anything the matter with the man, I listened to the circumstantial report he made to me of these depredations, and having heard them, I went down on deck to investigate the matter; I there found no confirmation of the evidence given, and on going to the side, was told by the Kroomen what was the cause of his illusions. I dealt with it in a semi-judicial way, allowing the man to suppose I had been convinced of the charge, and, promising to have it formally dealt with, left him. I wrote to his brother, who was some sixteen miles away, giving him particulars of the case, and asking him to come at once to the rescue; he was unfortunately too late, as twenty-four hours after his brother was carried down to Rough Corner, the impromptu cemetery of so many lives which had been lost from the same cause. It is a very distressing record, and such as to leave a very lasting impression on one's mind, and becomes particularly so to me when remembering the many of my countrymen whose bones are resting there in unhallowed ground, without anything to mark their resting-place, except wooden crosses with names painted thereon, which would only withstand the sun and rain for a very short space of time. A funeral cortege was a rude coffin covered by the British Ensign placed in a boat towed by another, with a procession of boats following in slow time down the River for six miles, a hasty funeral service read by some personal friend, the coffin lowered only some two or three feet below the surface, and hastily covered, when the sails would be spread to a fresh westerly breeze, and everyone eager to get back to their daily life, with the memory only of the lost one as a memorial of a lost friend.

Occupying the position of Chairman of the Court of Equity in Bonny frequently brought me into contact and correspondence with many of the Consuls and other Government Officials who exercised authority in the administration of affairs in the Bights of Benin and Biafra. In this way I became acquainted with Frank Wilson, who acted as deputy Consul for a time with Mr. Hartley, who was duly appointed Consul; his career, however, was a very short and inglorious one, as he soon fell a victim to the temptations of the climate and paid the penalty of his weakness. Consul Livingstone, the brother of David Livingstone the traveller, performed the duties of this office for a long time, and had much to do in the settlement which was ultimately arrived at between the belligerents referred to on the subject of the Bonny War; he was frequently my guest, and at times would be a most interesting as well as amusing companion; he had travelled much, and had his mind stored with much that was interesting; his unfortunate failing was a vitriolic temper, which at times was uncontrollable, and often got him into serious trouble; it was in consequence of this that he was recalled, and died on his way home in 1873 on board one of the African steamers, which was infested with Yellow Fever. The mortality during the voyage was of such a nature that some thirteen or fifteen persons died from the time of leaving Bonny to her arrival in Liverpool. His deputy was a gentleman named David Hopkins, who had been engaged in commerce as a trader. He was, however, quite unsuccessful in this capacity, and was glad enough to change it for the easier duties of an official life. This gentleman was for a long time one of my best friends; he had been a soldier in his young days, having an appointment in the Cape Rifles, was a splendid shot, and had been the Captain of an Irish team of marksmen in some international competition, which had carried off the trophy for the year; a most genial and witty companion, full of fun, as most Irishmen are, and a 'bon camarade' with everyone; this characteristic was unfortunately his undoing, as he was out at all hours of the night, and contracted habits which brought him to an early grave; one of the brightest and most cheery men I ever met, and it was with a sad and sorrowful heart that I followed him to his last home at Rough Corner, and returned to his grief-stricken wife to tell her that the last rites of the Church had been read over him, and that he was at peace; she, poor woman, had used every effort to cure him of his besetting weakness, unavailingly, and returned home in the same steamer as myself to rejoin her family, whom she had left behind to follow the fortunes of her husband in a semi-civilised country like Africa. I have never seen the lady since we were fellow-passengers homeward in 1879, but it is most gratifying to know that her family have all turned out well; one of her sons as an artist attained considerable distinction in his profession, while another is holding a higher position in the British Navy. Succeeding to this gentleman came Consul Hewitt, of whom I saw a great deal, but without its being of any great advantage to either of us; he had at some time of his life been a schoolmaster, and was unfortunate in being unable to divest himself of his former associations, with the consequence that he always wanted to be tutoring or lecturing someone who was opposed to such treatment, and who was equally disposed to look on his pedantry as objectionable: during the time he officiated as Consul, changes were proposed in the method of administrating the River District which were ultimately effected, with his assistance, but other hands were entrusted with these changes, as they occurred, however, after I left Africa I do not intend to deal with them here. In the course of time Consul Hewitt retired from his position, and the Consular Service he did not long survive, the climate having made such inroads on his constitution that, notwithstanding the best advice in London, he passed over to the great majority. During one of his temporary absences from his post, his duties were undertaken by a Doctor McKellar, who while being a most rigid teetotaller, was even more erratic or peculiar than some of his predecessors, who were quite the opposite in this respect. It was another instance of clothing an Official in a little brief authority, or further example of putting a beggar on horseback and his riding to perdition; as he lived among us and we saw him daily, we had too much Consul and too little medical attention to suit us, and I don't think many of us put ourselves much out of the way to conciliate or assist him.

After my leaving Africa, the changes in administration previously referred to were brought about, and were no doubt accelerated by the discontent engendered by the Government giving to the Niger Company a Royal Charter,[37] under which instrument they became an administrative body, as well as a trading company, to which the River Merchants were bitterly opposed as prejudicial to their individual interests, and in consequence the British Government established a protectorate over the part of Nigeria not governed by the Niger Company, inaugurated an administration, placed it under the control of a High Commissioner, and finally, after rescinding the Niger Company's Charter,[38] incorporated the whole territory under one administration, now known as Southern Nigeria, Sir Claude McDonald being the first, while Sir Ralph Moor succeeded him as second, with Sir Walter Egerton as present High Commissioner.

It will be seen that from 1863 to 1910 the country of which I am writing has passed from a condition of barbarism and chaos to a settled form of government, with improvements in the condition of Natives, and more security to life and property, without disturbing the trade, or without producing any revolution except of a peaceful and beneficial nature to all concerned.

During the years I passed in West Africa the insecurity to life and property was never anything more to me than of a merely nominal character so far as Natives were concerned, as I cannot call to mind any instance where either the one or the other was endangered except that it had been provoked by wrongdoing or indiscretions on the part of those who suffered the consequences arising from such folly. I never found it necessary to have recourse to arms, or indeed to any other method of protection than provided with by nature. My recollections of Bonny men, among whom I lived so long, are therefore pleasing ones, and I acknowledge a debt of gratitude to them for kindly interest and assistance repeatedly given to enable me to attain the prosperity I now enjoy.

Bonny being the principal port of call for steamers, and one of the duties of the Chairman of the Court of Equity being to act as Post-master, I had to visit them on their arrival to distribute the letters to whom addressed; in this way I became acquainted with everyone passing to and from other places outside Bonny, so that my circle was a large one, and I had opportunities of meeting notabilities who were journeying out or home. In this way I knew Captain Cameron, who arrived at St. Paul de Loanda, having crossed Africa from the East, H.M. Stanley on one of his journeys to or from the Congo, and Captain Burton, who was known as one of the greatest travellers of the world. Sometimes there would be white lady passengers, who were accompanying their husbands, but these were rare indeed, as very few white women ventured beyond Sierra Leone or the Gold Coast Colonies; two or three were bold enough to brave the life, among them being Mrs. Hopkins, Mrs. James Hemingway, and one or two others, whose husbands were masters of sailing ships; the isolated lives and other inconveniences, such as poor food and uncomfortable quarters, were generally a sufficient reason for their making their visits as short as possible. An amusing incident occurred on one occasion when one of these ladies was present at a breakfast given by an Agent, when a principal Chief of Bonny was one of the guests; he was answering a question put by the host as to the number of wives he had, and his reason for having so many; without going too much into detail as to the reasons given, one of them was that if a wife offended him he could flog her; this so worked on the feelings of the English woman present that she indignantly asked the Chief if he ever flogged women; on his replying in the affirmative, she got up from her seat, and walking over to the man said, 'So you flog women do you?' and gave him a smack first on one side of his face then on the other, whereon the Chief jumped up and fled ignominiously down the companion ladder into his canoe, cursing the lady in the choicest Bonny language he could find to express himself in, and I may here parenthetically remark that from my knowledge of the Bonny language it has the most comprehensive vocabulary of a vituperative, invective, and sulphurous nature that I am acquainted with: he declared he would bring one of his wives to resent the insult put on him, it being a law with them that an insult or offence can only be expunged by a process of retaliation similar to the insult received, and consequently one of his wives would treat her husband as she had treated him. Nothing more was heard of it, as I have no doubt the host squared it by some more material compensation than revenge.

The Man of War on the Station used occasionally to come in on a visit to us, and when they did so it was again my duty as Chairman to pay a visit of courtesy to the Senior Officer to ascertain the object of his visit, and to arrange for any business interviews or meetings he desired with the Native Kings, Chiefs, or Supercargoes; in this way I met Commodores Wilmot, Domville, and Hewitt, besides other Officers of minor rank who attended the Consul on his periodical visits.[39] On these occasions it was customary to invite the Officers to dinner, and the store rooms were ransacked to provide the best obtainable food, requisition being made on the poultry yard of our brother agents to make up a dinner suitable for our guests. One cannot do much in the way of providing sumptuous repasts in a country that only furnishes scraggy goats for mutton, attenuated fowls and ducks for poultry, and a chef whose ambition does not rise beyond rice puddings, pancakes and such food as would be considered delicacies by persons accustomed to salt beef and yams as ordinary food; still, the best was done, and as it was accompanied by a hearty welcome, with plenty of fluid, our guests would not be too critical even if it did not come up to their expectations, or their own mess.

When it was necessary to have meetings with the Kings and Chiefs, these were sometimes held on board the Chairman's hulk, or on board the Man of War, depending as it did on the matter to be discussed, Consular Courts being held on board the Man of War, while trade matters were relegated to the Court of Equity. The King and his Chiefs would avail themselves of these opportunities to come out in their war canoes, and parade around the cruisers to show off their skill in steering or war manoeuvrings. On such occasions the Chiefs would rig themselves out in the most grotesque costumes one can imagine; full suits of cast-off livery, naval and military uniforms, and even dress suits were used to improve their appearance, and to show respect to their visitors.

My official capacity as Chairman of the Court was instrumental in giving me some work to do outside my ordinary duties, as I was entrusted by a large German Fire Insurance Co. to investigate the cause of a fire which had occurred in New Calabar, upon which a large claim had been made on them for loss under a policy only a short time in existence. The circumstances were sufficiently suspicious to justify them in resisting the claim made on them; the policy was, however, in the hands of a third party, who held it as security for advances made to the suspected incendiary, and even though the charge could have been proved against him, it was held in law this would not annul the claim; it was, therefore, compromised just before going into Court, and as the person effecting the policy had died, no further steps were taken in the matter. I was well paid for my services by the Insurance Company, who were satisfied with the part I took in it. Another case was to obtain evidence from Natives to enable an Agent to obtain a settlement with employees for salary and commission due to him for services. This enquiry took a long time, as Natives could not understand what it was all about, nor could they be kept to the point. I succeeded, however, in establishing the Agent's case, which led to his making a settlement on the evidence. My time and trouble over this brought me nothing but disappointment and vexation that I had spent so much of it in support of a Man's interest who was weak enough to throw his advantages away after possessing them.

I have referred to the kings whom I met in Africa; it must of course be understood that 'king' is simply a means of identifying the principal chief of a town as occupying that position, and that it carries nothing with it beyond a right to preside in such a capacity at native palavers or councils. They were entitled in the years of my African life to collect what was called 'Comey' on each ship that arrived in the River as a kind of import due; this was assessed at 2/6d per registered ton and was paid to the king before the ship was allowed to trade. To the King of Bonny it meant a large amount per annum: as some 20 to 30 ships would arrive during the year, the king's income derived therefrom would be from £3000 to £4000 a year, out of which he had to subsidise some of his chiefs; beyond this, I do not know that he held any official status or recognised position.

King Amachree, of New Calabar, was an old man when I first went into the River, and I only saw him on one or two occasions, but with his son William who succeeded him I had more frequent opportunities of meeting: he used to sit in semi-state on such days as the white men visited him, and was hospitably inclined, entertaining them to the country dish of 'palm oil chop' on the 'Calabar Sundays', when such visits were general.

In Old Calabar, King Archibong reigned, and I had many opportunities of seeing him during my residence in that River, as I was a frequent messenger from Captain Mullen to obtain the influence of the King in assisting him to recover the 'Trust' which was due to him from some of the Chiefs, who were always out of the way when importuned for their debts: poor Mullen had been too confiding, and found that it was easier to lend money than to get it back again.

In Creektown there was a King called Eyo Honesty, about whom I knew but very little, except that he was enormously stout, and dressed himself in the most extravagant costumes.

With the King of Bonny – Pepple – I was much more intimately acquainted than with either of the other two persons named, as I had to see him many times on business matters, and to arrange meetings. He had been to England, and had become impressed with his dignity and importance by the sycophancy of the English people, who had treated him in ignorance as being a person to whom royal honours were due; in fact, he had so impressed himself on the English people whom he visited in 1862 that they persuaded him that his state required him to take out with him to Bonny persons to fill the position of state officials, such as secretaries, maids of honour, gardeners, and other occupations: the poor deluded creatures were engaged, and taken out to Bonny in a small brig chartered for the purpose, and on arriving in Bonny discovered that the 'king's palace', as represented to them, was a mud-walled house, that the gardens were to be created from swamps, and that the duties of the maids of honour would be to look after a lot of women whose ideas of clothing were of the most elementary description, if indeed they could be said to have clothing at all, except such as was necessary to cover their nakedness only. It was a cruel awakening to people who had left home with such expectations, to find that they were literally without homes or means of subsistence. Fortunately, they found good friends among the supercargoes, who provided them with the necessaries of life, and arranged for their passages to England in the sailing ships which were returning home; not, however, before some of them had paid the penalty by the loss of their lives. As the last of this party left for England the day of my arrival in Bonny, the subject was one of common knowledge and conversation, and it is very much to be regretted that some action was not taken against the king to compensate the victims of his ambitious ideas for the losses they sustained by a too-ready confidence in his regal pretensions.

I have a lively recollection of being present at an audience given by King Pepple in the early part of 1863, on some occasion of importance, when he was surrounded by his personal suite, as well as his principal chiefs; it was held in the compound known as the King's House, His Majesty being seated on the 'throne of his ancestors', as it was designated. There was nothing pretentious about this piece of furniture, which forcibly reminded me of something of the kind I had seen before as a necessary adjunct to a sick room; it was, however, covered round the bottom by some highly coloured handkerchief, and could not, therefore, be identified positively as the article I had in my mind: I subsequently ascertained that I was not mistaken in my supposition, as, owing to a physical weakness on the part of the dusky potentate, it became necessary for him to use this accessory as he was doing, lest uncomfortable consequences should result from its absence. I was certainly not impressed, either with the King or his surroundings, and less so when I realised that the lady sitting on her haunches at the foot of the throne was his Queen Alliputa, the mother of Prince George Pepple, who had put on such airs in our passage out to Africa.

The Queen, who had accompanied her husband to England, and had the advantage of knowing how persons of distinction usually dressed and comported themselves in high society, was dressed in a print gown loosely made and bound round the waist with a belt; her knees were drawn up towards her chin, with her hands locked across them, her legs showing an amount of white stockings, while her feet were encased in goloshed-shaped shoes with elastic straps across the instep, such as I remember schoolgirls used to wear when I was a boy. There were a number of other women present, none of whom had anything more on than the usual waist cloth, in which by this time I had become accustomed to see them.

When Prince George succeeded his father he was somewhat disposed to give himself grander airs, and to presume on his title; he once or twice visited Europe, and had a good time, being regarded as a potentate of distinction; he had received a good education, and certainly knew how to behave himself in good society; he was consequently taken up by some of the people of position in London, who trotted him out as a celebrity, among other of his patrons and patronesses being Lord and Lady Brassy,[40] of whom he used to speak with great familiarity, and I recollected seeing an announcement in one of the Society papers of a ball given at Allmacks, where the dancing commenced on the arrival of the Prince Imperial of France and King George of Bonny! He used to talk very grandly of the alterations and improvements he intended to make in his kingdom by the introduction of a police force, and other matters, following on the lines of European usages of civilisation, which however came to nothing more than the intention as the secession of Ja Ja altered his position in Bonny, and left him as a kind of puppet in the hands of his powerful chiefs, on whom he ultimately became dependent for his living; he did not live long, and a kind of regency was afterwards established with Oko Jumbo as the chief.

Ja Ja, who was after some years recognised as the King of Opobo, came to trouble with Consul Johnston, who deported him, with the sanction of the British Government, first to Accra, and ultimately to one of the West India Islands, where he died and was buried; his body was ultimately exhumed and re-buried in Opobo among his own people.

The 'Onward' was a rendezvous for many of my personal friends, who, in passing through Bonny, were always entertained there as my guests; they were mostly men of the same habits and character as myself, not given to either drinking or card-playing, and contemporaries who indulged in these amusements, we were considered a kind of puritanical lot, but this did not in any way interfere with the friendliness and good-fellowship which always existed between us, as I can truthfully say that even where differences existed there was never anything of such a nature as to create bitterness of more than a temporary character. Some of my best friends were those who were active and zealous competitors against me in trade, while others were equally so by reason of our having a common interest in each other's welfare, and a willingness to help in each other's success. Friends made under such circumstances as here related are usually lasting ones, each of us realising how much one becomes inter-dependent on the other for comforts and amenities of life, and doing everything possible to promote and secure such friendships by every means they may have of doing so.

I have confined myself in the foregoing pages to a simple record of my own life, without touching on anything connected with my family, as the object in writing at all has been taken up for the purpose of giving my children these particulars, which I am sure they will read with interest. With my own domestic life, they are familiar, as it was left to them to cheer and console their mother during my long absences from home, to which I always returned with increased love, and never left without the bitterest regret, and each time with greater pain and reluctance than previously. My wife and I have been singularly fortunate in having no heavy burden or domestic trouble to bear with; each of us knew that our separation called for special fortitude and patience, if our efforts were to be rewarded by seeing our children fitted to fill their stations in life by the means which my success enabled them to attain. That this has been so is one of the proudest feelings of my heart, and the dearest realisation of a long life filled with much work, and greater happiness.

Sport

During my many voyages to and from Africa I met many interesting persons as fellow-travellers some of them of the official class who held appointments under the Colonial Office, while others were as myself, traders, or in some way engaged in commerce, as also masters in charge of the steamer in which I would be travelling. There was nothing, however, of sufficient interest in these journeyings to and fro to make record of, beyond the facts of doing so as a pleasant way of remembering old friends, with whom a large part of my life was passed. The Captains were always anxious to do anything for us, and in this way I received many kindnesses and messages from home.

During one of my voyages out to Africa I was staying a short time at Miles Hotel, in Funchal, when a gentleman was announced as desiring an interview with me. I was greatly surprised to find a French gentleman named Count de Semele waiting in the Drawing Room to pay me a sum of £800, which I had feared was a bad debt. Some two and a half years before this gentleman had come out to Bonny with a companion named Burdo, with the intention of exploring the River Niger. He presented his letters of introduction and credentials from the Minister of Marine in Paris to Consul Hopkins, who was staying on board the 'Onward' with me, and as he required materials, provisions etc., for this expedition, I undertook to supply him with them, and did so to the amount named, for which I received a Bill on the Minister in Paris; this, however, was not honoured, and I feared the money was lost; it was, therefore, a very pleasant surprise when I received from him some £200 in cash, and another Bill on a commercial firm in Paris for the balance, also, a cable message telling me it would be met on presentation; he had arrived in Funchal that morning, and learning I was there also, came up at once to settle his debt.

On our voyages (which lasted a month generally) we had to amuse ourselves as best we could with cards, chess, backgammon, and sometimes with shooting; this became a pastime many of us indulged in, and I became by practice a very good shot; our targets in such places as Lagos and other ports on the windward coast would be the sharks that were continually keeping watch round the ship while at anchor. In Bonny I used to go out in the evening shooting curlew or wood pigeons, and sometimes had a shot at larger game, as I seldom went out in my boat to go through creeks without taking a rifle with me. On one occasion I saw a huge elephant get up from the creek where it was wallowing, and as the noise of my oars had disturbed it, it got up; I managed to hit it with a rifle ball, but, being in a less vulnerable part than the head, the beggar went on bellowing, and got away. We often used to shoot alligators, particularly in Old Calabar, where they were very plentiful, and would sometimes snap a black boy off a ladder when washing. A great cobra came on board the 'Onward' with some staves, and on the cooper knocking them to pieces, this reptile moved out; there was very soon a clear deck, and I went out with my rifle, to find it gliding across the bowsprit; I shot and knocked it into the water, where it was soon captured by the Kroomen, as it was powerless in the water.

On another occasion I found a rifle very useful. I used to make a tour of inspection down to the bale room and shop every Sunday morning, to see if everything was all right, and while doing so I saw a Krooman trying to remove a plank with a crowbar to obtain access to the bale room; looking round, I picked up a rifle, and having charged it, fired through a plank over the man's head; while he was running up on deck I did so too, to find him coming up through a hatch upon which some of his accomplices were lying to cover it: there was no necessity to ask questions, as the man was so pale with fright that he stood self-convicted, and being taken red-handed, got his punishment over as soon as possible.

I discontinued going to Africa in 1881, having made my last voyage in that year to establish the business bought from John Capper and Company by Mr. John Holt and myself, with whom I worked in partnership until 1889, when our business was taken over by the African Association Limited, with whom I am now working as Managing Director. I still continue to take the deepest interest in everything connected with the scene of my former labours, and have been instrumental in assisting both natives and white men by the influence of the position I occupy, as representing the most important Firm in the trade, comprising as it does all those Firms and Companies which were established there in the early part of my career.

The foregoing particulars or reminiscences of my life brought me up to the year 1881, when I retired from the Coast, and took my seat in the office of John Holt & Company, with whom I had been working in joint account in several ventures connected with West Africa. After the failure of John Capper and Co., Mr. Holt and myself bought the remains of the business, and entered into full partnership in Bonny and New Calabar as African Merchants, and continued together in this relationship until 1889, when our business was taken over by the African Association Limited, who had for its first Chairman, Mr. Stanley Rogerson, and as its Vice, Mr. Edward Cookson. The Board consisted of all the principals of the several Firms whose business had been taken over by the Company then formed, numbering in all fifteen members, of whom Messrs Tunnicliffe, Gilbertson, and myself were also Managers.[41]

The first six or seven years were a grievous disappointment to all of us, as on coming together after the valuations had been taken and properties transferred, the Company found itself saddled with a lot of obsolete factories which were taken over as going concerns and valued on this basis, notwithstanding that some of them for the purposes of trade were a burden rather than a help, and until the whole system had been re-organised there was little hope of doing a profitable business, over-burdened as it was with the expenses of carrying on the whole of them without adequate trade to meet them. It, therefore, became a vital question as to which were the least profitable places, and what should be done with them. The Managers strongly recommended the closing of some of them which were considered redundant, as also a complete change of policy in respect to the manner in which the trade was being conducted. The first three years were taken up in re-organising, during which time we became more acquainted with the people with whom we had been brought into partnership, and it was not long before we realised that our Chairman was quite unsuited to the position to which he had been elected. It also came to our knowledge during this time that those who had been credited with financial strength had very little of such foundation to rest on, and that they were under such monetary obligations to others as to be unable to exercise independent influence or judgment on questions of policy affecting the welfare of the trade, and the interests of their shareholders.

In 1894 Mr. John Holt was elected Chairman, and as he exercised influence on the minds of the majority of his colleagues the more peaceful policy advocated by the Managers was disregarded, and an active competition with those who were opposing the African Association in Nigeria was instituted and carried on rigorously under the supervision of Mr. John Holt.

We had been for several years carrying on trade in the River Niger under such circumstances as to make it impossible for us to do otherwise than make heavy losses, inasmuch as the Niger Company who were our principal opponents were a governing as well as a trading body, carrying on their business under such favourable conditions as to enable them to harass and oppose us in such places where we were trading, while, being free from opposition in others, they could make profits without our affecting them. After repeated attempts, the Board finally realised the futility of continuing opposition under such circumstances, and notwithstanding that the Chairman and others with him were opposed to such a policy, a resolution was passed to open up negotiations with the Niger Company with a view to selling our factories to them, Mr. Cookson and myself being authorised by the Board to take this course. We finally succeeded in coming to terms with Sir George Goldie,[42] and the whole of our assets in the Niger were transferred to that Company for shares.[43] During the process of these negotiations, the hostile faction on the Board of the Association threw every obstacle they could in the way to prevent a settlement, and I found myself at variance with Mr. George Watts to such an extent as to create an estrangement, and almost an open rupture with a friend with whom I had been in such close and intimate relations as he and I for twenty-five years, while it was so opposed to Mr. Holt that he did not satisfy himself by passive resistance only, but retaliated in such a way as to cause me to think of him as one who would not hesitate to give little consideration to his most intimate friends in order to gain his own ends. The Agreement entered into and arranged by Mr. Cookson and myself was ratified and confirmed by the Board of the African Association, notwithstanding the dissent of Mr. Holt and his supporters, and in this way the first step in the direction of harmonious working was accomplished, with the result that where it was predicted our heritage had been sold for a mess of pottage, it proved to be a mine of wealth, as the shares taken over in exchange for our goods, goodwill, and factories, on the basis of £6 for each £10 share, were ultimately liquidated and realised £32 per share, giving the Association a profit of nearly £200,000 on the transaction. The Niger Company reconstructed its share capital, and has continued to pay good dividends from that time.

In 1894, in consequence of the treatment I received, I decided to withdraw from the active management, and did so, going abroad for six months to Egypt and certain Mediterranean ports. On my return, I was idle for some months, and got into ill health from want of occupation, and worry caused by the shares of the African Association falling in value from £10 to £4/10/-, and other matters in connection therewith. I do not propose to refer more directly to this, as the episode is a painful one, and I cannot do so without exposing things which I would prefer should be considered as past.

I continued to attend the Meetings of the Board, and in this way kept in touch with the other Directors who were in accord with me, hoping that a time would come when I should be listened to, and my policy adopted as opposed to that which had brought disaster to so many of us. In due time this came about, in a way quite unexpected, as at the end of 1896 Mr. Holt resigned the Chairmanship and his Directorate, without a moment's notice, on an adverse vote being given against him, and thereafter followed peace.[44] His resignation was followed by Mr. Cookson, and notwithstanding that each of them offered themselves for re-election at the next annual meeting, they were unsuccessful, and having left the Board under these circumstances did not appear again on the scene for some years, and only then at a general meeting.

It now became necessary for me to give effect to my policy, and with this object in view I was authorised to approach one of our principal competitors, which I did, with the satisfactory result that a working agreement was entered into between us, which paved the way for a more complete unification of our interests at a later date.

It was confidently predicted as a consequence of the withdrawal of these gentlemen from the Board of the Association that the Company would become a failure, and that the shares would go even lower than they were at the time that their influence was withdrawn; it is, therefore, gratifying to think that the contrary was the case, as from 1896 to 1910 the Company has enjoyed a term of exceptional prosperity, having paid to its ordinary shareholders over a million pounds in dividends, while the founder shareholders have received about a third of this amount, the former being readily saleable at 100% premium, and the latter at £120 for each £8 share, the Reserve Fund being close on to £200,000, with an equal amount in value of assets over liabilities: so much for prophecy!

I am constrained to refer to this episode with considerable modesty, inasmuch as I was mainly instrumental in instigating and carrying through the many agreements which produced this result. These agreements were made after long and careful negotiations with the Steamship Companies for the sale of the fleet, with the Niger Company for the sale of our Niger business, already referred to, with the Steamship Companies again for carrying, and lastly with the Niger Company and other Merchants with whom we are now working under Agreement for twenty years, following a previous term of 10 years just recently completed.

The Board of the African Association originally consisted of:—

W. Couper	1
Stanley Rogerson	x
Thomas Harrison	x
John Tunnicliffe	x
Hahnemann Stuart	2
Mazzini Stuart	3
John Moore	x
I.C. McKinnon	
R.P. Gilbertson	x
Mervyn King	4
E. Hatton Cookson	
W.S. Tobin	x
George Watts	x
John Holt	
J.C. Holt	x
Harry Cotterell	5 [45]

Of these, eight have died, and three retired, leaving only five of the first number remaining. The altered circumstance of the Company, as related, so improved the financial position of each and all of us that those who have been removed by death have left their families well provided for, while those who remain have no longer to bemoan their fate, or to be unduly anxious lest the vicissitudes of the African trade should again place them in such a position as during the first seven years of the Company's existence.

Since my leaving the Coast in 1881 the British Government have incorporated the whole of Nigeria with Lagos as a Colony and Protectorate; it is, therefore, now governed as a Crown Colony, and where formerly there was only Consular protection for British subjects, there is now complete administration, with its attendant advantages to life and property. The interior of the country has been opened to commerce and industrial enterprise; intertribal raids have been stopped; the natives themselves, realising the security they now enjoy, have with energy opened up free markets, become interested in new products, while developing and increasing their former productions to such an extent as to provide the Government with revenue more than sufficient to cover the expenditure, out of which is provided schools, hospitals, and the many accessories of more civilised life.

My long and close friendship with the late Sir Alfred Jones led to my having from him frequent invitations to accompany him on trial trips of new steamers from the Tyne or Clyde to Liverpool. The first of these was in 1872 when a party of us were taken down the Irish Channel in the 'Africa'.[46] I afterwards sailed in this vessel on her first voyage to Bonny. We were to leave on the 29th February, but on embarking on that day it was found that through the negligence of the Secretary to the Company the Builders' Certificate had not been received; consequently, we were obliged to return to our anchorage, and I, therefore, returned home unexpectedly to my wife and children, to undergo on the following morning the same trying ordeal as had to be got through on the previous day.

I was several times on the trial trips of steamers which took us round the North of Scotland, and lasted for several days. On these occasions I met many old friends who were connected with West Africa, and as we were always most hospitably entertained, they were most enjoyable outings. Sir Alfred gave me frequent opportunities on these and other occasions of relating some of my experiences to himself and his guests, and I found them interested in many of the incidents which I have set down here as my reminiscences of African life.

I went out with him to Las Palmas, together with my wife, and as he had large commercial interests in the Canary Islands,[47] he held receptions, and gave dinner parties to the principal people in the Island, to which my wife and myself were always invited.

I had often been asked by him to accompany him to Jamaica, and having promised to do so, the matter was seriously entertained in 1906, when a large party were invited to go out to Barbados and Jamaica,, under the auspices of the Cottongrowing Association, of which Sir Alfred was President.[48] We were all taken to Bristol: we embarked the next morning on board the 'Port Kingston',[49] one of the Imperial Direct West India Company's steamers. We left England on the 29th December, and expected to be away about six weeks: we were favoured with excellent weather, and got out of the roaring forties without much discomfort. Business Meetings were held in the morning, to discuss subjects connected with cotton cultivation, and other subjects, the afternoons and evenings being devoted to less serious matters. The passengers' recreation was catered for by a Committee appointed for the purpose, and as there was plenty of talent on board, the fun was fast and furious; what with Concerts, Dances, Bridge-parties, and Music, besides games such as are usually played on board ship, time passed very quickly. We arrived at Barbados, and were there joined by about fifty delegates from the West India Islands, all of whom were interested in cotton cultivation, and added much to our knowledge of this industry. While there, the Merchants and others provided us with carriages, and took us around the town and its outskirts, to show us objects of interest, and otherwise entertain us.

After leaving Barbados, we got into stormy weather, and the first of our misfortunes began the day following, when a poor sailor doing something to the hangway was washed overboard, and drowned, notwithstanding everything was done to try and recover him: this accident created a feeling of gloom over the ship, which lasted some days. We arrived at Kingston to our appointed time, and were soon housed in the Constant Spring Hotel,[50] all of us dining and living together as a huge family. We made our call on the Governor, and were entertained by him to a Garden Party, and to dinner in the evening, where we met his wife, and many of the leading inhabitants of Kingston. My wife and eldest daughter had been invited to join us on the ship, and we were all having a good time until the following Monday, when an earthquake occurred which had far-reaching effects, and converted our pleasure party into one of mourning and disaster.

My wife, daughter, and myself, with other friends, took a trip on the morning of January 16th to Spanish Town, distant about eight or ten miles from Kingston: we then made an excursion to Bog's Walk, to see this place of interest. On our return to Spanish Town, we were walking from the railway station when a noise like reverberating artillery was heard, and on looking around us, we were horrified to see the buildings beside the road collapse like a house of cards; the earth trembled and oscillated under our feet, making it difficult to stand, we then realised that an earthquake had occurred of a terrible character. After getting over our fright, we began to think what we were to do to get to Kingston; some of our friends had gone into the Cathedral, and on hearing the noise had fortunately got out before the shock; they had a narrow escape as the Cathedral itself was damaged considerably, and was a wreck as compared with its peacefulness in the morning when we went through it. A gentleman and myself went to the railway station, to learn that there could be no train communication with Kingston; we, therefore, decided to return by road, and re-engaged our buggies for this purpose. On our way towards Kingston, we met multitudes of people who were escaping therefrom, and from whom we learned that Kingston itself had been practically destroyed, and many people killed: we ultimately arrived at Constant Spring Hotel, to find the place abandoned, with all our friends camping in the gardens. A portion of the Hotel having been destroyed and rendered uninhabitable, we passed the night lying on the ground, and went through the terrorising experience of feeling some fifteen shocks of greater or less intensity. When morning came we saw what devastation had been caused, and heard the reports of dreadful catastrophes and escapes. Several of our fellow-voyagers who were in Kingston itself were seriously injured, but fortunately those who were in the Hotel had escaped.

In the course of the afternoon, carriages were sent up for us to be taken down to the ship, as we were under the escort of Sir Ralph Moor, Lord Mountmorres, and other friends who had arranged the cavalcade. We passed through miles of streets, where the houses were all demolished, their former occupants sitting on the open road bemoaning their fate and so awe-stricken as to be incapable of action. We got on board the 'Port Kingston' to find our friends from whom we heard the details of what had taken place during our absence. Sir Alfred Jones and others had marvellous escapes, while many others had been less fortunate.

It was a most providential escape for us, as although the shock as felt by us in Spanish Town was great, had we been in Kingston, as we should have been, the consequences might have been such as to prevent even this account being written.

There was to have been a Ball that night at the Hotel, and my wife was anxious to get back to Kingston by a train which would have arrived there just about the time the earthquake occurred; this was frustrated by the negro drivers who took us to Bog's Walk assuring us before we started that there would be plenty of time to get back for the train, which was a delusion, as we found it impossible, and therefore reconciled ourselves by having lunch and intending to get home later, as we did in the way related.

When again on board the 'Port Kingston', we felt more safe, but even then, surrounded as we were by such devastation, it was a most trying time, and glad were we when we could leave the place behind us.

I did not commence this with the intention of giving more than an outline of this occurrence, but its far-reaching effects on my friend of whom I am writing more particularly were such as to impress the details on my memory. and I find it difficult to refer to it only as a passing incident.

Sir Alfred Jones was never in my opinion the same man after the earthquake as before; he seemed to be impelled forward to such activity and restlessness as to make it impossible for him to recuperate his wasted energies, and I am sure this exercised some influence on him, which brought about the illness from which he died.[51]

He and I had been intimate friends for thirty-five years, and notwithstanding that our separate interests as shipper and shipowner did not always coincide, I never had any difference or dispute with him that was not readily settled by short personal interviews and negotiation.

He died in December of 1909, a Memorial Service being held at Mossley Hill Church, which was attended by all the leading Merchants, and others connected with Liverpool.[52] For thirty years I had made a point of calling to see him on the 1st January, and on the one preceding his death, he had come down specially from 'Oaklands' to see me, knowing I should be disappointed if he had not done so. He was a kind-hearted many-sided man, and took a great interest in me and my family generally. At one of his Garden Parties his sister, Mrs. Pinnock, invited my wife into the conservatory to partake of refreshment, to find him there, and as the band struck up 'Should Auld Acquaintance be Forgot', he came forward and said to my wife 'I don't think it should be', and asked her to accept as a token a beautiful jewelled brooch of great value, and laughingly said to her 'Don't tell any of these women that I've given it to you, or they will be expecting me to do the same for them'.

His Partner, Mr. J.W. Davey,[53] was also a great personal friend of mine. I had known him almost as long as I had Sir Alfred, but there was not the same personal relationship between us. He had predeceased his partner by a short time, so that the great Firm of Elder Dempster & Co. passed into other hands, who came in to reap where they had sown, and shortened their lives while doing so.[54]

As I am writing for my children's amusement and information only, I will relate here an incident which occurred on one of our excursions on the trial trip of a new steamer. We went up to Glasgow, and were dined at the 'Central Hotel'. I had obtained an invitation for one of my personal friends, and found that we were to occupy the same bedroom. I retired to bed earlier than my friend, and was awakened by his snoring, which became recurrent each time he fell asleep after being awakened by different devices. On getting on board the steamer I found we were to occupy the same cabin, and with the previous night's experience in my mind, I asked my friend Picton Jones if he could not find me a berth somewhere, making the excuse that my room-mate was not in very good health, and I would like him to have the room to himself; I was, therefore, doubled up with a gentleman whom I knew very well, with the following result: he, being a very methodical man, retired to bed about 9.30; I did not go until two hours later; in the morning he told me that I had disturbed his rest when getting into bed, as I occupied the top berth. In the course of the day he found there was another room in the ship with only one occupant, and proposed to toss up who should go there; I, however, relieved him from this dilemma by taking my quarters in the Captain's room, leaving him to retire as early as he liked. I pointed out to him that people did not generally make excursions such as we were on to spend the best part of the time in bed, and, where I had retired at 11.30, if he had been so unlucky as to lose the toss he proposed, he might have found himself doubled up with someone who remained up later than myself.

It was on this same ship that an incident occurred which was partly serious as well as amusing. I had rambled into the Smoke Room late in the evening, to find an altercation going on between some gentlemen playing cards; for some reason, I was appointed referee, and on hearing the cause of the dispute, I suggested to the gentleman whom I considered to be in the wrong that he should apologise, which he did, and offered his hand at the same time to the person aggrieved, which was indignantly rejected. The person here referred to was an ex-Commander in Her Majesty's Navy, and being in his cups was more forcible than polite to the apologist, who appealed to me again, and I had to tell him to put his hand in his pocket, since the other man refused it, and, retaliating on the Naval Officer, told him the whole scene was due to the abuse of the hospitality they were enjoying, with which remark I went to bed. In the morning one of the gentlemen, an American, implicated in this squabble, came to breakfast very late, when a note was passed to him referring to his last night's condition upon which he got up and explained that the note he had received stated he had to get to his room in a cab. He denied this, but stated he 'found the way to this room pretty rocky', which was a candid acknowledgment that created a good deal of laughter.

In my wanderings I have travelled over 500,000 miles of sea, fortunately without meeting any serious accident. On our return from Jamaica, we were all publicly entertained by the Lord Mayor of Liverpool at a Reception given by him in the Town Hall, when each of us present had to give some account of our experiences to the assembled guests.

In 1894 my wife and I went to the Mediterranean, and arrived in Algiers very early in the Season. We put up at the Hotel Splendide, which was almost empty; we remained there about six weeks, and while there were joined by other parties; one gentleman, a Mr. Jackson, M.P.

for Bristol, arrived with his wife. The lady was a bright, vivacious French woman, who appeared to take very much pleasure in talking to a young clergyman who sat next to her at table. The husband had not much liking for the clergy, as he repeatedly made cynical and unpleasant remarks to the man to whom his wife was showing favour. One night he came to dinner very much flushed, and more offensive than usual. He was relating to us all how, being free from his wife's supervision, he had been having a good time, with plenty to eat and good wine with it; while relating this he was seized with an apoplectic fit, from which he died in less than two hours. The lady had been French governess to the late King's daughters. The poor clergyman was called on to perform the last rites to the dead man who had been so ungracious to him.

Algiers is a place that did not appeal to me except from its barbaric splendour, as, like most places, it is dirty, smelly, and swarming with mosquitoes, which even a bower of Eucalyptus hanging over our pillows did not prevent from devouring us. This remark applies to all the places I visited on the Mediterranean, and Naples, Messina, and other places were in all respects similar.

During our holidays my wife and I have visited the Continent of Europe, Madeira, Grand Canary, England, Ireland, Scotland and Wales, getting a good deal of pleasure in these journeyings, and some few adventures, but nothing calling for any special reference.

In my journeyings and residence abroad I have met many distinguished persons, and had much to do with them, being brought into personal communication and business relations with them. Having held the position of Chairman of the Court of Equity in Bonny so frequently gave me opportunities of meeting, and in many cases entertaining them. In this way I became acquainted with Consul Burton, who was one of the greatest travellers and writers connected with Africa and other parts of the world: he came to Bonny in 1865 to settle the disputes then existing between the Government and Natives in respect to certain breaches of Treaties for which they had been fined.

Consuls Hartley, Hopkins, Livingstone, Hewitt, and Johnston followed Burton, until 1889, when the more settled form of administration was introduced under the regime of Sir Claude Macdonald, Sir Ralph Moor, and Sir Walter Egerton, who is at present High Commissioner and Governor of Southern Nigeria. The Men of War on the African Station used to make periodical visits to the Rivers, and the Senior Naval Officer in command would convene a Meeting on the flag ship to which we were summoned, when a big palaver would be held to enquire into anything which might require investigation from the trader's or native's point of view. Commodore Wilmot came to

Bonny with an imposing array of War Ships to enforce a fine levied on the Bonnymen. Commodore Hewitt came on the more peaceful errand of presenting medals and distinctions to those Natives who had volunteered to serve us in our campaign against the Ashantis in 1873, while Commodore Commerell visited us when the palavers between Oko Jumbo and the Chiefs of Bonny and King Ja Ja, of Opobo, were being enquired into, and settled. Commodore Cameron passed through Bonny on his return from crossing Africa from East to West, and Henry Stanley also passed through on his return from a similar journey.

Winwood Reade and other travellers I met as fellow-passengers to and from Africa, and from whom I learned many things connected with their African travels, not always related in their books. I also had the good fortune to meet Mary Kingsley after her return from one of the most daring and interesting journeys ever made in Africa, while her description of her travels is given in one of the most instructive books I have ever read.[55]

In the course of my travels I have met with some incidents that may be interesting to my readers, and give them here with this object.

On my return from Africa in 1866 I was invited to visit an elder brother who resided in Brampton, and took train to this place in Northamptonshire. On arrival, I found we had made a mistake, and should have gone to Brampton in Huntingdonshire, but as we could not get farther on our way than Thrapston, we put up at the Hotel there, where we were treated as distinguished persons travelling incognito, and were charged accordingly, the whole retinue of servants being drawn up to line the hall on our departure, and on referring to the bill, we were told that charge for the boots was not included thereon. To cap all, on our arriving at the railway station, and about to get into the train, the driver came up stammering that he hoped I would remember the driver, which I have done to this day, as well as the extortionate amount charged us for our accommodation. Having got to the right Brampton at last, we had a walk of about three miles from the station to the village, on a broiling hot day in August, along a country road without shelter of any kind. In this place we put up at the village inn, and after inspecting our quarters, which were clean and comfortable enough, we left, to return to them late at night, to find that we could only get to our bedroom by going through a large barnlike room filled with about thirty or forty harvestmen, who were all sleeping there, but as they were all away to their work before we were up in the morning, we suffered no inconvenience therefrom.

On another occasion, we were going to Norway, and had booked our passages some time before the steamer left; in the meantime, my wife was taken ill, and notwithstanding that she was not fully recovered, we proceeded to Newcastle-on-Tyne to embark on board the 'Midnight Sun'. What with the travelling and the weary waiting before we got on board, my wife was completely exhausted; she, however, managed to crawl up on deck, when the Captain, bursting with indignation, asked me why I had brought a lady in such a condition on a pleasure voyage. I did not pay much attention to him for the moment, but requested him to send for the doctor. When this gentleman came, I left my wife in his charge, and then returned to the Captain, who was irritated and annoyed to such an extent that he insisted on my disembarking: to return, knowing the condition of my wife, and also realising the possible consequences to her if I did so, I positively refused, and left it to the Captain to take such steps as he liked; fortunately, at this juncture, the doctor came to report that the matter was not so serious as the Captain had supposed, and there it ended. We had a favourable passage crossing the North Sea, and as my wife's health became restored, we had a most delightful and enjoyable passage, the Captain being one of our best friends, and anxious to make amends for his ungracious reception of us at first.

On another occasion my wife and I were going for a trip to the North of Ireland, and as one of Elder Dempster's steamers was leaving Liverpool for Londonderry, we took passage in her. On going on board we found there were only a few 1st class passengers besides ourselves, but she had some 600 steerage passengers going to Montreal. After sailing, the emigrants made many complaints of their treatment by the stewards, who were surcharging them for water and other necessaries included in their passage. This culminated in a lot of them coming on to the upper deck in a very menacing manner to make their complaints to the Captain, and for a time it looked very much like having a mutiny and bloodshed, as the men, mostly Polish Jews, were armed with knives, and looked as though they would use them on very little provocation. The Chief Officer had brought up the hose charged with hot water, which he intended to use if necessary to drive back the malcontents. I was able to give some assistance to the Captain by investigating their grievances, which were such as they had a right to have removed. While parleying with the Captain, one of the ringleaders humbugged the Chief Officer by talking to him while another slit the hose pipe with his knife, and rendered it useless for any purpose of defence. Fortunately, it was not required, as arrangements were made to appoint persons among themselves to receive and distribute their daily rations as received from the stewards: notwithstanding this, there was barefaced cheating between themselves, as some of the more crafty ones got double rations, while others were left without. We got to Londonderry safely, and the ship to Montreal, without anything more than these repeated scenes during the voyage.

We travelled round the Donegal Highlands in an elongated jaunting car, carrying about twelve persons. We stayed during this tour in some of the most primitive hotels I was ever in. One in particular was at a place called Dunfaglonby, where we arrived at about six o'clock, and were told that dinner would be served at 7.30. The hotel itself was Post Office, Grocery Store, General Wares Shop, Pub and Hotel combined; the bedrooms about twelve feet square, diminutive furniture, locks, doors and windows of the same description; there was, however, a large Salle a Mange as an annex, where dinner was laid out: the landlady and her daughters had cooked it, and waited on us, and we were regaled with a six or seven course dinner which would have done justice to any of the leading London Houses. Our party was augmented by eight gentlemen who were there for fishing, and as they were out all day, the landlady knew for whom she was catering, and we came in to share the good things with them. We finished up at Bundovan on the West side of Ireland, and from thence we went across to Newcastle in County Down on the East, and when taking a drive in a public char-a-banc to Rostrevor, my wife got into conversation with the driver, and on telling him she had never seen a real shamrock, he volunteered to show her; a little farther on he got off the car, and plucking a handful of green stuff from the hedgeway, assured her that it was the real shamrock. Excepting my wife and myself, all the other occupants were Irish: a dispute arose amongst them as to its being the real shamrock or not, and so vociferous did they become over this question that it looked as though it were going to end in a free fight all round before the matter was settled; fortunately, it did not come to this, but it was an object lesson to me of the trifling things upon which Irishmen are willing to quarrel, and fight if necessary.

On another occasion we were taking holiday in Scotland, making Pitlochry our headquarters. We arrived there late at night, having engaged our rooms at the Pitlochry Hydro, went there, and were not favourably impressed with the place. I asked the Proprietor before going to bed if they had the usual Hydro Baths, upon which I was informed there were only private bathrooms on each of the landings; I made no demur to this, but stated I wanted a bath at such a time in the morning. We came down to breakfast, which was laid out in a large barnlike room, with slatternly waitresses, very grimy and rough table-appointments, and altogether not very inviting-looking. Before proceeding to breakfast the Proprietor, from an alcove which covered the serving-room, gave out a long Scotch Grace, which contrasted very much with the provisions on the table. After breakfast, my wife went over to the other Hydro called the Atholl, and on my returning home in the afternoon, told me that she had taken rooms there, and had told the Proprietor we should leave the following day; he, however, said we could not do so, as the rooms had been taken for three weeks, and we should have to pay the full term whether we remained or left: I came on the scene at this point, and told him that I would pay him whatever he was entitled to when the time for settlement came. The next morning I asked to have the luggage removed from the hall to the cart waiting to take it away, upon which he presented me with a bill for thirty-five pounds, being two nights' accommodation for my wife, daughter, and myself. Before disputing the bill, I insisted on having the luggage removed; when this was done, I told him I would not pay the amount demanded, upon which he presented me with a paper stating his willingness to commute the amount to £10/10/0 if I would sign it, withdrawing any imputation against the establishment for not having Hydropathic Baths: on my refusing to sign it or pay the thirty-five pounds, he told his men to take the luggage off the cart; as it was then out of his possession, I warned him against doing so, when he found himself in the wrong. By this time, the altercation had brought a number of the visitors around us, and calling one of them I asked him to witness that in his presence I offered to pay such reasonable sum as the man was entitled to for the accommodation we had received while staying, but I was not going to be blackmailed beyond that; I then gave him the name of the Solicitor whom I had consulted, and told him to apply there for his money when he had arrived at a more reasonable frame of mind. I never heard again from the man, nor have I paid him a halfpenny, although I wrote after arriving home to express my desire to be out of his debt. He certainly finished up by saying he would stop my luggage at the railway station, upon which I told him to go to a warm place and stop it where he liked. My wife in writing for the rooms had told him we knew nothing of Pitlochry, the house, or its surroundings, and it would depend on how much we were satisfied with any or all of these how long we stayed; if we were satisfied, we should require the rooms for three weeks. We were not satisfied with this result.

While we were lying in Kingston Harbour in Jamaica after the earthquake the 'Port Kingston' was boarded by a fillibustering American in charge of a torpedo boat, who, with his boat's crew armed cap-a-pie, asked Captain Parsons if he could tell him where the Governor was to be found. Captain Parsons suggested Government House as the most likely place, whereupon the American wanted to know how many people had been killed by the earthquake; Captain Parsons being a simple-minded mariner said, 'God only knows, I don't', whereupon the fillibuster said,'Well Captain, can you tell me who next to God-almighty can give me the information?' I think the Captain might well have told him to go to the antipodes of the power referred to for what he wanted.

I am nearing the close of the reminiscences and incidents of my life. As compared with many other travellers, they are nothing, but still, it may afford some of those who know and love me an opportunity of reading with interest what I have written with this object.

I have enjoyed good health, a fair measure of success and have been singularly fortunate in making many friends. I have interested myself in many things connected with Church Missions, business and sports; in each and all of them I have filled important positions, from Chairman of Court of Equity in Africa, offices in Church and Missions, Directorships in many different Companies, and President of many Sporting Clubs, in each of which I have made many friends, some of whom have given me very substantial proof of their goodwill. Among these is an illuminated address, presented to me by the staff of the African Association on my retirement from the management in 1894. About the same time I was calling on a Firm with whom I had done business for some years, when the Senior Partner indicated the desire of his Firm to make me a present for some information I had given them, out of which they had made a good sum of money by acting on it. This came to me as a pleasurable surprise, as I did not know anything of what they had done. On my expressing myself as being satisfied with their acknowledgment of the service rendered them, they insisted on a more substantial recognition, and as this occurred on the anniversary of my wedding day, they sent a beautiful gem ring to my wife, and a diamond ring for myself, which I prize greatly for the spontaneity of the gift.

Another friend gave me a beautiful pair of Crown Derby vases for a similar service, while the diamond ring I generally wear came to me in much the same way. One of the Native Chiefs in Bonny sent an order home for a diamond ring to cost about £50, which was bought and sent out to him but on realising that he had to pay so many puncheons of Oil for it, and looking at the bulk of the one as compared with the other, he decided not to buy it. It was, therefore, sent home again, and on our business being transferred to the African Association, this was the only asset left to be realised for distribution between Mr. John Holt and myself; my partner withdrew any claim of his share in it, and I, therefore, became its sole owner. In addition to this, Mr. John Holt and his brothers presented me with a silver tea and coffee service, as also other table equipments, all of which I appreciate and look on as heirlooms. The watch I now wear had also a little history attached to it, which may be interesting. In the earlier pages of these reminiscences, I have referred to the Count de Semele's voyage up the Niger; among other things sold to this gentleman was my watch, which they wanted to use as a chronometer in navigation; I sold it for thirty-five pounds, which amount formed part of the bill which was at first repudiated; the Count, being in want of ready money on his return from the Niger expedition, pledged it for £10 to a friend of mine in Brass, from whom I redeemed it by paying this amount. When my bill was ultimately paid by the Count, I tendered him the watch, upon which he relinquished any claim to it; I therefore, got my watch for the £10, having repaid myself the £35 it was originally sold for. My friend Oko Jumbo, on my leaving Bonny, presented me with some valuable coral beads, six of which I had made into waistcoat buttons, and the remainder I gave to my wife, which she still wears.

Notes

1. James Hatton set up in business in 1800 as a wholesale ironmonger and anchor-smith. His premises were at 1-3 Mersey Street, Liverpool. On his death in 1838 his son, Edward Hatton, and his son-in-law, Thomas Worthington Cookson, changed the character of the firm and it became an extremely prosperous West African trading house. By 1854 Hatton and Cookson owned twenty-four sailing vessels and apart from occasional voyages to India and America these were constantly engaged in the trade with the Coast. The ships ranged in size from 200 to 850 tons with one larger vessel of 1339 tons (*U.A.C. Hist.*, p. 74).
2. This was Edward Hatton Cookson, born 1838, who was Chairman of the African Association in 1892–3. He remained in business for sixty-five years and only retired when Hatton and Cookson became part of the African and Eastern Trade Corporation in 1920. He died, two years later, at the age of 84 (*U.A.C. Hist.*, p. 75).
3. s.s. *Palestine* was a well-known vessel of the period. Of 1,377 gross tons and measuring 245 x 34 feet she was built by Steele at Greenock in 1858 and remained in service with Cunard until 1870. (F.E. Dodman, *Ships of the Cunard Line*, Adlard Coles Ltd., London, 1955, p. 133 and F.E. Hyde, *Cunard and the North Atlantic, 1840 1973*, Macmillan, London, 1975, Appendix 6.)
4. The s.s. *City of Baltimore* was a screw steamer of 2,368 tons and measured 325 x 38 x 25 feet. She was built of iron at Glasgow in 1855. (*Lloyds Register*, 1866, C.545.)
5. Tyson, Richmond and Jones had their premises at 4/6, Blackstock Street, Liverpool. They are listed as 'soap boilers' or 'soap manufacturers' at this time. (*Gores Directory*.)
6. *Iphigenia* of 848 tons measured 161 x 34 x 20 feet. She had been built at Quebec in 1859. (*Lloyds Register*, 1866,I, 136.)
7. Captain Andrew McIntosh traded to the West African Coast in sailing ships

for many years and for a short period commanded various vessels of the African Steam Ship Company including the s.s. *Hope*. His eldest son, David, was also a trader in West Africa and became the first Agent-General for the Royal Niger Company. The younger son, Andrew, decided to follow a career at sea and served as a Captain with Elder Dempster. (*U.A.C. Hist.*, pp. 16 and 19; see also Supplement to the *West African Review*, 1939, p. 43.)

8. See below, pp. 98 and 185.
9. A shook is a cask that has been broken down into its component staves and packed into the smallest possible bundle.
10. *Osprey* was formerly a fully rigged ship of 465 tons. She had been built at Bristol in 1835 and until hulked had operated on the West African route for Tyson, Richmond & Jones. (*Lloyds Register*, 1858, 0.172.)
11. See above, p. 24 and note 7.
12. *Celma* of 772 tons had originally been built as a barque in Quebec in 1847. She was then operated by Horsfall's on the West African route. (*Lloyds Register*, 1848, C.244.)
13. See note 10.
14. *Merlin* was formerly a fully rigged ship of 489 tons. She had been built at New Brunswick in 1852 and until hulked had sailed between Liverpool and West Africa for Stuart & Douglas. (*Lloyds Register*, 1858, M.730.)
15. For a fuller account of the loss of *Lottie Sleigh*, see 'Builders of the West African Trade', *Elder Dempster Magazine*, Christmas 1927, pp.133–4.
16. s.s. *Athenian* was built of iron by Smith & Rogers of Glasgow in 1854. Of 1,107 gross tons she measured 241 x 29 x 20 feet. She was owned by the African Steam Ship Company until sold in 1871. (*Trade Makers*, Table 85, No. 9.)
17. James Irvine was born in Langholm, Dumfriesshire in 1835. He first sailed to West Africa in 1858 and six years later set up business as an African Merchant in Liverpool with Woodward. Irvine and Woodward were John Holt's sole agents from 1867 until Holt returned to England and established his own home office in 1874. James Irvine and Company is later listed as 'General Brokers' at 13, Rumford Street, Liverpool. James Irvine died in Birkenhead at the age of 91 in 1926. (*Gores Directory*, 1900).
18. *Calcutta* was a barque of 430 tons. She was built of teak in 1837 and was sheathed in felt and yellow metal. (*Lloyds Register*, 1866, C.25.)
19. The inauguration of regular steam-shipping services in 1852 led to a number of significant changes in the organisation of West African trade. Until then the merchants operating on the Coast had of necessity to own or charter a vessel in order to provide transport. This could, of course, be done in co-operation with other traders but in practice it meant that only firms with substantial resources took part in the trade. Once the African Steam Ship Company began to provide frequent sailings, the established merchants gradually utilised its services to supplement their own vessels and in time most came to rely entirely upon them. More important, however, was the large increase in the number of small traders. For the first time these individuals could order and receive goods from Britain quickly and cheaply, and could also transport the produce received in exchange in a convenient manner. The more successful of these were able to return to the United Kingdom after only a few years' hard work. They could then build up their business still further through the contacts they had acquired while on the Coast, the ease of communication enabling a satisfactory control to be maintained. John Holt of Liverpool was an outstanding example of a merchant who developed his business in this way. (*Trade Makers*, pp. 29–30.)
20. For another view of the trade in spirits, see below, pp. 116 and 159–161.
21. *Onward* was built at St. John in 1850. Of 911 tons, she measured 152 x 32 x

22 feet. (*Lloyds Register*, 1866, 0.138.)

22. This, of course, was only a small section of John Holt's interests in West Africa. See: *U.A.C. Hist.*, pp. 75–85; *Merchant Adventure* (Liverpool, John Holt, 1948); C.R. Holt (ed.), *The Diary of John Holt* (Liverpool, Henry Young & Sons, 1948) and Cherry Gertzel, *A British Merchant in West Africa in the Era of Imperialism* (Unpublished Ph.D. thesis, 1959, in the Bodleian Library, Oxford.)
23. The African Association Limited was formed by a number of firms whose business lay in the delta of the Niger – the region known as the 'Oil Rivers'. These firms were normally in violent competition with one another but the 'Ja Ja' affair drew them together and the example of the amalgamation that had resulted in the formation of the Royal Niger Company suggested a profitable form of collaboration. Alexander Miller, Brother and Company refused to join the proposed merger, but in spite of this the plan went forward and the African Association was incorporated in 1889. The constituent firms were Thomas Harrison & Co; the British & Continental African Co.; Couper, Johnstone & Co.; Hutton & Cookson; Holt & Cotterell, R. & W. King; Stuart & Douglas; Taylor, Laughland & Co. and George Watts & Co. (*Trade Makers*, pp. 94 and 425).
24. The formation of the African Association led to a tremendous fight with Millers in the 'Oil Rivers'. The African Association set up trading stations in the interior of the delta instead of waiting for native traders to bring produce to the coast. Millers were forced to do the same but both found these posts to be unprofitable and they were withdrawn in 1893. Partly as a result of these activities the African Association made very little profit in its early days and this led to a rift amongst its board of directors. One section, led by John Holt, was prepared to continue to fight its rivals but the other, led by Harry Cotterell, believed it would be better if co-operation could replace the existing state of cut-throat competition. Cotterell was able to persuade the board to sell those of its stations which lay within the sphere of the Royal Niger Company and so re-established good relations with that firm. Cotterell also wished to make peace with Millers, but could not get the board to make the necessary concessions and when John Holt became the Chairman of the African Association in 1894 this signified the ascendance of his opponents. Cotterell therefore resigned his position as a manager, although he retained his seat on the board. (*Trade Makers*, pp. 94–5.)
25. By 1896 the 'peace' party was back in power owing to a dispute between John Holt and Alfred Jones over the sale of the fleet of the African Association to Elder Dempster. This had the effect of forcing Holt to resign his chairmanship and, after a few months, Cotterell was reappointed a manager. The differences with Millers were then quickly resolved so that from this time the African Association began a period of ever-increasing prosperity. (*Trade Makers*, p. 95.)
26. The Sierra Leone Coaling Company – sometimes referred to as the 'Old' Company – operated in many parts of West Africa and dealt with many items besides coal. See copy of this firm's advertisement in the *Sierra Leone Weekly News*, 17 October 1891.
27. See below, pp. 180–2.
28. It was not until the end of the nineteenth century that a really scientific approach was made to the investigation of tropical diseases and it was 1898 before the British government appreciated 'that it was sending untrained doctors to work in the colonies'. It was only then that it became fully understood that, 'there was no place in Britain which was dedicated to the necessary disciplines and there was no specific reference to them in the medical curriculum, apart from the elementary parasitology'. (B.G. Maegraith, 'History of the Liverpool School of Tropical Medicine', *Medical History*,

Vol. XVI, No.4, Oct. 1972, p. 354. See also: Ronald Ross, *Memoirs*, London, John Murray, 1923, and *Trade Makers*, p. 162.)

29. West Africa was first connected to England by cable in 1886. Only Bathurst and Freetown were linked with the UK at that time and it took another three years before Accra, Lagos, Brass and Bonny were also connected. (*Message Communication Part I*, Standard Bank Review, October 1969, p. 5.)
30. Ajai, a Yoruba boy, was liberated from slavery in 1822 and taken to Bathurst. He was re-named Samuel Crowther and, after a brief visit to England, was employed as a teacher – firstly at Bathurst and then in Sierra Leone. In 1841 Crowther accompanied the British Niger expedition 'to prospect for a mission' and on his return was sent to the Church Missionary Society's college at Islington. He was ordained in 1843 and returned to Sierra Leone, subsequently preaching throughout West Africa including Abeokuta where he was reunited with his mother and sisters. In 1864 he was consecrated at Canterbury, becoming Bishop of the West African countries beyond British jurisdiction. He died in 1891 at a great age. (C. Fyfe, *A History of Sierra Leone*, London, Oxford University Press, 1962, pp. 172, 221, 236, 327 & 472.)
31. The manilla was usually in the form of a small copper horseshoe of about four inches in circumference. Its value varied from twopence to sixpence over time and a few, larger manillas of greater value were also used. The manilla was accepted extensively throughout the nineteenth century and was so popular that it remained in regular use until 1948. (*Nigeria Handbook*, Crown Agents for the Colonies, London, 1953, p. 69. See also P.N. Davies, 'The Origins of Banking in British West Africa', *Sea*, Vol. 8, No. 6, July 1973, pp. 9–11 and below, p. 176.
32. See below, pp. 106, 114 and 122.
33. The correct name of this vessel was *Clangregor*. Of 838 tons, she had been built in 1853 and was owned by Tyson, Richmond and Jones. (*Lloyds Register*, 1858, C.476.)
34. s.s. *Retriever* was built of iron by Denny & Rankin at Dumbarton. Of 329 gross tons, she measured 159 x 22 x 12 feet. She was owned by the African Steam Ship Company from 1854 to 1867 and then she was sold to Laird Brothers of Birkenhead in exchange for a new steamer. (*Trade Makers:* Table 85, No. 8.)
35. Ja Ja moved to Opobo in 1867 but fighting continued for several years. A division of markets was then agreed upon with the assistance of Consul Livingstone and, under Ja Ja's strong rule, Opobo became very prosperous. In 1886 a dispute arose with a number of British merchants, but Alexander Miller, Brother and Company sided with Ja Ja and, as a result, secured a near monopoly of the trade. The following year Mr. H.H. Johnstone was appointed as Acting Vice-Consul and he took the side of the combined merchants. By a trick he persuaded Ja Ja to come on board H.M.S. *Goshawk* and took him to Accra for trial. Ja Ja was sentenced to five years deportation and was sent to St. Vincent in the West Indies. His sentence was later revoked but he died at Teneriffe while on his way home. (*U.A.C. Hist.*, pp. 61–4. See also C.N. de Cardi, in Mary Kingsley's *West African Studies*, MacMillan, London, 1899, Appendix I, pp. 526–9 and pp. 541 and K.O. Dike, *Trade and Politics in the Niger Delta*, Clarendon Press, Oxford, 1956, pp. 182–98.)
36. John Holt, wishing to extend his interests in the 'Oil Rivers', subsequently formed a partnership with George Watts. In 1889 George Watts and Company became co-founders of the African Association Limited and Mr. Watts became one of its original directors. (See note 23.)
37. At the Congress of Berlin in 1884 the British government began to appreciate that if it took no positive action both France and Germany would reap a considerable benefit. A policy was therefore evolved to

extend British sovereignty to inland areas. This was partly designed to increase trade but its primary object was to prevent the French and Germans from cutting off the coastal settlements from the interior. But the British government believed that the public would not support the undertaking of vast new expenses and responsibilities in West Africa, and so it adopted the expedient of creating a chartered company to do its work for it.

38. The formation of the Royal Niger Company in 1886 meant that it had the duty of ruling as well as the privilege of exclusive trading in enormous areas of the Niger basin. A gradual change in public opinion was then reflected by changes within the British government and these were confirmed by the advent of Joseph Chamberlain to the Colonial Office in 1895. Chamberlain was known to be in favour of a more vigorous colonial policy and an important aspect of his work came to fruition in 1900 when the Royal Niger Company lost its administrative functions. (*Trade Makers*, pp. 26–7; *U.A.C. Hist.*, pp. 19–31 and also J.D. Hargreaves, *Prelude to the Partition of West Africa*, Macmillan, London, 1963.)
39. An interesting account of life aboard a British naval vessel stationed on the West African coast at this time is provided in: *Cox on the JuJu Coast* (Journal kept on H.M.S. *Fly*). Published by Ellison & Co., St. Helier, 1968.
40. Lord and Lady Brassey were also very active travellers. See: Mrs. Brassey, *Around the World in the Yacht 'Sunbeam'*, Henry Holt & Co., New York, 1878.
41. See note 23.
42. John E. Flint, *Sir George Goldie and the Making of Nigeria*, Oxford University Press, London, 1960.
43. See note 24.
44. John Holt resigned because the Board of the African Association failed to support him in a dispute over the sale of their fleet to Elder Dempster. (*Trade Makers*, pp. 112–3.)
45. The five remaining directors of the original Board are numbered: those who had died are indicated by an 'x' and those who had retired have a blank against their names.
46. s.s. *Africa* was built of iron by Laird Brothers at Birkenhead in 1871. Of 1,717 gross tons, she measured 285 x 34 x 23 feet. She was owned by the African Steam Ship Company until 1899 when she was broken up. (*Trade Makers*, Table 85, No. 30.)
47. P.N. Davies, *Sir Alfred Jones and the Development of West African Trade*, Unpublished M.A. Thesis, University of Liverpool, 1964, pp. 147–51. See also *Trade Makers*, pp. 126–7.
48. W.F. Tewson, *The British Cotton Growing Association* (Golden Jubilee, 1904–1954), issued by the Association, 1954.
49. s.s. *Port Kingston* was built of steel by A. Stephen and Sons at Glasgow in 1904. Of 7,585 gross tons, she measured 460 x 55 x 33 feet. She was owned by the Imperial Direct Line until sold in 1911. (*Trade Makers*, Table 85, No. 211.)
50. As part of its agreement with the Colonial Office, Elder Dempster took over and refurnished the Constant Spring Hotel and the Myrtle Bank Hotel. (*Ocean Highways*, Illustrated Souvenir of Elder Dempster & Co., Published by Shipping Gazette & Lloyds List, Liverpool, 1902, pp. 48–52. See also below, p. 199.
51. A.H. Milne, *Sir Alfred Lewis Jones, K.C.M.G.*, Henry Young, Liverpool, 1914, pp. 105–6.
52. The remaining private papers of Sir A.L. Jones are in the possession of his great niece, Mrs. F.N. Mocatta. (*Trade Makers*, p. 498.)
53. Mr. J.W. Davey was born in Cornwall in 1853. In 1871 he moved to Liverpool and obtained employment in Elder Dempster's office. He made steady

progress and became a partner in 1879. From then until his death in 1908 he was Alfred Jones' right hand man. (*Journal of Commerce*, 2 November 1900, and *African World*, 26 September 1908.)

54. Alfred Jones' commercial interests passed into the hands of Sir Owen Philipps – later Lord Kylsant – and Lord Pirrie. (*Trade Makers*, pp. 169–73. See also P.N. Davies and A.M. Bourn, 'Lord Kylsant and the Royal Mail', *Business History*, Vol. XIV, No. II, July 1972, pp. 103–23.
55. Mary Kingsley, *West African Studies*, op.cit.; see also Olwen Campbell, *Mary Kingsley. A Victorian in the Jungle*, Methuen, London, 1957 and Cecil Howard, *Mary Kingsley*, Hutchinson, London, 1957.

2. AUTOBIOGRAPHY OF JAMES DEEMIN

INTRODUCTION

James Deemin was born on the 4th of May, 1863, at Berkeswell, near Meriden, Warwickshire. Little is known of his background except that his father, William Deemin, was a farmer, and that his mother's maiden name was Astley.

Family tradition suggests that James Deemin left school at an early age and obtained employment in a Coventry cycle works. He is said to have been ambitious as a child and, finding that prospects of advancement were extremely limited at home, determined to try his luck abroad.

We will probably never know how he came to apply to John Holt and Company. Perhaps it was one of a series of applications or there may have been some personal connection that now eludes us. At any event in 1882, at the age of 19, James Deemin travelled to Liverpool and began his career as a West African merchant.

It is at this point that the present narrative begins. It is in no sense a complete autobiography but a very full and detailed account of Deemin's early days in West Africa. The period covered is that of Deemin's first tour which lasted from 1883 to 1887 – no less than four and a half years spent in extremely difficult and, at times, dangerous circumstances. The record has a general chronological pattern but there are any number of fascinating digressions. There are also a number of repetitions. Deemin wrote the three sections which follow at different times and for different purposes. Some of the overlapping items might, with advantage, have been removed but, perhaps, more might have been lost than was gained.

James Deemin spent his entire business career with John Holt's. From 1883 to 1914 he was a vital part of their Coast staff and eventually became Agent-General for the Company. Eight of these years were utilised in fighting Holt's case against the 'concessionaire' policy of the French Government at Libreville – an activity which eventually resulted in substantial compensation. In 1914 Deemin was captured by the Germans in the Cameroons. Fortunately his captivity did not last long and he was rescued by the Royal Navy and subsequently repatriated to England. By then the effects of long exposure to a severe tropical climate together with the shock of imprisonment had weakened his health and he was taken to a Nursing Home in Gambier Terrace, Liverpool.

Once fully fit he left the Home and, soon afterwards, married the Assistant Matron – Sister Edith Evans. Deemin was then aged fifty-two and this was his first and only marriage. From this time onwards he was subject to frequent attacks of malaria but, nevertheless, he was able to play an active and responsible part in John Holt's Liverpool Office. Deemin retired in 1931 and from then till his death in March, 1939, lived quietly in Prenton, Birkenhead.

In 1967 I was approached by Mr. Ian Holt of John Holt and Company (Liverpool) Limited. It appeared that the Company had been making some re-arrangements in their office and had come across Deemin's desk which had been untouched since 1931. The desk contained a great number of letters to and from Deemin together with other papers and artifacts. In due course these were duly catalogued by me and now form part of the John Holt Papers which are held at the Rhodes House Library in Oxford. The interest generated by this task then led to a further investigation of Deemin's career and to the present work. In addition, under my supervision, Miss R. Glover of the Department of Economic History, University of Liverpool, is currently preparing an M.A. thesis on certain aspects of Deemin's career in West Africa.

Sources John Holt Papers.
Obituary in *West Africa*, 1 April 1939.
Obituary in *Birkenhead News*, 25 & 29 March, 1939.
Correspondence with Mrs. C.P. Bodenham Cowley, (niece of James Deemin).

TRIBUTE TO MR. JAMES DEEMIN

By Mr. Robert Holt

I find some difficulty in putting down in a concise manner, even a brief résumé of Mr. James Deemin's life and activities in the service of the Company. He is the only living Member who can claim a right to be called one of the 'Founders' of our Company.

He entered the service of JOHN HOLT in 1883. In 1884 the name of the business was changed to JOHN HOLT & COMPANY, as it was at this time that Captain Jonathan C. Holt became a partner with his brother.

In 1897 the Company was incorporated as a private Limited Company.

Mr. Deemin's service therefore covers each stepping stone of the Company's progress. No other individual in our employ can claim this honour. His early Coast life was one of hardship and discomforts, and few men without his courage, endurance and patience could have withstood the conditions which existed at that time. The late Mr. John Holt, when writing to Mr. Deemin in regard to the fight he was carrying on in the Company's interests against the French Concessionaires, used these words:–

"Your tenacity of purpose is excellent, – you have
"suffered enough to daunt the most courageous."

and this quotation applies to many stages in his career with the Company.

For eight continuous years he stayed at Libreville, fighting the Concessionaires in the French Courts for the rights our Company claimed. It was finally in the Court de Cassation, – the equivalent to our House of Lords, – that the success of his labours on the Coast received their due reward. It was due to Mr. Deemin first, and foremost, with the guidance and help of Mr. John Holt, at this end, that we received compensation for the wrongs we suffered by the policy of the French Government granting concessions to French Nationals of rights over territories, and trading, in Districts we had been established for so many years. Some day, I hope Mr. Deemin will find time to write us the inner history of this unfortunate Concessionaire policy of the French Government, and how it affected the Company.

Mr. Deemin always had the misfortune to be sent to those of our Establishments which needed straightening out. When just out of his teens he was sent to Cape Lopez to clear up a muddle made by the Agent in charge, and all through his career, it has been his lot to create order out of chaos. Lagos, Cameroons, Nigeria, Dahomey, all in their turn have received his attention, and the foundations of sound trading in all those Areas were instituted by him. He lays no claim to the modernising of our organisation, but the foundations on which our present mode of trading has been built, were created by him. When he eventually gave up his Coast life, he entered the Home Management, and became a pillar of strength in bringing the Coast mentality into Head Office. He voiced the difficulties of climate and conditions under which our employees lived and worked in Africa and taught us patience and forbearance towards them. To say that we hold him in the greatest esteem and respect is only a common form of expression. It is with sincerity we use such words, and in addition we say he has the affection and friendship of all of us.

We trust he will be with us for many years to come, – and give us all the benefit of his wonderful and exceptional experience, which is so essential to our progress and welfare. As a junior to Mr. Deemin I appreciate to the full the wise guidance he has always given to me during my business life.

ROBERT HOLT

AUTOBIOGRAPHY OF JAMES DEEMIN

I

I signed my first Agreement in April of 1883 in the Firm's small Offices in Preesons Row, when, if I am not mistaken, the whole office staff – including the three Brothers – did not exceed 7 to 8 men. The terms of the agreement were to serve John Holt and Company on the Coast for three years with free passage out and home, food and lodgings, and such medical attention as obtainable, and Salary at the rate of £40,0.0., £50.0.0. and £60.0.0. I was instructed to sail per s.s. *'Gaboon'*[1] to Sette Camma, now forming part of the French Congo, but then unattached. My age was 19, and the only formality I had to fulfil, apart from furnishing references, was to obtain the consent of my parents, as the idea of having applicants medically examined had then not materialised.

I duly sailed as instructed and found the s.s. *'Gaboon'* had a small passenger accommodation right aft, and the only promenade was on the poop over the Saloon. So far as my memory serves, the accommodation consisted of 8 small Cabins and as there were upwards of 30 passengers, most of them bound for the Congo, a number of us had to make shift on the stern sheets of the Saloon right over the propeller until we got into the Bay where it was no longer possible to prevent getting rolled off on to the saloon deck so we had the beds made up in the latter as being less dangerous. The main drawback to this was we had to turn out at 5 a.m. to allow the stewards to scrub down, and the majority of us lined up on the main deck for our morning bath which was served by the Quartermaster playing the hose on us washing down decks. As there was only one small bathroom provided for passengers this served to relieve the congestion which would have been more acute had the whole of the passengers insisted on bathing in the orthodox manner.

The food provided was, to say the least, of a somewhat monotonous nature. For breakfast we usually had porridge served with water slightly coloured with condensed milk, Salt Beef curried, and Bacon, and an oily substance which was supposed to be butter. Lunch usually consisted of salt beef or pork, hot or cold, and dinner of beef or mutton (killed on board), Sweets and Cheese.

The whole question of passenger traffic to and from the Coast was then of minor importance and I have certainly no recollection of being met at the end of my voyage by Elder Dempster's Agent with an offer of a £5. note as some slight compensation for having to accept the

Saloon Deck as sleeping accommodation.

Our first port of call on the Coast was the Island of 'Goree' then the principal trading station of Senegal, Dakar being only a small native village. We then went on to Sierre Leone and afterwards called at numerous villages along the Kroo Coast between Monrovia and Axim where we picked up large numbers of Krooboys destined for the Oil Rivers and Plantations of Fernando Po and St. Thome. At the latter places they were handed over to the highest bidders and in some cases as much as £5.0.0. per head was paid for them, the price varying according to supply and demand. The decks were absolutely crowded with these men and how they managed to sleep was a mystery to me. It is not difficult to imagine the noise and odour which existed, and the fights which daily occurred when their rations of boiled rice were served twice daily were, to say the least, exciting until one became accustomed to them.

What is now known as the French Ivory Coast was then unattached and there were no trading stations established in the whole district. The small trade which was carried on was by means of sailing ships mainly hailing from Bristol which sailed out with a cargo of goods and anchored off the main coast villages, Natives bringing off produce through the surfs by means of Canoes, and bartering this for goods. When the goods were exhausted the vessels sailed home with the produce and returned to the Coast again with further goods the following season. It must have been a somewhat monotonous existence lying off an exposed coast for many months subject to the constant Atlantic rollers which kept the vessels on the move the whole time.

To-day this Coast is served with Wharves, Railways, excellent Motor Roads, and an efficient Administration under the French Government, and is renowned for the excellent quality of Mahogany it exports in large quantities, in addition to Palm Oil, Kernels, and Cocoa.

On the Gold Coast the vessel called at numerous ports below Axim and Elmina landing a few packages here and there and picking up Coopers and Carpenters to meet requirements in Lagos and the Oil Rivers. At this time Cocoa – now the main export – was quite unknown in this Colony, the exports consisting of Oil and Kernels and these only in comparatively small quantities.

I must not omit to mention one small port of call and that was Quittah, then known as Jella Coffie. It was of considerable importance as it was the port where steamers then obtained supplies of fresh food in the way of Chickens, Ducks, Turkeys, Eggs and Fruit. As soon as the steamer anchored hundreds of small Canoes came alongside, many of them half full of water, and for some few hours after pandemonium reigned with the bartering for the provisions they brought, and although the poultry was not of first quality and many were killed to save their lives, they formed a very welcome change of diet.

The next port of call was Lagos Roads as the present Wharves and flourishing towns of Lome and Cotonou were then undreamt of and in fact there were no signs of even a native village on the beach between Quittah and Lagos.

Leaving Lagos after spending a couple of extremely unpleasant days owing to heavy seas we made for the Oil Rivers, calling at Bonny and Old Calabar. In all these rivers the trade was then conducted on Hulks – i.e. old sailing ships with masts dismantled and roofed in with Galvanised Iron. It was in Old Calabar I made my first acquaintance with Palm Oil Chop, my host being Mr. George Watts, on the Hulk 'Amsterdam'.[2]

The British Government was, at this time, represented in Old Calabar by a Consul in the person of Mr. Hewett, who, at the moment was very much perturbed at the activities displayed by the Germans in the Cameroons.

After leaving Old Calabar we made for Fernando Po where we landed Mr. J.E. Gibney[3] for the firm. Although from a trading point of view this picturesque Island is of minor importance it has particular interest to the firm as being the spot where Mr. John Holt received his initiation into the West African Trade, and it can therefore be looked upon as the foundation stone of the present important business. In his days it was the headquarters of the British Consul whose main duties consisted in suppressing the Slave Trade, and it was the terminal point of the first line of British Steamers which served the African Coast.[4] Goods destined for ports South West of this point were landed here and transported to their destinations by means of Schooners, and Captain Holt who joined his brother after he had established on his own account commanded the Schooner 'Maria', the figure-head of which now adorns the Board Room in Liver Buildings.[5] It was by this means the factories of Elobey and Gaboon were opened and supplied with goods. Its main trading importance in those times was due to the fact that it was one of the Depots and Coaling Stations of the British Fleet which was actively patrolling the Coast with the object of suppressing the Slave Trade, and at the time of my first visit Messrs. Holts were actively supplying Coal to one of these Coasting Vessels.

From Fernando Po we went across to Ambas Bay (Victoria) where Mr. Harry (now Sir Harry) Johnston was acting as British Vice Consul, and our visit was mainly to carry mails and stores for him.

We afterwards proceeded up the Wuri River to Cameroons and anchored off Bell Town. Here, as in the other Rivers, there were no factories established on the land, all trading operations taking place in Hulks anchored in the stream. We were represented in this respect by the Hulk 'Rajah Sarawak'[6] the remains of which being still in evidence near our present beach. Another Hulk which I remember very well was the 'Robert Burns'[7] belonging to R. & W. Kings of Bristol, with a well-known old Coaster in charge in the person of Captain Buchan. For many years after these Hulks disappeared the various Agents were always known by the Natives as Captains, and even to this day some of the older Natives use this denomination when addressing them. At the time of my visit the German flag had not been hoisted nor the territory proclaimed as a German protectorate. This took place 2 years later.

On leaving Cameroon after spending 3 days there we wended our way to Elobey. Here, apart from Hatton and Cooksons who had a Hulk anchored off the Mouth of the Muni River, the few factories working the trade were established on a small Island about two miles from the river mouth. It was here Captain Holt had the unpleasant experience a few years prior to my visit of being seized by Natives on board the 'Maria' and taken up the river where he was held as prisoner until ransomed by Hatton & Cookson's Agent, Mr. R.B.W. Walker. The main export from this District was then Barwood which was used in this Country for the extraction of a red dye. It was exported by sailing vessels who came out loaded with Coal for Fernando Po and Gaboon where the French Government had a Coaling Station for their fleet.

The following day we arrived in Gaboon where we landed from the steamer's deck the 'Oviro' a 30 ton river steamer on account of the firm who were then opening out factories in the Ogowe River. This craft, I believe, was the largest up to then carried on the deck of a West African steamer and it was built to the full dimensions of its deck space. Four years later I had this craft under my control on being transferred to the Ogowe and she was in commission until 1906, a period of 23 years, which is not a bad record for a timber built craft in the tropics.

Three days were spent in Gaboon fitting in the Boilers and Engines of the 'Oviro' and we then left towing a small Schooner 'Bakali Bangue' loaded with cargo and building material which the firm was sending to Fernan Vaz where they were opening a Trading Station. We took on board Mr. Findlay who was going there as Agent, and I remember his astonishment the next morning when he found the schooner missing. It was, however, afterwards discovered that the Native Crew on board had got frightened during the night and had cut the tow rope. Ten days later the schooner arrived safely at Fernan Vaz under her own sail, although the crew had a very rough time being short of food and water.

We landed Mr. Findlay at Fernan Vaz along with the cargo destined for this port and then proceeded to Iguela, where Hatton & Cookson had a small Trading Station, but were unable to land cargo owing to the heavy surf running.

The next morning we arrived off Sette Camma after a voyage of 46 days, without voyage pay or any expenses allowance such as enjoyed by employees at the present time.

The vessel anchored about 4 miles from the beach off Holt's factory which was 5 miles to the South of Hatton & Cookson's, and from the manner in which she rolled there was every indication that the surf was none too good. However, after several attempts the boats safely negotiated it and after a couple of hours waiting they got alongside bringing with them the firm's Agent who instructed me to get into the first boat and get on shore which I had considerable difficulty in accomplishing owing to the manner in which the Ship was rolling. One minute the boat would be nearly level with the ship's deck and the next appeared to be near its keel, and one had to swarm down a rope ladder and wait a propitious moment to jump for the boat. However, I managed to get in with nothing worse than bruised shins, and an hour later was waiting with considerable trepidation outside the surf for a favourable moment to negotiate it. During this waiting nothing could be seen but a huge wall of water racing for the beach and showers of spray as it broke on it and one had to hang on to the thwarts to prevent being pitched out. It was only after waiting half an hour that an opportunity occurred and we then shot toward the beach on the top of a breaker and arrived safely although the boat was half-filled with water and my Kit was floating about in this.

Altogether I was not feeling particularly happy being drenched to the skin and with no one to meet me and no dry clothes. All I could see were two White Buildings and a few native houses erected on dazzling white sand about 100 yards above high water mark, which one of the boys told me was Holt's factory. On approaching them I found that at the end of one of the buildings was a small Bungalow consisting of two small bedrooms and a sitting room, all very sparsely furnished and not overclean. My luggage was deposited in the sitting room. There was no alternative but to wait the Agent's return which only took place shortly before dark, and during this time I was both empty and cold. Unfortunately the Agent was in a quarrelsome mood, having from all appearances sampled a good many glasses of liquor on board. Apparently he had quarrelled with a Mr. Martin who had arrived by the same steamer to open a factory for Edward Bros. and immediately after landing he buckled round his waist a heavy revolver and stuck a bowie knife in his top boots and insisted on my accompanying him 5 miles along the beach to settle his quarrel, at the same time informing me of the number of people who had been recently carried away by Leopards. Every few yards he would fire off his revolver to frighten these beasts away, but fortunately we had not proceeded very far when the liquor took effect and he became helpless. I then took charge of the revolver and after dragging him above high water mark returned to the factory for boys and a hammock and eventually got him back to the factory and put him to bed, retiring myself to the spare room where I lay down on a bare mattress. Fortunately one of the stewards lent me a dry cloth and made me a cup of tea which was all I had from breakfast until the following morning.

The next morning the Agent passed me out a few tins of meat and some biscuits and went off in a canoe to visit one of Hatton & Cookson's Branches up the Lagoon, promising to return the same evening, but as he took with him a liberal supply of liquor obtained from the 'Gaboon' it was 5 days before I saw anything of him again, and I was reduced to paying a visit to Hatton & Cookson's Factory 5 miles to the north to beg a few more tins and a little tea but even with this I had a very thin time of it, and heartily wished myself back again in England.

As the whole Factory was locked up and desolate with the exception of a few Krooboys I had plenty of time for reflection, and I began to think there might be some truth in the weird stories with which I was regaled on the voyage out. In any case I began to wonder what was meant by the firm undertaking to provide food and lodging and such medical attendance as obtainable. Both the former were of an exceedingly primitive nature, whilst I soon learned that the nearest doctor was 300 miles away and the only manner of communicating with him was by mail boat which rarely called at the port homeward bound. There was certainly a Doctor on board the steamer but he usually knew too much of the risk of passing such a surf to venture ashore, and as a matter of fact I never knew or heard of any one of them doing so during my stay in the District.

In so far as medicines were concerned, we were provided with such lines as Cockles Pills, Castor Oil, Epsom Salts, Chlorodyne, and sulphate of Quinine in powder form. The latter was usually taken wrapped up in tissue paper, but with no scales for weighing out a dose we had to simply guess at it. We had no knowledge then of the mosquito transmitting fever, and that taken in moderate doses regularly quinine acted as a preventative, and naturally we only resorted to it when fever was actually present.

No one in the place wore a helmet and during the whole of my stay in the District, nearly 4 years, I usually wore a small Cap and occasionally a trade felt hat when I wanted to appear well dressed.

To revert to my introduction to the Coast, immediately the Agent returned he instructed me to get ready to proceed to NGousa Island where we had a small branch and which I was to take over from the Assistant in Charge and carry on the trade. I was packed into a small and cranky canoe along with as much luggage as it could conveniently carry and told I should arrive at my destination in about 3½ to 4 hours.

As we passed through creeks infested with Hippos and Crocodiles the former popping up frequently quite close the the Canoe, and afterwards had to cross open stretches of rough water my journey was not at all pleasant, and I was heartily glad when the Island appeared in sight, but I got another shock when I was introduced to my future quarters which consisted of an extremely dilapidated native-built house, half of which was used as a shop, and the other half a one roomed bungalow, which served as bedroom, sitting room, dining room, bath room, &c. The only thing that could be said about it was that it was extremely well ventilated, particularly through the roof. My bed consisted of a rough bamboo couch upon which was placed a native grass mat. No mosquito curtains or pillows were supplied and it was with some difficulty I could obtain a trade cotton blanket. The furniture consisted of a very antiquated Madeira Chair, a canvas deck chair belonging to the Assistant in Charge and two wooden chairs, a small table and the bamboo couch referred to. There was a table lamp, but no Kerosene, but we were fortunate enough to possess a few candles and some empty bottles to serve as candlesticks.

It did not require any degree of intelligence to come to the conclusion that unless prompt steps were taken the factory would collapse, and in pointing this out I was instructed to build a new one and sent at the same time a few axes and Matchets with which to build it. I was also authorised to engage a few more native labourers to assist in this operation.

The nearest native town to the Island factory was at least three miles away. The island itself was covered with trees, and thick undergrowth, with the exception of about 100 yards square which had been cleared and I soon found out that it was infested with a variety of snakes, many of which were actually killed in the shop and house, and my first step was to make a bigger clearance round the buildings.

After some trouble I eventually got the Agent to give me a rough plan of the building I was to erect. This consisted of two rooms, one to serve as a shop, and the other as dwelling quarters, and he went so far as to supply sufficient galvanised iron sheets to surround the shop and enough native sawn planks to make the shop doors. All the remaining material had to be obtained from the bush.

I was really expected to erect the building without shewing any extra working expenses except for the few extra boys, and as these only cost about 5/- per month each it was not a considerable item.

As the rainy season was approaching it can be imagined I lost no time in setting to work to get some building erected which would be at least water-tight, and I was very proud when it was completed at no extra cost beyond the usual labour account of a few pounds. It would have been more comfortable if I could have obtained a few planks or a little cement to form a deck, but frequent requests for this luxury were turned down. Even my request for a decent mattress was not listened to, except that it was pointed out there was plenty of straw in the Earthenware Casks which would serve to make a Mattress if I really needed such luxury.

In so far as regards food, I was not so badly off as Chickens, eggs, fish, and goats, were quite plentiful and cheap. Bread I rarely had but occasionally was given a tin or two of Cabin biscuits. Butter and lard were always at a premium and for cooking purposes Palm Oil was the usual medium. As a matter of fact we had to depend mainly on local supplies for food and the average cost of living in this manner did not exceed £40.0.0. per annum, covering servants' wages.

One of the worst features was the excessive loneliness of the existence. It was very rare one could get a supply of Kerosene and for long periods one had to be content with a home made Palm Oil lamp, or native made bush light. As for society, frequently a couple of months would pass without seeing an European, and then only for an hour or two. Sometimes when the surf was unworkable three months would pass without getting the slightest news from outside and when papers did arrive they were usually kept on the beach for a considerable time before distribution took place.

Fortunately the Natives were of a peaceable nature so long as they were sober, but one of the main articles of trade was cheap German Rum and this was frequently the cause of considerable excitement and the letting of a little blood, mostly amongst themselves. If this took place in the factory it was the usual custom to put them into irons and lock them up until sober again.

Labourers employed were always drawn from another part of the Coast, mainly from Loango and the Congo, except the beach boys which were from the Kroo Coast. On Sundays these labourers were collected together from the different head factories on the beach and dressed up in second hand officers' tunics, and regularly drilled and taught to shoot. The arms used were old Snider rifles and on several occasions these had to be utilised when some of the smaller chiefs got troublesome. A demonstration outside their villages was usually sufficient to clear them out into the surrounding bush and the most drastic punishment it was found necessary to use the burning down of their village.

Personally I had very little trouble with them, although I had frequently to use the hand and leg irons. So long as there was justification for the punishment inflicted they bore little, if any, malice and it must be remembered there was absolutely no outside protection and we had to entirely depend upon ourselves for this.

The District I had to open and work was considerable in extent. It comprised the whole of the extensive river and lakes and 20 days march inland from the south of this and 2 days walk North. To visit the whole of my District it therefore took the best part of two months, partly by canoe, but mostly footing it. In many districts I visited I was the first European to penetrate so far inland. It meant marching through the enormous Equatorial forest day after day, and at night making camp and plucking leaves from the shrubs to make the ground somewhat soft to sleep on. There was no such luxury as tents, camp beds, or even a rubber sheet provided. During trek a sharp look out was kept for Monkeys or birds to supplement the meagre larder, and many a time have I been thankful for a good monkey stew.

One of the main difficulties on these walking tours was the possession of boots, and on many occasions have I returned with the remnants of shoes tied up in strips of shirts or any other material found handy for the purpose. Matches were at an absolute premium. Safeties were not then invented and steamers would only carry the ordinary matches on deck at high rates of freight. Apart from this, when we got out a consignment it not infrequently happened they were lost in the surf. On Canoe trips a fire in a tub filled with sand was usually carried, and when one wanted a smoke a piece of fire was passed along from one man to another. In the bush a flint and steel were carried and it took some time to get a fire started with these. It was very essential to have fires surrounding the camp to keep Leopards and other beasts and reptiles away.

The interior tribes up to then were totally ignorant of European goods and the extremely scanty clothing worn was woven by themselves from grass, but very few indeed wore any vestige of clothing at all. Tobacco was locally grown and local pipes made from Clay were used. Game was killed by poisoned arrows, and food cooked in well made earthenware pots, many of which were quite artistic in design. The older men were extremely difficult to approach and would cover their heads under their grass cloth when I came near them, but the younger generation were full of curiosity at seeing a white man and in fact their attention was somewhat embarrassing especially at night time when they would insist on singing round my Hut the whole night through. Up to then the only trade they had was in the sale of slaves (domestic). These they took to the Coast where Natives produced salt through the evaporation of shallow pieces of sea water, and the slaves were exchanged for this and it was through the men who were engaged in this trade we were able to obtain interpreters and make ourselves understood.

Their villages were well made and kept quite clean and free from grass and there appeared to be no lack of food and drink. The latter consisted of a kind of beer brewed from ripe plantains and palm wine.

They expressed themselves quite willing to produce rubber if I would send in goods to purchase it, and arrangements were made for them to build shops and dwelling houses for traders who were afterwards sent in, but it took some time to get any profitable trade established amongst them and in most cases it meant sending men in to teach them how to tap the trees and make the rubber.

The whole of the trade of Setta Camma was confined to the production of rubber. The usual system was to give out to the headmen of the various villages a quantity of goods according to the number of the inhabitants of the village. These he distributed to them and was held responsible for the payments. There was practically no free trade existing as every man in the whole Country was owing something and the collection of these debts was no easy task. It necessitated frequent raiding of villages and the catching of men and women who were held as prisoners until the debts were paid, and I have had as many as 40 to 50 of these on many occasions. The debtors had to pay for their keep and it usually proved an effective means of obtaining prompt payment.

The buying and selling of Slaves[8] for domestic purposes was actively carried on and these slaves were usually sent into the forest along with two or three headmen to work the rubber and the whole of the work of the factory was carried on by Slaves, their masters turning up regularly to draw their wages. In some instances I was able to arrange to purchase the slaves and the men would then work off the amount and would become free men, but even then they would not have the local standing of freemen, but in any case they would be entitled to the money they earned and some of them became fairly wealthy and owners of slaves themselves. The more wives and slaves owned, the wealthier the individual, and some of the chiefs had as many as 150 wives and upwards of 100 slaves. The master had full power over the lives of his slaves and I have seen many a man killed for very trivial offences when the master was intoxicated and the bodies were simply thrown into the river as of no account.

On one occasion, soon after my arrival, I had a good deal of trouble with the local chief known as King Cole, who, during my absence, had compelled my shop boy to give him two gallons of Rum. Upon enquiries I found he had been making a practice of this and I went across to his town by canoe in order to have the matter out. Fortunately he met me on the landing beach and was practically alone, so I pulled him into my Canoe and we made tracks for the factory as hard as we could go, with 20 or 30 Canoes following us. We, however, managed to get to the Island first and I effectually persuaded him to order his canoes to clear off. We then talked the palaver, and he admitted having compelled the boy to give him various goods. It was arranged for him to send for produce to pay for the goods, plus a heavy fine, and I kept him prisoner until the whole payment was made.

The news of the trouble reached the beach and a dozen well armed canoes came up, but prior to their arrival the whole matter was settled and we parted quite friendly as he had sense to realise that he had merited punishment.

During the whole of my stay in the District the Old Chief was my best trader and never gave me the slightest trouble afterwards. It was from this incident I got my native name of 'Eboe' Iron bar.

I had another rather serious palaver with the Makaga of the District (Native Judge) who was responsible shortly prior to my arrival, for brutally killing a Portuguese trader, by the name of Gavier.

Unbeknown to me, he had induced one of my traders to marry one of his daughters and persistently levied toll on the factory, so I visited his town which was a days pull in a canoe from the factory and met him in all his war paint and surrounded by a large number of Natives. Fortunately for me King Cole happened to be present and during the free fight which took place it would have gone against me had not the old King taken sides with me. As it was I got a nasty cut on the shoulder and most of my crew were cut in the mêlée, but we managed to get the judge tied up and I took him away with me until he had paid for the stolen goods and the fine imposed. For some time afterwards, however, I gave his town a pretty wide berth. There were hundreds of instances of this nature, but of minor importance, but these two will give some idea of what trading consisted of in those times.

I may mention that some little time after my trouble with the old Makaga he visited Woermann's Factory[9] near his town and tried to get hold of the European, threatening to serve him as he had the Portuguese, but the European managed to get away during the night. The various chiefs were called together and a big palaver held when it was decided that the judge should be banished, and that if he shewed his face at any factory he was liable to be shot at sight. After this he disappeared from the river altogether, and in any case he took good care to keep clear of my factory. The Chiefs, knowing themselves supported by the Europeans, confiscated the majority of his wives and slaves, and his successor took care to confine his attention to Native affairs and leave the factories alone.

Although the Island upon which my factory was built was, to say the least, lonely, being in the centre of a lake, it was not altogether devoid of excitement. On the East side was a shallow bank where Hippopotami were fairly plentiful, and these used to come on the Island to feed at night time and left their traces even on the Verandah, and although we dug pits covering them over carefully, we never succeeded in getting them to fall in. I, however, managed to shoot two of them on a moonlight night. It was a common occurrence to be wakened up at night by snakes getting amongst the chickens, and without exaggeration I think I killed considerably over 100 of these reptiles on the Island, amongst which were many large pythons. Crocodiles were also fairly numerous. These used to crawl out of the water during the day and sleep in the sun with their mouths wide open, and many were killed and eaten by the Natives.

Deer and pigs were frequently seen swimming across the lake from one Island to another, and in the mainland were large numbers of Gorillas and Chimpanzees. The former frequently attacked unarmed natives and many of the latter came to me to have their serious wounds doctored. I remember one day meeting a big male Gorilla on a narrow bush path standing on his legs and beating his chest with rage. I had, at the moment, only a single-barrel gun loaded with small shot, but I let go at him only a few paces away and ran for my life, but after loading up again returned cautiously to find him dead. He measured 5'10" and his skeleton was sold for £10 with which we bought potatoes and other luxuries on one of the mail boats.[10]

Another exciting incident I remember very well was having my small dog taken from my heels at night time by a leopard whilst I was walking along a narrow path bordered on each side by long grass. These animals frequently came right into the factory yard after the goats and many of them were caught in traps.

Elephants were plentiful in the forests, and it was by no means rare to have our camps disturbed by troops of these passing too close to us to be at all pleasant. On many occasions have I seen them crossing fairly wide rivers and although I have shot at them when swimming,never succeeded in killing one in the water.

As I had about 150 traders to look after, spread over a wide area the most of my time was spent travelling. This was not so bad during the dry season, but during the rainy season there was nothing pleasant about it, as it was rarely one was dry from one month end to another and during the tornado season many risks were taken crossing wide stretches of water in a laden canoe, or spending a night in the forest with the wind, and thunder and lightning playing round to the extent unimaginable outside the tropics.

II

(James Deemin landed at Sette Camma on the West Coast of Africa in the year 1883 at the age of 19.)

This port is situated 2½ degrees south of the Equator and at that period the territory between 1 degree south and the Portuguese Colony at the mouth of the Congo had not been annexed by any European Government and the nearest Government Official was stationed at Gaboon ½ degree North of the Equator.

The South Coast was served by the Elder Dempster line who sent one steamer per month as far south as Landana, but it not infrequently happened that the heavy surf at Setta Camma prevented any communication with the steamer, and our supplies and correspondence were landed on the homeward passage at Cameroons and the following outward steamers would pick them up. In some cases we were without supplies and news for periods of three months.

There were two factories established in the Sette Camma District which extended roughly from Ngoue to the north and Nyanga to the south, a distance of 100 miles and the European population totalled 8. The two trading firms were Hatton & Cookson's, and John Holt's, and a distance of 4 Miles separated their two Depots on the Beach. The nearest Native village to Holt's factory was 5 miles away and this was the only village within a radius of 20 miles.

The main factory consisted of one Galvanised Iron Building and a few native built houses for the boys. The Iron building served as store, small shop and European Dwelling quarters (two small bedrooms and one living room) all of which were extremely scantily furnished by the local Carpenter, with the exception of 2 Iron bedsteads and 6 Windsor Chairs.

No trade was done at this place and it simply served as a receiving and shipping Depot, and it was only on rare occasions it was visited by any stranger.

The day after my arrival the Agent decided to visit one of Hatton & Cookson's Branches about 20 miles distant per canoe, promising to return the following day, and leaving me a few biscuits and a couple of tins of boiled Beef to carry on with. He was, however, absent for seven days and I had a very thin time mainly existing on Crabs caught on the sea shore and a little rice obtained from the Kroo boys washed down with rain water.

Immediately on his return I was verbally instructed to proceed to NGousa Island where we had a small branch factory situated about 30 miles up the Lagoon and was given a small and cranky canoe for the Journey. To reach the factory we had to pass through narrow grassy creeks infested with Hippopotami and Alligators, the former popping up their heads close to the Canoe at frequent intervals and although I did my best to try and appear indifferent to these episodes I was very far from feeling so, and was to say the least relieved when we reached our destination safely.

This latter was a wooded Island of about one mile in circumference situated in the Lagoon about 1½ miles distant from the Mainland. A small clearing had been made in which I found a very dilapidated Native made house divided into two rooms, one serving as a shop, and the other dwelling quarters, and a few tumble-down Native Shimbecks which served for galley and native quarters. Anything more dilapidated and lonely it would be difficult to imagine. The furniture consisted of two native made chairs, a table made from packing cases, and a native made bed with mattress stuffed with straw from an Earthenware Cask, and the roof was so well ventilated that during rains one had to use an umbrella to keep dry. Per return of canoe these conditions were pointed out to the Agent who replied by sending a few axes and Matchets with instructions to start building a new house, and in spite of requests for further details this was all I got, but as it meant either sleeping in a wet bed or making a new shelter I set to work and was exceedingly proud when succeeding in erecting a new place without any outside assistance, obtaining all the material from the Bush. It of course had no fancy glass windows, nor any wood or cement flooring, but it was at least rain-proof.

One of the main troubles I had was with regard to snakes, the Island being infested with these and without exaggeration some hundreds were killed during my residence on it. We were also troubled with Hippopotami which came on to the Island at night time destroying the vegetable garden I had taken so much pains to start, and I eventually killed two of these within 20 yards of the premises.

As to Society, two and three months would frequently elapse without seeing any Europeans.

My first fever was a pretty severe one, but all the nursing I got was from the boy who acted as Cook and Steward who got hold of some limes and dosed me with hot lime drinks until perspiration set in and I then took doses of sulphate of Quinine of which there was fortunately a supply in the factory. My Medicine Chest consisted of:–

1 bottle of Sulphate of Quinine in Powder
1 box Cockles Pills
1 bottle Chlorodyne
1 bottle Epsom Salts

No one at that period took Quinine as a preventative of fever, and it was only used when fever was present, and then the dose was usually guessed at as there were no means of weighing it out.[11]

During the dry season drinking water had to be obtained from the main land a mile and half away from the factory, whilst during the rainy season it was collected from the thatched roofs into casks and it was with considerable difficulty I eventually managed to get a charcoal filter.

The food question was not a particularly difficult one as Chickens, Goats, and Eggs were plentiful, whilst the Lagoon yielded a plentiful supply of fish and the forests game in the way of Deer, Pigs, Bush Cows, Monkeys, etc. Bread and Butter were however luxuries only indulged in on rare and special occasions, and for fats generally we had to depend upon Palm Oil both for edible and lighting purposes. Plantains and Kank (Manioc) formed our staple diet.

News from the outside world was always 5 to 6 weeks late in reaching us as we were of course not connected by any cable and had to solely depend upon the monthly steamer which was always a week to a fortnight late, and on many occasions was unable to land anything when they did call.

Literature of any kind was at a high premium, whilst recreation such as Tennis, Cricket, Golf, etc. was entirely out of the question. In fact it is hard to picture a lonelier existence than I had to bear on this Island.

The Trade consisted of bartering goods for rubber, the only produce exported, and the general method adopted was the establishment of small branches in charge of Natives throughout the District. These traders were visited each month, produce collected, and stocks taken in so far as regards those established on the banks of the Lagoon and small rivers, and each three months for those established in the interior. To visit the river side stations per Canoe usually occupied 5 days, whilst the interior trip took from 3 to 4 weeks hard walking. During the dry season the Canoe trips were not too bad, but during the rainy season especially when tornadoes were prevalent they were not only dangerous, as stretches of 10 miles of water had to be crossed, but also extremely unpleasant as one was more or less wet the whole time, and on more than one occasion my canoe has capsized and I had had to cling to her for upwards of an hour before we could get her righted.

The interior journeys were by no means pleasure trips as it meant walking the whole distance through the Equatorial Forest along narrow footpaths which were formerly used for the slave trade, and except on rare occasions where rough rafts existed for the crossing of rivers the only way of getting across was by swimming and as they were all infested with Alligators there was a certain amount of excitement when this had to the mode. In other cases small trees had been felled across narrow and deep ravines and considerable amusement was caused to the Natives by seeing me straddle these and hitch myself across.

The gear taken on these trips was necessarily limited, as everything had to be carried on the heads of Natives. It was suggested that a camp bed would be of service, or, failing this, a waterproof ground sheet, but these were considered unnecessary luxuries, and had there been any suggestion of a tent I am afraid the Agent would have had a fit. All the bedding carried was a mosquito Curtain, Native made Grass Mat, couple of white cotton Blankets, and a pillow, and these, with a Frypan, Tea kettle, Enamelled Teapot and Cup and Saucer, a few tin plates and spoons, and a couple of Marmont pots, completed the outfit.

As for food, we had to mainly depend upon what we could shoot in the way of birds, monkeys, or other small game, or what we could purchase from the Natives, and it generally meant either a feast or a famine, and on very many occasions we had to start off for a 20 to 30 miles walk without a bite or sup.

When opening up new Districts we generally camped in the forest as we were never quite sure of the reception we should get from the Natives, and in many instances the distances between villages were too great to accomplish in one day. The routine was to start at daybreak after having a cup of tea when this was obtainable, and walk steadily until 11 a.m. when a halt would be made for a meal and rest, starting again at 1 and walking until 5 p.m. We would then camp near a stream and at once set to work to collect a quantity of firewood as it was necessary to build fires round the camp to keep Elephants, Leopards, and other uninvited guests away. One boy would be told off to pluck leaves for my bed with the view of making the ground somewhat less hard, and fix up my mosquito curtain, and another to prepare a meal if there was anything to cook. Then it was necessary to set relays of watchmen to keep the fires going. In many instances we passed sleepless nights through the passing of herds of Elephants near the Camps, and often had to change our camp through the visit of driver ants, these latter often proving more troublesome than the former.

In one instance when the watchmen had let the fires get low the camp was visited by a Leopard which took a goat we had bought for the next day's meal. It was perhaps fortunate we had the Goat, or it might have taken a fancy to a Native or myself.

After I had served six months and was then 20 years old, I was instructed to visit a district which had not been previously opened to trade and which had never been visited by any Europeans. It was estimated to take six weeks to do the trip, but owing to considerable trouble with Native Chiefs who had acted as middlemen between the Interior tribes and ourselves, it actually lasted 9 weeks for although, after being kept a prisoner for several days, I was eventually permitted to pass through their District, I had to make a big detour to avoid returning the same way. A short time prior to my attempt a Portuguese trader from the Congo had tried to get through, but I was shown the spot where he was killed along with several of his people, and had considerable trouble in persuading my porters to continue their journey, and it was only by promising them increased remuneration they finally consented to do so.

During this journey we came across several campments of Pygmies who lived entirely in the forest and subsisted mainly on the game they shot with poisoned arrows, and who were generally feared by the village dwellers. In this part of the forest two of my porters who had lagged behind disappeared, and although we camped for two days and made a search for them they were never heard of again. It was presumed that the Pygmies had something to do with their disappearance as these had also vanished from their encampments we had passed the previous day.

On the whole we were well received by the Natives who had established villages, and being the first European they had seen I was the source of considerable curiosity, which was not altogether pleasant, and in fact, in order to get any rest I finally had to camp at some distance from the villages.

On our way through the forest we met several caravans conducting slaves. These were bound for the coast where the slaves would be exchanged for salt produced by the evaporation of salt water, and again sold to the wealthier natives in Sette Camma, Feenan Vaz and Gaboon, where they were utilised for the making of Native Food Plantations etc. The cost of these varied according to sex and age. The price of a girl was 50 fathoms of cloth, whilst an older woman could be bought for 20 fathoms, and a boy would cost about 30 fathoms. As a general rule these domestic slaves were not ill-treated. They lived mainly on the farms and were allowed to marry amongst themselves, and frequently they intermarried with the free natives. The children of slaves were the property of their masters, but the children resulting from marriage between slave and free native were given their liberty. The owners of slaves had full control over their lives and on several occasions I have seen them killed for what we would consider very minor offences, and their bodies would simply be thrown into the river. Labourers on the factories were mainly slaves who had to hand over wages earned to their masters, but on many occasions I was able to purchase them outright and after working the cost off gave them their freedom.

The natives of the Lagoon District were on the whole peaceable, but shortly prior to my arrival some of them got out of hand and killed a Portuguese trader by the name of Gavai, and on several occasions these same natives, led by a turbulent Chief were inclined to be troublesome and truculent. On one occasion this Chief visited one of my branches and stole a quantity of goods and in order to recover these I caught one of his sons and put him into prison which resulted in the old Chief coming to my factory in all his war paint accompanied by 20 canoes to release him. I however got wind of his preparations and transferred the prisoner to the beach and obtained a force of armed canoes to meet him. With the aid of these and only a few minor casualties I managed to get hold of him and put him into irons where he was kept until his people had returned all the stolen property, plus a heavy fine. This kept him quiet for a spell, but he broke out again by looting other factories and his town was finally burnt and he was driven into the interior where he remained until I left the District. There were frequent minor scraps with various towns, mainly in connection with the payment of debts, but it was rare that anything worse than a few bruises or small cuts resulted therefrom.

Apart from these incidents the life in the Factory was dull and monotonous and what local trade existed was usually done at night time, as the natives were afraid of crossing the wide stretch of water which separated the Island from the Mainland, during the day time, when usually a stiff breeze was blowing and the water troubled. It was nothing unusual for me to spend the whole night in the shop whilst during the day no single visit was paid to the Factory.

The labourers employed on the Beach Depots amounting to – between the two factories – from 80 to 100 men were drilled and formed into a regular fighting force. The drilling usually took place on Sunday morning. They were supplied with second hand officers' tunics whilst the headmen or captains were furnished with a second hand admiral's rig-out and very proud they were of it. It was an amusing sight to see these troops with their bare legs and multi-coloured tunics strutting about carrying old Snider Rifles which very few of them could use effectively. The main thing however was to form a shew of force and so long as they made a terrific noise with the beating of drums and blowing of trumpets it was quite enough to overawe the inhabitants and create the effect intended. Occasionally several large canoes would be manned and with flags flying and drums beating make a naval demonstration up the Lagoon just to show that they were prepared in the case of any emergency arising, but on no occasion was it necessary to arm them with guns for any offensive or defensive operations.

During my residence in Sette Camma (3 years and 9 months) I saw no single European wearing a helmet, the usual head covering being either a trade felt hat or an ordinary tweed cap, nor did I see or hear of any doctor setting his foot on shore.

I may mention I was upwards of 20 years on the coast before I wore a helmet, and then only donned it for state occasions, but would not by any means advise anyone to follow this bad example as there is little doubt that I should have escaped many a dose of fever had I been more prudent in this respect.

During my first tour I served 4½ years and despite the hard and rough life and fairly constant exposure to sun and rain was only off duty from illness a few days.

III

From questions which have been put to me from time to time by those now (1931) employed in the West African trade, an entirely wrong impression seems to be rife as to the general conditions attached to, and methods adopted in connection with the trade in its early stages. I received my initiation into the real conditions in May, 1883, in a district 2½° south of the Equator known as Sette Camma, a name given to it by the Portuguese Slave Traders.

Although at that date the export of slaves from West Africa to foreign ports had been put a stop to it may prove of interest to learn that a fairly active local trade was still prevalent, particularly in this district, which supplied such places as Gaboon, Fernan Vaz and Loango with their requirements, and in Sette Camma itself more than half the population consisted of slaves.

By far the larger number of these slaves were purchased in the first instance in exchange for salt which was locally manufactured by the evaporation of sea water, the whole beach for a distance of 30 to 40 miles being dotted with small salt producing works.

The value of a slave varied according to sex, and age. 100 lbs of salt would be paid for a girl in her teens, whilst a boy of the same age could be bought for 50 to 60 lbs. Resale took place through the payment of what was locally termed a 'Slave Bundle'. This was made up of a certain number of fathoms of domestics and a quantity of rum which varied according to the recognised value of the slave. The actual sterling cost of the goods varying between £2.0.0. and £3.10.0.

Sometimes the slaves passed through several hands prior to reaching their definite owners, and each intermediary would make a profit out of the transaction.

Even in this class of transaction, credit and middlemen played an important part, and to show its local importance generally it may be mentioned that fines inflicted in settlement of Native Palaver were always fixed in terms of 'Slave Bundles'.

I think it will be readily understood that the natives found business of this nature more attractive from every point of view than that of spending long periods in the forest on the production of rubber, and one will not fail to realise the difficulty we were faced with in establishing a legitimate export trade in this produce.

The general inception of trade in its early stages is that it was only necessary to produce a few bunches of beads and other gaudy trifles for natives to flock in with the proceeds of their labours, but I can assure you this is entirely wrong as it was found utterly impossible to get them to take any interest in it without first giving them credit and afterwards harassing them in every possible way for its settlement.

The main credit attractions were undoubtedly rum and tobacco, the former being by far the most popular article dealt with, and without this I doubt very much if any production of a serious nature would have been possible so long as they had any trade in slaves to fall back on for other requirements.

Credit was usually given out just prior to the setting in of the Dry Season, as tapping for and the preparation of rubber only occurred during this period. As soon as the dry weather commenced it was necessary to visit all the towns holding credit to ascertain what steps had been taken to meet obligations, and it was by no means unusual to have to take strong measures in order to get them to make any move. These measures took various forms. In some instances hostages would be caught and imprisoned, and in others the villages would be raided and all movables of value to the inhabitants seized and held until the debts were paid.

In the former case, the value depended upon whether the hostage was of free parentage, or slave. If of free parentage considerable energy was displayed in getting his release, particularly if it happened that he was of a different family to the actual debtor, but it was not always the same if the person caught was a slave, the amount of the debt governing the whole matter.

These raids not infrequently resulted in free fights, but fortunately, beyond a few cuts and bruises, from matchets and sticks, it was rarely any serious damage resulted as no fire-arms were ever used by either side.

In most cases the native canoemen would, in their songs, give due warning of the approach of a European, and the natives would clear out into the forests which surrounded their villages. When this happened it meant the removal of property which was usually stored in the 'fetisch' house under the guardianship of the Medicine Man, which resulted in my having to force an entrance as no native would dare to do so.

In one instance, the Medicine Man, after threatening me with dire calamity, spat in my eyes some substance he had been chewing which must have been mixed with chilli peppers, and which for the moment completely blinded me.

During my 2½ years service on the Island upon which my factory was established I held a large number of hostages for debts, including the King of the NDogo Lake, and it was rarely any trouble resulted from their retention for legitimate reasons.

In addition to the large number of credit customers on my books, I had some 15 branches spread over a wide area to supervise and keep supplied with goods. Their stocks were taken by me regularly each month, and produce bought by them collected and transferred to headquarters. This had to be done partly by canoes, and partly by trecking through the forest, both in the wet and dry season. This was a far different proposition to the present day facilities for travelling by comfortable motor cars, luxurious trains, and even river steamers.

Even a camp bed was a luxury unheard of in those days and it simply meant either sleeping on native mats spread on the bare ground, or in a native hut on a bare bamboo bed. From purely sanitary reasons the former was generally preferred, except, of course, during the rainy seasons.

Travelling by canoe may sound all right to those who have spent their holiday in pleasant reaches of the Thames, or paddling about on the Norfolk Broads, but it is a far different proposition when exposed to a tropical sun or strong tornadoes and tropical rain for ten to twelve hours a day and crossing wide stretches of water infested with crocodiles, hippopotami, etc. with frequent risks of swamping. On several occasions this latter has happened to my canoe necessitating in some instances swims of upwards of two miles to safety.

Apart from the effort of swimming this distance, even in light clothing, there was the probability of coming up against a hungry crocodile or ferocious hippo, and on many occasions I have experienced unpleasant thrills of apprehension when colliding with floating objects during these enforced immersions.

Nor was trecking through the huge Equatorial forest without tent, camp bed, or any protection except that afforded by an old Snider Rifle, anything in the way of a picnic, as elephants, leopards, gorillas, snakes etc. were plentiful. In fact, it was not often that I possessed even a box of matches and had to depend upon the primitive flint and steel to start a fire, without which it was positively dangerous to pass the night, although during the heavy rains I have had to do so on numerous occasions.

I do not suppose that many of my readers will have spent many (if any) nights in a tropical forest during a Tornado without shelter of any kind, but if so, they will, I am sure, agree with me that it is at least an awesome experience. In fact, I know of nothing more so, as, with the rapid flashes of vivid lightning followed by tremendous claps of thunder, the howling of the wind and rain amongst the trees, accompanied by crash after crash of broken branches and falling trees, a regular inferno exists, and although drenched and cold, and feeling anything but happy on its termination, one's relief at having escaped any serious accident can be realised.

It will, of course, be understood that no roads existed through these forests but simply narrow uneven tracks made by natives and broken up with the spreading roots of gigantic trees. Streams and rivers had either to be forded or crossed by swimming, and during the latter operation one had to reckon with crocodiles and water snakes, both of which were very unpleasant bathing companions.

These forests were the real home of the gorilla, and I have seen and met hundreds of them during my various journeys, but only on rare occasions have they caused any trouble. However, I remember on one occasion suddenly meeting an enormous bull standing on the path and beating his chest with rage. He was only two or three yards away from me when I let him have the contents of a double-barrelled muzzle loading gun I was carrying charged with slugs, which put him 'hors de combat'. His skeleton, which measured 6'1" high found its way to the Cambridge Museum, and I believe it is still there. He must have weighed between 400 and 500 lbs, but it was surprising how quickly the flesh was consumed by my native staff.

Snakes were my pet aversion, and they were both plentiful and varied, from the small green whip snake, to the python which, in some instances, measured over 20' long and 2' in circumference.

Fortunately the flesh of the latter was considered a great delicacy by the natives and they were constantly on the 'qui vive' for them.

Although many of the snakes were of the poisonous variety, and amongst these the 'Horned Serastis', it was rarely that any deaths occurred from their bites, and I only remember losing two men from this cause during the many trecks of fairly long duration which I made.

It must be realised that all this work had to be accomplished with the aid of natives who had only recently come into contact with Europeans and practically none of whom understood a word of English. As the district had not then been annexed by any foreign power, it is obvious that no Government protection could be looked for, and not even a Missionary or Doctor could be found within a radius of 300 miles.

As regards diet, fish, chickens, eggs, and goats were fairly plentiful and cheap. The former consisted mainly of a specie of carp, 20 of which could be purchased for a bottle of rum or a head of tobacco costing about 2d. Chickens cost about the same, whilst a small goat could be obtained for 10 heads of tobacco. One egg could be bought for a leaf of tobacco, and game, such as deer, bush pig, bush cow, etc. could be obtained on the mainland, but it was only when on treck and existence depended upon such supplies that I had much opportunity of this variation in diet. Many have been the times when I have been thankful for even a monkey or snake stew.

As for bread, this I rarely tasted, plantains, yams, and manioc taking its place. With regard to fats, palm oil usually took the place of butter and lard. As a matter of fact, we lived mainly on local supplies, and having to depend upon a real 'bushman' as cook with exceedingly scanty and primitive cooking material (mainly three legged iron pots) this was perhaps just as well.

Apart from this, however, the question of economy was looked upon as a factor of more vital importance than exists in the trade at the present time. My house a/c, for example, which covered all food, service, lighting (which, more often than not consisted of a home-made palm oil lamp), laundry, replacements of gear (sic) etc. never exceeded £50 per annum, and the whole cost of a European was less than that paid for a second-class native clerk to-day.

As regards recreation, on the lines now considered so necessary it simply did not exist, and as I rarely saw a European more often than two or three times during six months, social life was equally non-existent. As a matter of fact the only conversation which took place from one month end to another was through orders given to native staff, or in carrying on the trade when native dialect was used. Although somewhat better off than poor old Robinson Crusoe in this respect, the situation was one which enabled me to fully sympathise with him and his joy when able to converse with Man Friday.

Although golf and tennis were unobtainable it does not follow that no exercise was taken, and it is indeed probable that I took a good deal more than the majority who have the advantage of being able to indulge in those sports as I rarely missed taking a swim of a couple of miles each morning before six o'clock, whilst any spare time during the day was occupied in a kitchen garden which was established from seeds obtained locally, or in making bits of furniture from packing cases, etc. Usually the days appeared to be exceedingly long as the trade was mainly done after sunset, it being very dangerous for loaded canoes to cross the big stretch of water necessary to reach the Island until after the sea breeze had fallen.

What one missed the most was the lack of literature there not being more than a dozen readable books in the whole country, and the occasional receipt of a two months' old newspaper or a few magazines was in the nature of a real 'Godsend'.

The accountancy work attached to the business was not of an onerous nature, but at the same time detailed accounts had to be kept showing the exact dealing with each line of goods received, and stock accounts had to be correctly balanced. I have very distinct recollection of having to pay a sum of £5.0.0. for goods I could not account for (which was equal to more than one month's salary) although I was quite certain that the loss was due to failure to water the rum sufficiently to cover leakages.

Apart from the Europeans there were probably not more than three or four men in the country who could read or write, and these hailed from the Gold Coast, so no outside assistance in clerical work was at all possible, but I admit that this part of the business did not worry us. What we were out for was to establish a profitable trade and capture as much of this as possible.

The fact that only two or three firms were trading in the District did not prevent keen competition, and jealousy of each other taking place, but fortunately this was shown in other directions than that of cutting down margins of profit to a vanishing point.

The assortment of goods carried, although not so wide as at the present time, was just as important and constant trials of new lines were being made with considerable success, particularly in small fancy articles appealing to the women folk. It was in this direction that initiative and competition took place, and during my tour of 3½ years the number of lines handled had been considerably more than doubled and the trade increased more than threefold.

It may be mentioned that the word "initiative" used above had some real significance in those early days, as the cost end of the business was left entirely in the hands of those appointed to manage it, and the total correspondence with Liverpool would not exceed a couple of ordinary letter pages per month, whilst cable communication was, of course, out of the question altogether.

Produce shipped home was sold on their behalf and Account Sales rendered to them exactly as would have been the case if sold on behalf of any other third party. From these it was possible to see the exact result of the venture It was entirely up to them to order the goods they required, and beyond sending out occasional samples, only these were bought, shipped, and consigned to the District headquarters from whence they were invoiced and distributed to the various inland trading stations, who, in their turn, accounted for them to headquarters where the final accounts for the venture were made up.

The actual system of trading varied in different localities, as in some rubber was bought by weight and in others by the piece. In the former the exchange price of each article of goods was fixed in dollars and cents, the natives having been used to this denomination from the old slave trade, and the exchange price was so fixed to bring the actual cost value of the dollar at an average of 1/-, some articles costing a little more and some less, according to their popularity. Some system such as this was necessary not only for the determination of the first cost of produce, but also for the payment of labour and purchase of food.

A labourer received 5 dollars of goods per month plus his food which would cost another five dollars, which totalled 10/- per month. A cook and steward combined would be paid at the rate of 7 dollars, or, with food, 12/- per month, and a shopman 10 dollars, equal to 15/- per month.

Of course, this appears to be a low rate of wage, but it must be understood that goods were not subject to any import duty and were altogether cheaper than at present. For example, a gallon of rum only cost about 1/-, and a six-leaved head of tobacco cost 2d, whilst lines of cotton goods handled rarely cost more than 3d. per yard and the average would not exceed 2½d.

Three classes of rubber were dealt with, ball, mixed, and flake, each one being obtained from the latex of different species of vines, the best

(Ball) being from the 'Landolphia'.

It is needless to say the natives were great adepts at adulteration, and one had to be constantly on the 'qui vive' to avoid paying for stones, clay, etc. placed in the middle of the rubber balls. Although all adulterated rubber was confiscated, the practice still continued. Apart from this they were fairly honest, for although goods were stored in cheap and flimsily built shops, it was rarely they were looted.

With regard to this, however, it may be mentioned that the native custom of dealing with arrant rogues and thieves was of a drastic nature, consisting of the slicing off of their nose and ears. The same penalty was inflicted for adultery between a male slave and a free woman, and it was no uncommon sight to see men parading about with this disfigurement.

On several occasions I had the greatest difficulty in preventing the penalty being inflicted on men in my own employ, and on one occasion it was only by capturing and holding as hostage the chief wife of the King of the district that I could get the man, who was a slave, released. I am afraid, however, that my efforts did him no good as he disappeared from the factory and his body was shortly afterwards found floating on the lake.

As a general rule the slaves which formed an important percentage of the Lake population, were not badly treated. Their duties consisted in providing food for their masters, and producing rubber, for which the owner took the proceeds, but so long as they performed their duties in a satisfactory manner they were well fed and clothed, and many of them provided with wives. These latter were, of course, slaves and any children resulting from the union were claimed by the owner, but they were rarely sold by him.

The worst feature was the power of life and death the owner held, and on many occasions I have seen this power exercised for trivial offences. For instance, an owner shot his slave within a few feet of me simply because – when handing him a glass of rum – he stumbled and spilt the rum over him. Although he would carry to his grave the marks of the thrashing he got from me it would not deter him from doing the same thing again, but I do not think he would try it on in my presence.

Frequently free men would unite with slave women,and children born from such union were known as "Bambas" or "half slaves" and were free from slavery, but were generally looked down upon by those born in freedom, and the males were not permitted to wed with free women. Many of these men, however, achieved wealth and became slave owners themselves, and they were amongst the best of my rubber producers.

Some of my best and most faithful servants were slaves whom I bought and freed and who afterwards saved enough money to purchase wives. On my return to the Ogowe they followed me there and continued to render loyal service.

As regards health, the cause of malaria and preventive measures against this were, of course, undiscovered. The only quinine taken was after the fever had got a hold, and the manner of taking it was to screw up powdered sulphate in a cigarette paper and swallow it, guessing at the dose. The only other medicines procurable were Epsom Salts, Chlorodyne, Friars Balsam, and Cockles pills.

No one wore a helmet, and protection against mosquito bites was only considered necessary when they prevented sleep. A few yards of cheap print were then made into a curtain.

The only filter I had was an old worn out Teneriffe Drip Stone, and it was not often that the water I drank was filtered or boiled. On treck it was consumed as taken from the rivers and streams.

During my 3½ years in the district I do not think I took twenty doses of quinine, and I only remember being laid up one week with a bad dose of fever, which was the only time I was really incapacitated from work, although, of course, I did not escape the usual small doses many of which were probably due to long exposure to the sun without adequate protection.

What furniture I possessed, with the exception of one dilapidated Madeira chair, was made locally including bedstead and mattress, the latter as well as a pillow, being stuffed with moss. Sheets and tablecloths were made from cheap Croydon costing 2d.per yard. In fact, the whole of my table gear was made up of trade articles and a value of £5. for the whole lot, including furniture, would be excessive.

The living quarters consisted of one room devoid of any flooring except baked clay, which, although not particularly comfortable, certainly saved the expense of washing down with soap and water. My bath tub was half a rum puncheon, but as these were used for the shipment of rubber I got into serious trouble for taking one for this purpose.

The walls of the sitting-cum-dining-cum-bedroom were made of bamboos tied on the upright sticks, and my principle pastime at night – when able to light up – was the spearing of huge rats which amused themselves by running up and down between the bamboos. Through frequent practice I got quite adept in this sport, but some of the rats I missed had their revenge by getting into my bed and nibbling my toes during the night. Other pests upon which I made constant war were hordes of cockroaches as large as locusts, centipedes, scorpions, and snakes, the island being absolutely infested with these latter much to the detriment of my stocks of poultry and goats.

On one occasion, on returning from one of my stock-taking tours, I found a couple of pythons under my bed where they had coiled up to sleep and digest the chickens they had eaten. On another occasion I found a horned serastis, the most poisonous snake in Africa, coiled up on the top of my mosquito curtain having got in through a hole in the thatched roof. It was a fortunate thing for me the curtain was there as, otherwise, he might have made himself at home in my bed. Needless to say, careful search was made each evening for uninvited guests of this nature, and particularly for scorpions and centipedes. A favourite place of abode for these latter was the thatched roof, and it was by no means uncommon for them to drop down on to the dining table as the person was sitting at it, and stings from them were frequent and exceedingly unpleasant, although not particularly dangerous, the effect being a swelling of the glands and high temperature which would last for several hours.

An equally unpleasant inhabitant of the island was a small red ant, known by the natives as 'Sangera Ugenda', and it was surprising how painful the sting of so minute an insect could be. They seemed to be literally charged with formic acid, and even the thick-skinned natives often had to remove their villages in order to escape from them. In order to keep them away from food, my table legs were set in small iron pots half filled with coal tar, and the legs of my bedstead were treated in the same manner.

It may perhaps surprise some of my readers who have come into actual contact with the well known 'driver ant', to learn that regular visits from these were welcomed by me, and it was mainly thanks for these visits and their activities in clearing out of the premises snakes, rats, cockroaches and other vermin, that the place was at all habitable.

Far less pleasant visitors were hornets, but fortunately these were less frequent. These insects build huge nests from branches of trees overhanging waterways and only become really offensive when disturbed, but when they really get on the war path they become positively dangerous. Unfortunately my island seemed to take their fancy and on several occasions when passing canoes disturbed them they simply took complete control driving every human being into canoes and away into the centre of the lake, and all poultry and animals into the forest, but not before they had inflicted severe discomfort and damage.

At the North end of the Island was a small muddy inlet which was utilised by crocodiles as a breeding place, and during this season the natives used to gather their eggs which were esteemed by them as a delicacy. On one occasion they brought me three of these eggs which I intended to blow and conserve the shells as a curiosity, but forgot to do so leaving them tied up in the dirty piece of cloth in which they were wrapped. Some little time afterwards, hearing a croaking noise I traced it to the cloth and on opening this found three young crocodiles. These I kept in a tub of water for some months, feeding them on cockroaches and small fish. Eventually they were bartered on board one of Elder Dempster's steamers for a bag of potatoes, and this was one of the few occasions on which I tasted this luxury during my stay in the district.

Drinking water was a real problem on the Island, as the nearest source from which anything of this nature could be obtained was on the Mainland, five miles away. Two boys were employed daily in bringing across supplies in jars and demijohns, and it was a case of rationing this.

In the foregoing I have endeavoured to draw a true picture of the conditions under which pioneering work was carried on at the headquarters of the district under my control, and after trying to picture for yourself what life must have been like under such circumstances to a youngster of 20 years of age, I think you will readily understand that any change could hardly fail to prove attractive, however arduous and dangerous this might be, and it was undoubtedly fortunate that my duties necessitated frequent and prolonged absences in the endeavour to open up and establish trading relations in new areas.

My first serious expedition was made at the age of 21 when I started on a treck calculated to take two months through the Equatorial Forest, with a view to ascertaining trading possibilities in the hinterland between Sette Camma and the Congo, and I was the first European to penetrate that country.

This district was the main source of the domestic slave trade, and I was therefore able to secure from amongst those actively engaged in this trade a capable guide and interpreter, and amongst my own people I had several slaves who had also a knowledge of the country and some of the dialects used therein.

As my camp equipment only consisted of a few native woven grass mats, mosquito curtain – also native – woven from fine grass fibre, 3 cotton blankets, one pillow, a few honeycomb towels, a few pillow-slips and sheets made from grey baft, a few tin plates and some mugs, trade knives and forks, iron cooking pots, fry pan, and kettle, the whole lot costing about 25/-. The expense in this direction could not be termed high.

Such luxuries as a tent or camp bed, or even a waterproof ground sheet were not to be thought of.

In so far as clothing was concerned, this consisted of a few suits of blue dungaree made locally, cotton singlets, pyjamas made from cheap prints, cotton hose, and a dozen pairs of plimsoll gymnasium shoes (rubber soled), one felt hat and one tweed cap, a couple of dozen C.B. handkerchiefs (costing 2/- per dozen) the total outfit costing about £3.0.0.

The remainder of my baggage was made up of an assortment of goods (30 loads weighing each 50 lbs) and carriers' rations for one week consisting of rice. The total number of porters amounted to 40, who were paid at the rate of ten dollars in goods per month, equal to 10/- sterling, which was the regulation scale for this class of work. The whole of these porters were selected from men who had an intimate knowledge of the tapping of vines and general preparation of rubber and, with the exception of the guides and interpreters, they were all slaves.

As the expedition was into an unknown country in so far as Europeans were concerned, and was entirely through the dense Equatorial Forest inhabited by tribes of savage pygmies, leopards, herds of elephants, etc. it was considered prudent to provide some means of defence and this was made up of ten men armed with old Snider rifles, each carrying twenty rounds of ammunition, whilst I had a Martini Henry rifle with fifty rounds of ammunition.These men carried lighter loads (25 lbs in weight) mainly consisting of my personal effects, camp equipment, and provisions.

The day of setting out, although upwards of 46 years ago is well remembered as it happened on my 21st birthday. All the loads had been prepared the previous day and duly allotted to each porter. These latter were mustered at "Cock Speak" i.e. about 5a.m. which was the usual practice when on treck, and before 7a.m. all were under way, myself leading and a responsible headman bringing up the rear.

For the first two hours we passed over plain land, and I was fortunate enough to kill a small deer before entering the forest. The sudden change from brilliant sunshine to the sombreness of a dense forest through which the sun rarely penetrated was a very welcome change, but after plodding along a narrow foot path for a few hours in a semi twilight with the constant necessity of keeping one's eyes glued to the ground in order to avoid tripping over roots of the gigantic trees, in a hot and humid atmosphere one began to long for the open spaces, a glimpse of the run, and the breeze which usually sprang up in the afternoon.

The first village, near which our camp was made, was reached after a walk of eight hours duration, and as the natives of this village complained of having been seriously troubled by leopards for some time past it was necessary to guard against any attack by keeping fires going throughout the night. This was by no means my first experience of camping in the forest, and many of my porters were quite 'au fait' with the routine of fixing camp and the arrangements for fires, etc.

One of the first duties after fixing camp was the plucking of fresh leaves from the thick undergrowth as some little protection against the hard and uneven ground upon which my bed was made, and the fixing of mosquito nets. Whilst this was going on and the evening meal was being prepared, a bath was taken by me in the stream near which the camp was pitched. That night I dined sumptuously on roast venison and plantains, followed by a cup of tea sweetened with condensed milk, and as I had not stopped for a mid-day meal it was all very acceptable.

The following day I spent in the village talking trade, and as there happened to be a caravan carrying rubber down to Nyanga – after a good deal of talk and judicious dashing to the headman – I succeeded in diverting it to our factory at Copa at the head of the Ndogo Lagoon, which had recently been established, and then made all arrangements for opening a branch in the village which was named Lisboa.

The next day we broke camp at daylight and, after an arduous walk of nine hours, reached the town of the Chief of the Bayaka country who had the reputation of being a fairly rich slave merchant and who levied a pretty heavy toll on all trade passing through his country.

Here I was met by at least a couple of hundred natives armed with bows and arrows, and spears, with the express object of preventing my proceeding further inland. They were a ferocious-looking lot all covered with war paint, each one wearing a string of leopard teeth and little else, and although I tried not to show it I felt anything but happy.

It was perhaps very fortunate for me that my interpreter was connected with the chief through marriage, and after a long palaver succeeded in calming him down and finally getting him to agree to provide us with quarters for the night, and food for my porters. However, my quarters were carefully patrolled and I was virtually a prisoner.

The following two days were passed in palavering, from which I gathered that what the chief was after was the payment of a heavy tribute on all trade passing through his territory, and his demands were too exorbitant to be taken into consideration. His consent to my passing was finally obtained after making him a present, part of which consisted of an admiral's second hand tunic and hat, along with the promise of a factory at a later date.

Although the day was well advanced when consent was given, I decided to take immediate advantage of it and after four hours walk came across a fairly wide river with no visible means of crossing, except by swimming. This, however, would not overcome the difficulty of getting the loads of goods and personal effects transported without serious damage, so there was no alternative but to set to and make a raft by cutting down small trees and lashing these together with bush rope, an abundance of which could be easily obtained. As my native porters were as eager as myself to put the river between us and our late hosts, this was soon accomplished and we were able to camp on the opposite shore.

The succeeding day was pretty well filled with anything but pleasant incidents. We had to pass through fairly hilly country and to cross numerous deep and precipitous gullies on primitive bridges made by felling trees across them, some of the trees being not more than 1½ feet in diameter, and it was really wonderful to see the porters walking across these small rounded surfaces. The only way in which I could tackle them was to get myself across straddle-legged, much to their amusement.

It was on this day that I came in close contact with the pygmy tribes for the first time. These small people had no settled abodes, but wandered about the forests living mainly on game which they killed with poisoned arrows, and what other food they could loot from the plantations of regular native settlements. They were exceedingly dirty and repulsive looking individuals. The only covering for their bodies was clay and other dirt, and with their long matted hair they resembled animals more than human beings. Several groups of about half a dozen each were met with during the day, and although we managed to get hold of two of them they refused to open their mouths, and even had they attempted to speak it is doubtful whether any of my men would have understood them.

A very unfortunate incident occurred in the loss of two of my porters along with their loads, and although a whole day was spent in searching for them, they were never heard of afterwards, and I was only able to assume that they had lagged behind the regular caravan and fallen into the hands of the pygmies.

In addition to the pygmies, this District seemed to be a favourite resort of elephants as, not only did we meet many traces of them during the day, but at night a whole herd of them passed close by our camp and from the noise they made and the number of small trees broken down and uprooted, there must have been at least thirty or forty of them.

By this time my own food supplies were getting very low, and supplies for the native staff were entirely exhausted.

Fortunately, early during the day we emerged from the forest on to a fairly large plain and I was lucky enough to drop a sable antelope from the only herd of this type of deer I ever saw. Later on we came across a large native town which received us in an exceedingly friendly and hospitable manner, and in fact, being the first European the natives had ever seen, their attention became somewhat embarrassing as I could not move without a crowd of entirely nude women and children following me. It was with the greatest difficulty they were prevented from assisting at my bath.

The village itself was exceedingly clean with symmetrical and well built houses, and the natives were well built and nourished. They had important herds of goats and sheep and abundant supplies of chickens, eggs, and plantains, and their liberality with all of these was both astonishing and gratifying. A happier and more contented crowd of natives I do not remember meeting. Although their general custom was to go about in a state of nudity there were many of them actively employed in weaving cloth from dried grasses, and I was given an exhibition of a fetisch dance by men on stilts wearing grass cloths completely covering them, and most weirdly painted wooden masks. Their agility on these stilts was remarkable.

In addition to large and flourishing food plantations mostly consisting of plantains and manioc they grew a quantity of tobacco and manufactured their own clay pipes and cooking utensils, brewed their own beer from plantains, and obtained a plentiful supply of 'Mimbo' (Palm Wine) from the numerous palm trees surrounding their village.

Their salt supplies were obtained from the selling of slaves whom they obtained from towns further inland, and several small convoys of these were encountered prior to reaching their village on the way to the Salt Works in Sette Camma.

The Chief of the town was a very old man who, along with some of his older councillors, absolutely refused to meet me, they being afraid that some undue calamity would happen to them if they set eyes on a white man, but they expressed their willingness through my interpreter to produce rubber if there were any means of disposing of it locally, and arrangements were made to leave men with them who would teach them how to make this with the promise that a trader with goods would be sent at a later date.

During my stay of two days in this locality I was fortunate in being able to kill two bush cows, the meat of which I had dried and smoked for future requirements.

During the three days it took to cross the plains we passed through several large villages, the inhabitants of which treated us most hospitably and arrangements were made to open up trading relations with them.

We were warned by these natives that on entering the forests again we might expect trouble from the pygmies who had been raiding their villages, and we certainly got it as our first night's camp was raided by them and a dozen sheep and goats we had collected together for future supplies were stolen, along with my chop box which contained the balance of my tea and condensed milk, and a number of bunches of plantains.

This forest was honeycombed with elephant tracks and unfortunately we got very much astray in following one of these instead of the regular tracks. Instead of taking three days to reach the next village it took us six days, without meeting a single human being.

Fortunately we came out on to another plain upon which we found several villages, but miles away from the direction in which we had planned to go. All the food we had had for the last three days was provided by three bush pigs we had managed to kill out of a herd which crossed our path, but this did not go far amongst forty hungry men, and we were all completely at the end of our tether by the time the plain was reached.

Our progress through this part of the forest was exceedingly slow as a good deal of it was of a swampy nature through which we had to wade, and I had considerable trouble in preventing my porters from abandoning their loads. Ten of them had to be left behind at the previous night's encampment, along with a couple of men with Snider rifles, with which they were able to kill a few monkeys.

I was lucky enough to meet a Sette Camma man who was there in connection with some slave transactions, and it was in a great measure due to his good offices that we were favourably received and hospitably treated, and I was able to arrange for food and assistance to be at once sent to the porters who had been left behind, all of whom eventually arrived safely.

In this village food was not by any means plentiful, due mainly to their plantations having been raided by elephants who had destroyed the plantains, and leopards who had taken serious toll of their sheep and goats. Game in the way of bush cow and deer was, however, fairly abundant and I was fortunately able to kill three of the former and several of the latter, the meat from which was very acceptable as part of it was exchanged for plantains and manioc, of which we were in serious need. However, owing to the general scarcity I could only get two days' supplies.

Two men who were suffering from sore feet were left in this District to start the natives in rubber production, and after getting a guide a start was made for the next settlement which was reached after three days trecking (one day across the plain and two days in the forest). The country here was hilly and rocky, and going was consequently difficult and arduous.

This settlement consisted of five to six large villages situated on the bank of a fairly wide stream. As in other districts visited, the villages consisted of extremely well built huts, constructed with bark sides and roofs thatched with bamboo leaves. They faced a wide main road which was kept absolutely free from grass and weeds, and in fact perfectly clean.

The natives themselves were well formed and nourished, and although quite nude they appeared to be happy and contented. Their food plantations of manioc, yams, plantains, and sweet potatoes, covered a wide area, and during our stay we were ‘in clover’ as far as supplies were concerned.

Here I met several Fernan Vaz men who had come overland via Archira and Barama in search of slaves, and I was able to arrange with two of these men to start the natives on rubber production and chiefs promised to transport this to the Sette Camma Lagoon and bring back goods in return. As in the previous settlement visited, the natives complained of the depredations of leopards in taking their live stock, and I gained their gratitude by killing three of these animals during my stay amongst them.

As the Fernan Vaz men, who seemed to be well acquainted with the country spoke in glowing terms of trade prospects in the Barama District which was to the east of where I met them, and as one of them agreed to act as guide through it I decided to return by that route instead of going over the same ground twice. Before doing so, however, I visited a further important group of villages two days further south and known as Semi Congo, situated three days walk from the Congo River.

The forest traversed was of a mountainous nature and extremely difficult to negotiate in consequence. It was a case of either climbing steep and rocky hills, or descending same and passing through deep gulleys and numerous streams and rivers, and it was fortunate that my porters were travelling light with regard to loads, otherwise it would have taken at least double the time spent over the trip.

On the first night when camping we were again visited by pygmies, but fortunately they were detected by the watchmen before any losses took place and two of them were caught, but as there was no one present who could understand their dialect they were given their liberty after depriving them of their bows and arrows.

In the Semi Congo District I visited five or six villages, in all of which my reception was quite cordial and ample supplies of plantains and manioc were procurable, but meat of any kind was scarce although they kept me personally well supplied with chickens and eggs during my stay of three days amongst them.

The surrounding forests were rich in the Landolphia Rubber Vine, and demonstrations for the preparation of rubber were given in each village visited.

The natives struck me as being of a lower type than those I had previously met and their villages were not nearly as clean or as well constructed, but they gave me the impression of being quite happy and contented, and their general appearance clearly showed they were well nourished.

During the whole of my journey so far, the only natives I had met who appeared to be poverty stricken and suffering from malnutrition were the pygmies.

When talking trade affairs with the natives the article which appeared to be most highly prized by them was salt, and it was more with the object of obtaining supplies of this than anything else that they were prepared to work rubber.

It will, of course, be realised that trading operations so far in the interior with natives uncontrolled by any government were extremely risky. One of the most troublesome questions to solve was the one of transport and their desire for salt had to be utilised in order to cope with this.

Although fairly large quantities of salt were imported none of this was ever sent into the interior in the ordinary way of trade, and the only manner in which the interior tribes could obtain it was by carrying down to the main trading stations in Sette Camma the rubber purchased by other goods through the traders established in the various villages.

The exact arrangements made by me with the various chiefs were as follows:–

If they desired to open up trade they were to commence by producing rubber, and when they had obtained 50 'Matett' loads (weight about 1,000 lbs for the 50 loads) they were to transport this to the nearest main factory. The carriage of the rubber would be paid for in salt at the rate of one plateful for each 10 balls of rubber of a standard size, this being about 1 lb each.

A trader would then be appointed and would return with them along with a well assorted stock of goods, which they would carry in free of charge.

Within four months from the date of my trip upwards of twenty factories had been established on the above terms, and some 15,000 to 20,000 lbs of rubber collected at an inclusive cost of about 3d. per lb.

My return journey through the Barama Country – the whole of which was through dense forest – was accomplished in about 30 days, but for ten days of this I was hung up waiting for a fresh supply of shoes, the whole of my stock having been worn out, and I had sent runners through to our Bongo factory for a further supply as well as for some other articles of attire of which I was in most urgent need.

It was whilst waiting for these that I killed my first elephant on the plantation of the natives who had given me hospitality.

As I was extremely nervous and agitated when firing at him at a distance of about 20 yards I was more than astonished when he fell almost at my feet. It was, in fact, a lucky shot which penetrated his brain. Although at the time I was highly pleased and elated at the result, the native jamboree and orgy of feasting which followed and lasted for fully a week was anything but entertaining and pleasant. The stench of the putrid meat, and the millions of flies it attracted was unbearable, and necessitated my camping in the forest some distance away. The astonishing part of the business was that the natives did not seem to take any harm from consuming it.

As the smell of the meat proved a great attraction to leopards, I was able to kill a couple of them when prowling round quite close to my camp in broad daylight, and, needless to say, care was taken to see that good fires were kept going throughout the night.

Between twenty and thirty large villages were visited in this country and as a result a very prosperous rubber trade was established therein.

It must be borne in mind that long ere this my stocks of goods had become exhausted, and considering I had nothing to offer the natives in the way of presents, or even to barter against food supplies, the fact that we managed to exist speaks well for their hospitality.

There were times, however, when we were extremely hard put to it for a meal and a walk of some twenty miles with an empty stomach was by no means a rare incident.

One of the things I greatly missed was an occasional cup of tea, particularly the morning cup which I was deprived of during the last thirty to forty days of my trip, and during the last fourteen days I was reduced to smoking native grown and prepared tobacco, which was far from enjoyable.

I learned a good deal of the insect life of the forests which was extremely abundant and varied. On some occasions millions of driver ants would take charge of the encampment and it was by no means a joke to have to move the camp in the middle of the night. When a real attack was made by them there was no alternative.

Mosquitoes were not particularly troublesome, but on the other hand all forest clearings, and especially the native villages, were infested with sand flies from which between the hours of six and eight a.m. and five to six p.m. there was no escape, and stings from these minute insects were infinitely more painful and troublesome than mosquitoes.

Frequent stings from scorpions and centipedes proved both painful and troublesome also, and the necessity of sleeping on the ground laid one open to attacks from these.

Other insects which were troublesome were cattle ticks, and on one or two occasions I got up simply covered with them, and in negotiating swampy Districts one got practically covered with leeches.

Bird life in the forest was exceedingly small and we would go for days without either seeing or hearing a single one. In fact, I only remember hearing on one or two occasions the raucous cry of the hornbill, but on the other hand one saw large quantities of gaudily coloured butterflies.

Monkeys ranging from the gorilla down to the marmoset were seen in plenty and on one evening a whole family of the former came down to drink at a stream in which I was taking my bath after a long day's walk, but as soon as they spotted me they fortunately turned back. Numerous crocodiles were seen on the banks of the rivers and larger streams we had to cross, and fully a dozen were killed and eaten during the trip. The flesh of a young crocodile is as white as the breast of a chicken and is not to be despised when one is hungry and short of other food, and the tail of the reptile has provided me with many a welcome meal. As a matter of fact, fastidious ideas regarding food when starvation is staring one in the face are apt to disappear and there were many occasions when it was not a question of choosing one's diet but of being thankful for anything of an edible nature turning up at all.

The duration of the trip was 60 days during which time I visited between 50 and 60 villages and opened friendly trading relations with their Chiefs. The total cost of the trip was not more than £60 including my salary.

For fully forty days myself and native staff depended entirely upon local supplies for subsistence and my sole beverage consisted of unfiltered water drawn from the various forest streams. The medicine taken by me was nil, not even a single dose of quinine, and although I had walked over 500 miles and had lost upwards of a stone in weight, I was perfectly fit on arrival at my Island headquarters.

The whole of the native staff which accompanied me served me well and faithfully, the only loss amongst them being the two who had disappeared after meeting the pygmies.

A year later, when acting as Agent, and after serving three years, I made practically the same trip on a tour of inspection accomplishing it this time in about 40 days. Depending upon the aid of my traders I started away with only twelve porters including the interpreter. Five of these porters who were (natives of Loango) deserted, carrying with them the major portion of my kit and the whole of my provision reserves, including tea.

The only things I was left with in the way of clothing were two pairs of boots and what I actually wore – a blue dungaree pair of pants and a cotton singlet, nor was I able to get any renewals with the exception of a few singlets and a few pieces of cheap print which I had to wear 'a la native'.

On this occasion over 500 natives were sent down with rubber to my factory at Copa established at the southern end of the Ndogo Lagoon, and this result more than repaid for the many hardships and deprivations.

J. DEEMIN
1931

Notes

1. s.s. *Gaboon* was built of iron by John Elder at Glasgow in 1878. Of 1,863 gross tons she measured 302 x 34 x 23 feet. She was owned by the British & African Steam Navigation Company until 1896 and then transferred to the African Steam Ship Company. She was sold in 1898. (*Trade Makers*, Table 85, No. 43.)
2. There was no *Amsterdam* stationed on the West African Coast at that time. It is certain that Deemin was referring to the *Athelstan* owned by Stuart and Douglas. This vessel had been built at Maryport in 1850. Of 476 tons, she was rigged as a barque and measured 122 x 25 x 20 feet. She was hulked at Old Calabar in 1871. (*Lloyds Register*, 1866, A.1035.)
3. James Edwin Gibney subsequently had a long career with John Holt and Company. In 1891 he was stationed at Fernando Po and at the request of the Governor sent what was probably the first large consignment of cocoa seeds, 'sufficiently ripe for planting', to the Gold Coast. Ghana now supplies some 60% of the world's cocoa. Gibney eventually retired to Brisbane, Australia, and was still alive in 1945 at the age of 81. (*Guinea Gulf Line MSS*: History file Con/2a, Letter from Sir Brandford Griffith to Gibney, 2 June 1891; letter from John Holt to Gibney, 24 November 1891 and letter from Gibney to R.L. Holt, 10 January, 1945.)
4. P.N. Davies, 'The African Steam Ship Company', in J.R. Harris (ed.) *Liverpool and Merseyside*, Frank Cass & Co., London, 1969, pp. 212–38. See also 'The beautiful island – Fernando Po', *Sea*, Vol. 8, No. 5, January 1973, p. 20.
5. *Maria* was purchased in 1868. 'She was a two masted, fore-and-aft 65 ton schooner, Plymouth built with a length of 71 feet and beam of 16 feet. She was sixteen years old and cost £620.' She was sold for £600 in 1876. (*Merchant Adventure*, op.cit., p.22.)
6. *Rajah of Sarawak* was a ship of 484 tons. She was built at Bideford in 1850 and measured 118 x 25 x 18 feet. (*Lloyds Register*, 1866, R.25.)
7. The correct name of this vessel was *Burns*. She was a ship of 375 tons and measured 124 x 25 x 16 feet. She had been built at Annan in 1853. (*Lloyds Register*, 1866, B.582.)
8. See below, pp. 113, 115 and 122.
9. Carl Woermann established his firm in Hamburg in 1837. At first it was 'a general trading house for overseas products' but it quickly developed a specialisation with Africa. The trading activities gradually gave way to a concentration on shipping and in 1885 the Woermann Line was established. Since then it has always held a substantial share of the West Africa shipping

trade. (*A Short History of the German Africa Lines*, Published by the Company, Hamburg, 1967.)

10. This was a term applied to the regular vessels of the African Steam Ship Company and the British and African Steam Navigation Company. Both were managed (and later owned) by Elder Dempster and Company and both, after 1873, carried the Royal Mail. (*Trade Makers*, pp. 63–5.)
11. Quinine was more widely used as a preventative than Deemin suggests. It was used in the West African Squadron of the Royal Navy and in his account of his exploration of the Niger in 1854 Dr. Baikie makes specific reference to its prophylactic qualities. W.B. Baikie, *Narrative of an Exploring Voyage up the Rivers Kwo'ra and Bi'nue in 1854*, John Murray, London, 1856, Appendix G. Medical, pp. 452–5.

3. WILLIAM K. FINDLAY

INTRODUCTION

W.B. MacIver and Company was founded by two brothers in Glasgow in 1875 in order to trade with the West Coast of Africa. The elder brother, who gave his name to the firm, died in 1883 and left Charles MacIver as the sole partner. For a time the Company was highly profitable but difficulties followed the ending of the boom in forest rubber and in 1900 Charles MacIver was declared to be bankrupt. It was subsequently discovered that the business had always been operated in a proper manner and MacIver was given an unconditional discharge the following year. In the meanwhile the Assets Realisation Company had purchased the bankrupt firm from the Public Trustees and in due course it was re-sold to a syndicate of merchants led by W.K. Findlay.

William Findlay had been born in Angus in 1868 and 'served an apprenticeship to the law'. This career was not to his taste, however, so when a suitable post came vacant he moved to MacIver's office in Glasgow. The next year, 1889, Findlay went out to Lagos on a two year agreement. In fact, he was on the Coast for considerably longer than the stipulated period and then completed a second tour. It was at this stage that the Company got into financial difficulties and gave Findlay the chance of becoming his own master and such was his reputation that he was able to arrange the necessary capital without delay.

The resurrected firm retained the old name and under Findlay's guidance made good profits and new branches were established at Sapele and Opobo. MacIver's were also partly successful in organising direct shipping links with West Africa in spite of the deferred rebate system operated jointly by Elder Dempster and the Woermann Line. The two trips made by *Prestonian* in 1906 represent the only real incursions into the conference control of the trade in the period from 1895 (when regulation was introduced) to 1909 (when Alfred Jones died). These were of minor significance at the time but were to prove of some importance in the future for in 1910 W.B. MacIver and Company were purchased by Lever Brothers.

William Hesketh Lever was naturally interested in West Africa as it was a major source of the products that were vital to the manufacture of both soap and margarine. Consequently, in 1896, he had invested privately in the Oil Rivers and Exploration Company Limited (later the Company of African Merchants Limited) but following a visit to the Coast by Mr. H.R. Greenhalgh he had sold these shares. Greenhalgh's advice was that a substantial interest should be developed in West Africa but it was not until 1910 that Lever's actually entered the trade. The acquisition of MacIvers was then undertaken and it proved to be useful in two particular ways. Firstly, it secured the services of W.K. Findlay who had the necessary experience to guide Lever's future development on the Coast. Secondly, it gave Lever's a unique insight into West African shipping conditions for, as noted above, MacIver's were probably the only firm with recent knowledge of viable chartering in this region.

Thereafter Findlay's career lay with the Lever organisation. He played an essential role in extending both the trading and shipping activities of the Group becoming a Director of Lever Brothers, Managing Director of the Bromport Steamship Company and Chairman of the Niger Company. He retired to private life in 1931 and subsequently devoted himself to his estate at Castle Douglas.

In 1965 Findlay saw a picture of Frederick Cutts, Chairman of Henry Tyrer and Company, in the *Liverpool Echo.* He remembered that Tyrer's had been the firm which had arranged for *Prestonian* to carry cargo to West Africa for MacIver's in 1906 and decided to renew their friendship. Accordingly he wrote to Mr. Cutts and thus began a correspondence which was to prove to be of great interest to both men.

For the preceding twelve months the Editor of this work had been interviewing Mr. Cutts because of his long connection with the West African trade. Feeling that a meeting would be mutually beneficial, Mr. Cutts then suggested a discussion with Mr. Findlay and this took place at Tyrer's office in July 1965. Mr. Findlay was then 97 and Mr. Cutts was 84 and the two men had not met since the early thirties. The conversation which then ensued covered many aspects of the West African trade and proved to be extremely informative to the present author who at that time was anxiously preparing his Ph.D. thesis. Findlay subsequently sent him a transcript of a recording made with Dr. W.J. Reader, then of Unilever, in March, 1964, and it is this which is reproduced here.

The passage of time had inevitably weakened some of Findlay's memories of events which had taken place perhaps seventy years earlier. Nevertheless this is an historic document which deserves the widest circulation and is well worth its place in this volume. Mr. Findlay died in December 1966, at the age of 99; Mr. Cutts died in 1968 at the age of 87 – he was still in control of Tyrer's which he had joined as a boy in 1895.

Sources: *History of the U.A.C. to 1938*, op.cit., pp.56, 102–3.
Trade Makers, op.cit., p. 131 and p. 178,
Correspondence between Findlay & Cutts.
Obituary in *Liverpool Echo*, December 1966.
Author's interviews with W.K. Findlay
and F. Cutts in 1965.

INTERVIEW WITH MR. W.K. FINDLAY, LIVERPOOL, 4 MARCH 1964

Mr. Findlay: "I thought when I received your letter first, I ought to write to you and tell you that my memory wasn't as good today as it was 50 years ago. I didn't know what questions you were likely to put to me, but I decided I wouldn't say anything to you until I saw you. And then, if you asked me questions about certain years, I mightn't be able to tell you to within a year or so."

Mr. Reader: "Well we can, generally speaking, check dates. But we thought we would like to talk to you because you were in West Africa, presumably, for many years."

Mr. F: "I served my apprenticeship to the law. I didn't like law and I applied for a job in a West African merchant's office, and I got it. That was in 1888. In 1889 the manager of the office was going out to Nigeria."

Mr. R: "What firm was that?"

Mr. F: "McIver's."

Mr. R: "That was a Glasgow firm and latterly a Liverpool firm."

Mr. F: "I hailed from Angus so I went to Glasgow. In 1889 the manager, Thompson, was going out to Nigeria and he took me with him. I was only 21, I should have been 22 as that was the starting age then. We sailed. When we reached the Gold Coast the captain said he wasn't going in to Lagos, he was going straight down to the Congo and he landed us in Accra. So we waited for a steamer to come along to take us to Nigeria. We went into a native hotel and we stayed 10 days waiting for this steamer, and Thompson contracted malaria. The steamer came in and I got him on board and he died on board so I landed in Nigeria alone.

I remember that when I was in digs in Glasgow, my landlady, when I told her I was going out there, said 'Take your coffin with you!' "

Mr. R: "This was the general impression of West Africa at that time I suppose."

Mr. F: "Yes. So I landed in Nigeria, at Lagos. Lagos was not then part of Nigeria, it was a colony on its own on an island. Nigeria was formed of Northern Nigeria and Southern Nigeria and Lagos. That was around 1901–2. I landed there and I served two and a half years. I had a two-year agreement and the employer had the option of asking me to stay a further six months, and I did. At the end of the six months, he said would you stay a few months more? I said no, money will not keep me here now, I am going home. I had seen a lot of sickness, a lot of deaths and so I went home and worked six months before coming back again. On the way home, on board the steamer, we took on a man in Liberia and he died on board and was buried at sea. We went into (a port in) North Africa, and a stoker on board also died and was buried at sea."

Mr. R: "What kind of trade was it at that time?"

Mr. F: "Barter trade. Maybe 75–80% barter. A difficult trade. They'd bring in their oil in canoes, or on their camels and they were told the price against goods. They went to the warehouse store and picked out the goods they wanted and they would take so many pieces of this and so many pieces of that at such and such a price and these were all totted up and you maybe had to give them shillings or a pound to round off the value."

Mr. R: "What kind of goods would they have taken?"

Mr. F: "Principally cotton goods, textiles from the Bolton area. So then I came home for about six months and then went back again to be in charge of the produce in McIver's at Lagos."

Mr. R: "Was there a McIver in the business at that time?"

Mr. F: "Yes, there was one. Charles. W.B. was dead when I joined the business and then at the end of my second trip I was made partner. Both partners died and I was left in charge of the business. I formed a limited company, I had a share of the profits, quite a few thousand, and I was able to raise, amongst people in Liverpool, sixty thousand. I was then back in Liverpool. Whilst I was in Africa the firm moved from the Glasgow office and came to an office in Exchange Buildings. I was able to raise £60,000. One man gave me £26,500. That was John Holt. You see his name in the Holt Line today. That would be in 1901.

Then W.H. Lever approached us, I think maybe about 1910. Our shares were £10 shares and he paid us £16 a share, which I think included some of the preference shares. He paid us the bulk in shares, a small amount in cash. So I still have some of the same shares. I have had them all these years."

Mr. R: "They are presumably Unilever shares?"

Mr. F: "Yes. So I went across with one of the directors to see the then Mr. Lever. He approached us through Mr. C.C. Knowles and when we got up to a certain point we went across at Mr. Lever's invitation to his room at Port Sunlight. During the conversation, when he had confirmed the price, he said,'What about you, Mr. Findlay?' That wa how he talked. 'Oh', I said, 'I am under an agreement'. I was the only one with knowledge of the African side of the business. He said, 'What's the length of your agreement?' I said, 'It is a three year agreement and expires in about three months.' He said, 'That's not an agreement at all.' Before I could say anything more Mr. McDowell (not Unilever's McDowell, we had a director, a chairman named McDowell of W.B. McIver) said 'Mr. Lever, Mr. Findlay is going to leave himself in your hands'. That was the beginning, and, you know, the end."

I left him and he immediately put me on better terms than I had been working under. I continued with a share of the profits. I can't tell you now, my memory doesn't serve me, what salary I received, until he made me a director of Lever Brothers. Then he put me on £5,000 per year, and a share of the profits. With the capital he put into the business, I extended it by going into the Gold Coast. Then I closed the Gold Coast and extended it further in to Nigeria and he made me director in Nigeria. I went right up north, away as far as Kano."

Mr. R: "Was it mainly a Nigerian business?"

Mr. F: "Yes, mainly in Nigeria, dealing in palm oil and palm nuts. We were largely interested in mahogany also and I was in Lagos when the civil engineers arrived to survey the railway which now runs up to Kano (700 miles). I was in Lagos when the engineers came out and started to build the railway. I went across to the mainland to see the engineer in charge, and said to him, 'I want to go up country to see the king of Allaro, will you give me a lift?' He said he would. I said, 'How far do you go?' He said 16 miles so I said, 'Oh well, that's a start. How often do your trains go?' – 'Twice a week.' – 'What days?' (He told me the days but I forget them now.) 'What time?' – 'Seven in the morning' – 'All right', I said, 'I'll be across. I'll have sixteen men with me and be travelling by hammock.' We went across, small engine and five wagons loaded with rails. He says, 'Can you get up there?' I said, 'Not very well, on top of a wagonload of rails.' I got a lift up, and a box, and I sat on the box, feet on the rails. The men were in the other wagons, I had an interpreter with me and sixteen men. We started and as the sun came out, the rails got very hot and I was liable to get roast soles, so I had to get a board and sit on the box with my feet on the board.

After that we went across country to Allaro. Two fellows with flint lock guns and loin cloths on were standing at the palace gate. I said, 'Go and tell the king I want to see him.' They went away and left us standing outside. There was a gateway but no gate. We didn't wait long before they came back. I said, 'Go back and tell the king that I cannot wait as I have to sleep in the forest tonight and I want to be there before dark.' So they said that the king was getting his chiefs together. We were then ushered in. An old man was sitting on the throne, with four chiefs sitting round on the mud floor, and his principal wife at his left foot. I told him that I had about a 40 sq. mile mahogany forest and it had been reported to me that they were interfering, that men were felling the mahogany trees that belonged to me (my company). I didn't stay very long and said I would be back to see him in a week or two.

When I arrived in the forest, I actually caught the men felling the trees. They disappeared just like snow into the bush and I never saw anything more of them again, but I stayed there. I slept on a fallen tree with uprights on either side to prevent me from falling off on to the ground amongst the snakes.

I got back from the forest, and went to see the king again. I was ushered in pretty promptly this time and I told him what I had seen and briefly I gave him a present (a piece of gold cloth). He gave me two ostrich eggs and a live wild goat. I managed the ostrich eggs and Randall, my interpreter, said, 'What are you going to do with the wild goat?' One of the men carried it round his neck with its feet tied. I said,'We will eat him tonight', and we did.

On the way down from the palace I heard someone running and we stopped. Down came five young women, pretty girls (the King had many more). As they reached us, I said, 'What do you want?' They said, 'We are the king's wives, you gave the king a present but you didn't give us anything.' I said, 'Oh no, in my country we don't give presents to other men's wives, what would the king say if I gave you a present?' Those black hussies said, 'We won't tell him.' They had never seen a white woman so she didn't teach them, it was second nature – 'We won't tell him!' I said to Randall, my interpreter, one of the clerks, 'See what stores we have got now.' We were on our way back to the seaboard. He came back and said that we had a lot of stone ginger. So I said bring five bottles. He gave each of them a bottle of stone ginger and they went away from us carrying the bottles in their bosoms. The best champagne in the world. They were pretty girls, teenage girls who hadn't been long enough married to have a family. It is not generally known in this country but in these parts, the principal wife, the one who was sitting at his left foot, she is the one that selects the wives for the king and submits them for his approval. I don't know how many he had there, maybe something over 20, but I only saw the five, and the senior one.

Well, I got back to Nigeria and I reported the matter to the Governor of Lagos. He said the king was an old man and not able to travel very far, so the principal chief was sent down. Sir George Denton, the Governor in Lagos, sent for me and in my presence the chief got a thorough dressing down and was sent away back to Allaro and we had no further trouble. Then I'd be about 26 or 27, I am 96 now, and I went out in 1889 so that was about 75 years ago.

I remember Mary Kingsley, the traveller and writer who walked all over W. Africa – I travelled three weeks with her. She died when she was 34 years of age.[1] I have Mary Slessor's book, 'White Queen of Calabar.' She belonged to the same county as I did up north, Dundee. I saw a good deal of her, a wonderful little woman. The last time I saw her, I think, was 1895. I came down the Niger River in a launch, a wood-burning launch – we had no coal. The furnace was large and took the wood which was supplied by natives from the banks all the way down (wood stations) and when we got down near the mouth of the river I said to the pilot, 'There is an ocean-going steamer at anchor there', so we drew alongside. I remember the captain's name was Harrison. Harrison knew me and he said 'Come on board. I've got a friend of yours here.' I said, 'Who is it?' He said 'Come and see'. I went on board and it was Mary Slessor.[2] She was making for Calabar and I was making for Lagos. She had another Aberdeen girl missionary with her and she had been up as far as the Gold Coast with a sick missionary.

I was also down there, in the Benin district, when Philipps and two government officials and one of my men named Gardner went up to the city of Benin when the festival was on, to see Nana, the king of Benin.[3] Nana sent to assassinate them, they caught my man Gordon. Nana sent his finger down with his ring on to show that he had been assassinated and Philipps made for the bush and escaped.[4] The government sent a small gunboat up the creeks, all the way up to Benin city where they had been offering young girls, so many every year, to their gods who smothered them in a murder pit. A bronze god[lay]in each corner of the pit, I have two of the gods in my house."

Mr. R: "Have you?"

Mr. F: "Yes, I can't lift them, they are made of bronze and very heavy. And very valuable today. The colonel of the regiment got the other two."

Mr. R: "They sent an expedition to Benin, didn't they?"

Mr. F: "Yes, they sent the gunboat up the river and troops as well. As the troops were going up to the city, shots were fired from the trees. The captain turned his machine gun on the trees, and they dropped like nuts. Nana the king fled, round the back of Lagos.

Two or three weeks after that I was in Lagos. I went round to the back of the island to see a chief. He knew me, I was accustomed to just walking into his house. As I approached the chief's house, I said to my horseman, 'What are these policemen doing here this morning?' I got out of the trap and went through the gates, past the policeman and upstairs to see the chief. When I went in, there was a man sitting in the far corner of the room. His eyes looked through me. Then the chief came in. He says, 'Oh, Mr. Findlay, let me introduce you to Nana, the king of Benin.' I can see his eyes looking through me yet. He was apprehended and sent to the Gold Coast as a political prisoner, and he died there."[5]

Mr. R: "Did you spend most of your time in Africa up to 1910?"

Mr. F: "I spent most of the time in Nigeria but I took over the firm of Ratcliffe & Co. in Sierra Leone."[6]

Mr. R: "Was that a subsidiary of McIver? A subsidiary of Lever's?"

Mr. F: "It was a subsidiary of Lever's, nothing to do with McIver. We took them over. John Walkden & Co. of Manchester, we took them over too.[7] I knew all these people. In fact, I get a Christmas card every year from Dent, who was Ratcliffe's man in Sierra Leone. He was in the Liver Building, as also Manchester manager."

Mr. R: "When Lever's bought McIver's, you became a director of Lever's?"

Mr. F: "Oh yes, I became managing director of McIver's and also about 18–19 companies. I had the whole lot, including the Congo."

Mr. R: "Did you go to the Congo?"

Mr. F: "No. Mr. Greenhalgh, he managed the Congo, the Belgian side of it. All these companies, I think there were 18 or 19 of them, and the Bathurst Trading Company,[8] although I had never been to Gambia.

I was captain of the European Cricket Club in Nigeria. I played cricket. I remember the Queen Mother as a little girl. I played for Strathmore Cricket Club. Before I went to Africa, and when I was home, I used to be still interested. I'm going to tell you why I am telling you about this cricket. There is a reason for it. Sir Gilbert Carter, the governor of Lagos, was a great cricketer, and he and I we were quite friendly. He was a very good batsman and I a left-hand bowler so I kept up with him for two or three years. One day Sir Gilbert sent for me and said that he had just been up country. He said that he had a native of the Gold Coast with him and whilst they were travelling this native of the Gold Coast, who was a cook, said, 'Rubber trees plenty – rubber trees plenty.'

I sent a cable to the Head Office as a result of what Sir Gilbert told me, and said I had gone to the Gold Coast on business. I travelled 1,800 miles. I went to Cape Coast Castle and from there I travelled by hammock to Saltpond, where I stayed for a week or two. Rubber was brought in balls and put through not a circular saw but a circular knife, like a washing machine and cut into strips and then put through a mangle again to take all the dirty water out and dry it out. It was then put into cases and shipped to the rubber markets. I got to know all this, went back to Lagos, ordered machinery, put up buildings and started to buy rubber. I introduced the sale of rubber into Lagos. Sir Gilbert appreciated all that I had done. I got a snubby letter from the Head Office who thought I had gone off on a picnic. I made money in rubber. I introduced rubber into Nigeria and I still think that the government should have taken some notice of what I did, but they didn't. That was brought about through cricket. But I stopped as a player, and they made me President of the club."

Mr. R: "Unilever has a plantation now at Sapele and also there is one further up country."

Mr. F: "I opened the Sapele factory and sent a man named Gordon also. I have a picture of a tree that I sold in Liverpool by auction for £1,600. I wrote out to Sapele and said that the tree must have been about 100 feet high so the branches must be very thick. Go back into the forest, see if you can find the branches of that tree and send them home to me. I have got a table in my house made out of one of the branches. I had it made in Castle Douglas.[9] This was from the forest near Sapele, and shipped from Sapele, rafted down and shipped in one of the Elder Dempster steamers to Liverpool and sold in Liverpool by Gobells the brokers. I was deeply interested in the timber trade, my grandfather was interested in it and at weekends when at school I used to go into the woods with him. That caused me to take an interest in mahogany."

Mr. R: "There is a big timber mill now at Sapele, run by United Africa."

Mr. F: "John McNeill, he was in the timber trade in Sapele and originally he was with the African & Eastern. That was many years ago. The Sapele wood is a very heavy wood. I think I have one or two boards of the branches of that big tree lying in my garage. I had them about 17 or 18 years in Liverpool and I transferred them when I went up there (I have an estate of about 1,000 acres and they are up there now) 47 years ago.

We had our own steamers you see . . .Bromport Steamship Company[10] (Lever's). I was managing director of that company."

Mr. R: "Lever got steamers because he was afraid of the Elder Dempster monopoly?[11] Was that right?"

Mr. F: "Yes, that was it. We couldn't get our mahogany shipped and in what we call brackish water, salt and fresh mixed breed worms. The worms attacked the logs and they became useless if they were left in the river for a certain time in this water. The Niger River has about four or five mouths, all tidal. I visited all the British Colonies except for Gambia. I was never in the Gambia as it was groundnuts only. Gambia is a small colony a few miles only in width on either bank of the river. So I carried on a successful business with the Bathurst Trading Company but entirely groundnuts with Manchester goods – cash trade, not barter."

Mr. R: "At one time Lever was afraid that the West African trade was getting into so few hands that the price of these materials would be forced up against him. Do you think that was why he went into that business?"

Mr. F: "That was one of his reasons. He wanted to make sure that he would get a certain proportion of his requirements for the soap firms. He wasn't then in margarine."

Mr. R: "No. He didn't go into margarine until 1914. What was your impression of Lever when you first met him? What kind of man was he?"

Mr. F: "He was a very big-hearted man, far-seeing. I wouldn't like to say that he was a dictator. He knew what he wanted and got the men he wanted and he got them all around him. He was a very liberal-hearted man to his staff. We only had one strike in my time. His staff were all well paid. He introduced this co-partnership business whereby after a certain number of years, they all participated. He had annual meetings of all the co-partners in the big halls at Port Sunlight. I would rather work under Lord Leverhulme as I knew him than 999 others."

Mr. R: "Do you think that as he grew older his judgement began to fail?"

Mr. F: "Yes. The Congo didn't do him any good. His visits to the Congo killed him."

Mr. R: "He died after one of them, didn't he?"

Mr. F: "Yes, and he lost his wife when she arrived home from the Congo."

Mr. R: "Was it the Congo did that, do you think?"

Mr. F: "Yes. He shouldn't have taken her because she was a delicate little person, you know, a very small person."

Mr. R: "She was very tiny, wasn't she?"

Mr. F: "Very tiny. I'll give you an instance. His headquarters were in Bolton. His business was of course in Bolton when he entered the soap trade. He telephoned me from Bolton one day. I can't remember what it was about now, but he said, 'I want to see you about such and such a thing. Will you come out this afternoon and see me?' I said yes. 'I don't know about the trains.' He said, 'You will get the 2 o'clock train from Exchange Station. Lady Leverhulme will be on the platform. Bring her with you.' (She was travelling in the same train.) So I took Lady Leverhulme to Bolton and his car met me there, and I discussed matters with him. I delivered my message and I delivered her and we talked over the business and I was back later that evening. He never could do enough for me. He was very big-hearted with me.

When I was chairman of the Niger Company I used to go to London every week. I would be in the Liverpool office on Monday morning and the Port Sunlight board meeting Monday afternoon at 3 p.m. I lived in Cheshire. The directors' car or my own car would take me home from the meeting. There were three or four of us. I came over to Liverpool every Monday night to get the midnight train to London. I was in London Tuesdays and Wednesdays as chairman of the Niger Company and then back to Liverpool on Wednesday afternoon. In the summer season I used to go up to Scotland every Friday night, back to Dumfries, and return on Sunday night. I couldn't get to Liverpool on Sunday night so I had to sleep in Preston. I would be in the Liverpool office at 9 o'clock on Monday morning. I was a bit of a tramp then. I had my railway contract which cost £204. In addition to that, and my £5,000, he gave me £2,500 a year expenses. I'll tell you the funny side of this now. My accountant McGregor, a senior partner of Chalmers Wade, Liverpool and London, came into the office and said, 'The inspector has been at me about these expenses of yours.' I said, 'What about it, what has he got to do with that?' He said 'Can you justify spending £2,500 per year expenses?' I said 'No, I can't.' 'Would you take an assessment for £1,250?' I said 'Yes, I will' and that settled it. My expenses were free of tax, you see, but I accepted an assessment for £1,250. That was the big-heartedness of the man.

I'll give you another instance . . .have you been to Port Sunlight?"

Mr. R: "I know Port Sunlight quite well, yes."

Mr. F: "You know his house?"

Mr. R: "Yes."

Mr. F: "Coming down in front of the office one morning a few minutes after 9 o'clock, he saw three managers going into the office door. He went straight up to his room and rang for Mr. Fildes, who was then secretary. Fildes answered and he said to Fildes, 'Mr. Fildes, I saw three of the staff coming into the office this morning late as well as the chairman.' He was late himself a few minutes after nine o'clock. 'Will you find out who they were?' Fildes went down and saw the commissionaire, got the names of the men, and they were in the Export Department, then rang the bell for Miller, who was deputy director and Mr. Solomon who was a managing director. 'Mr. Miller, I find three of your men staff came in late this morning. Would you just give me their names.' He said 'Oh yes.' He went back and told the chairman who they were and Miller backed up the men and said they were very good men and this and that sort of thing. It took over a year or more before he forgave Miller for backing up his men as against coming in late. But that was his strong point. He seized the opportunity of being sure of what he was talking about. He saw these men coming in with his own eyes and he seized the opportunity of laying down the law by saying that he saw there were others besides the chairman come in late in the morning. He had to do that, with a huge staff such as they had there. If he had the chance of being severe and sure of his ground, he was severe. On the contrary, if you should, what I call, play the game with him, he didn't know how much to do for you. That's the man."

Mr. R: "You were chairman of the Niger Company after he bought it? What was your view of the Niger Company transaction, the way he bought it and the rest of it?"[12]

Mr. F: "There was a good deal of talkie talkie about that. They thought that he paid too much. But one of the difficulties of the Niger Company was the senior general manager. He didn't like the transaction and he made a great many difficulties."

Mr. R: "Was this before Lever's had got hold of the Niger Company?"

Mr. F: "No, afterwards. That was the difficulty. As chairman I used to go down there. I spent two days every week there but it would take more than two days to realise what was going on. But I think it was a very wise move. He may have paid too much for it but the Niger Company strengthened Lever's hand by the quantity of produce that they were able to buy and import as against opposition. They had the land and a monopoly, the land belonged to them. If you wanted to establish on the River Niger, you couldn't do it then without the Niger Company. I knew of a case of a man (I can't think what firm he was with now) but he started business on his own. He built a factory and started trading. The Niger Company stepped in and said, 'You are a poacher, what are you doing here, who gave you permission to come and put up these buildings and buy produce? Clear out!' So they cleared him out. It was their land, just the same as was all the land around the Niger swamps.

I have heard these reports about the Niger Company, about him buying it. I still think he was right in doing it because he had a monopoly. He didn't have the opposition that he had in other parts with the African & Eastern. I started the African & Eastern purchase."

Mr. R: "That would be in 1929?"

Mr. F: "Yes. I knew the chairman and the directors and I had a good deal to do with the African section of the Chamber of Commerce, I was on the Committee. Colonel Nicol and John Tunnicliffe, two of the directors, were on the floor above us in the Liver Building and I went up to see them and I used to talk things over a good deal with them. I started talking to Tunnicliffe and he lifted the telephone to Nicol in the adjoining room and we talked the matter over. That set the ball rolling about taking over African & Eastern. They reported the matter to the chairman of African & Eastern, I forget his name now, but it doesn't matter. He rang through to me one day to come up and see him after Tunnicliffe and Colonel Nicol had reported the conversation. So I went up to see him and got a thorough dressing down. He didn't take any leading part in the business, he looked nearer 70 than 60 but I may have been wrong. That was the beginning of the African & Eastern. I pointed out what an advantage it would be to Nicol and Tunnicliffe to be under the same umbrella as I was under."[13]

Mr. R: "Do you think that if Lever had not bought the Niger Company when he did, the African & Eastern would have bought the Niger Company in 1920? I sometimes wonder if that was what he was frightened of."

Mr. F: "No, I don't think so. The African & Eastern were too narrow-minded to expand. That's what was wrong with them. Tunnicliffe and Nicol were the two live men, the others were what I call guinea pigs. One of them was a city councillor. I can't remember the chairman's name. It would always take him twice the time to go downstairs that it would take me. That was the African & Eastern.

I still think, you know, that an organisation such as Unilever should not depend upon the market for raw material. I still think that they ought to have something of their own to fall back on even though it may cost them more sometimes. The law of averages will prevail and the benefits to be derived through having suppliers of their own makes the Buying Department independent. Knowles would ring through to me, he would say, 'We are running short of palm kernels now, what have you got afloat?' I could tell we had about 1,500–2,000 tons, some of it due in at such and such a time. He knew to a day when he could have his Port Sunlight lighters alongside Elder Dempster's or their own steamer when he could have that across to the mill, into the mill and then oil into the soap pans all within 48 hours."

Mr. R: "And this, you think, paid Lever's better than selling it on the open market?"

Mr. F: "Oh yes, they could make a ring against Lever's but with Lever's having their own suppliers it made them independent of the ring. They did get together, but they couldn't stop the machinery for supplying the margarine firm or the soap plant."

Mr. R: "What sometimes surprises me is that Lever went into West Africa buying palm oil when in fact the main material that he used in Sunlight soap was coconut oil, because he did not get any coconuts from West Africa, and I sometimes wonder why he was so interested in palm oil."

Mr. F: "I couldn't say."

Mr. R: "Because at that time I think palm oil was a rather low grade material which he couldn't use in Sunlight."

Mr. F: "Palm oil was inedible. If you saw it as I saw it being brought down in petrol tins, all sorts of tins, in all sorts of vessels and canoes, under filthy conditions, it would take a good deal to make it edible."

Mr. R: "Did you have anything to do with Lever's oil milling ventures in Nigeria? He set up crushing mills in Nigeria I think?"[14]

Mr. F: "Yes, that was after my time."

Mr. R: "So you didn't have anything to do with that?"

Mr. F: "No. You see my heavy work with Lever's stopped about 40 years ago and your mind gets a bit rusty. I have been looking at some books, I don't know if you edited them or not, the last two volumes."

Mr. R: "I didn't write the history, but I had quite a lot to do with the research. How did you find the two volume history?"[15]

Mr. F: "Very interesting. I have been looking through them with a view to trying to refresh my mind for dates before I saw you, because I felt a little bit guilty in not telling you that my memory is not as good now as it was 40 or 50 years ago."

Mr. R: "Well, it seems to be remarkably good anyway. You mentioned McIver's McDowell, what did you think of Lever's McDowell?"

Mr. F: "He was a very brainy chap. McDowell was a clever lawyer. But he was never in private practice. He came to Lever's without ever being in private practice, very soon after he took his finals."

Mr. R: "Yes, I think he must have come when he was quite a young man. I know I have heard it said that he could play fast and loose with Leverhulme to an extent that no other man ever could."

Mr. F: "Old man Lever was very fond of McDowell. Lord Leverhulme was a far-seeing man and so was McDowell, not to the same extent, but he was all the same. Lord Leverhulme took over many associated companies that would be of use to him for various purposes. One day, it must have been about 1912, Lever asked me to have lunch with him at his club in Liverpool. On the way there we came to Woolworths and he went in, so I followed. We walked around and when we came out again he asked if I thought it would be a good idea to set up stores like Woolworths in Africa. I had to tell him that Africa wasn't yet ready for anything like that. That was far-seeing, I admire Lever for thinking about that, but he was thinking away ahead of Africa as it was then.

Woolworths in Africa would need a staff sufficient to watch the monkeys going round the counters! To give you an instance, McIver's house was on the bank of a tributary of the Niger. We had a verandah round three sides of the house and on each side we grew mango trees and in the house we had a monkey. Matheson, the senior assistant, had a room in my house, the others were all in another house. Matheson was going out riding on a Saturday afternoon and he was dressing. The bedroom door opened on to the verandah and he was shaving, using a looking glass on the verandah and he put his razor on the rail. He went into the room and when he came out he couldn't find it. The monkey had been sitting up in the mango tree watching all that was going on, and when Matheson went into his bedroom, down he comes and whips the razor off the rail. Matheson came out and couldn't find the razor and as he looked up towards the trunk of the tree, he saw the monkey had gone up the tree with the razor and said, 'That's not going to be any use to me', so he dropped it. I was sitting reading another night and I heard glasses breaking. I went into the dining room and there was the monkey sitting on the sideboard lifting glasses and throwing them on the floor and breaking them."

Notes

1. See above, p. 82 and note 55 on p. 92.
2. W.P. Livingstone, *Mary Slessor of Calabar, Pioneer Missionary*, Hodder & Stoughton, London, 47th Edition, 1940.
3. After a gap of some sixty years, Findlay has mixed up two separate events. Nana was a famous chief who controlled the coastal district to the West of the Benin River estuary. His main town was at Brohemie and this was destroyed by a British attack in 1894. The Oba (or King) of Benin City at the time of the massacre was Ovonramwen. Part of the reason for the confusion is that Nana was sometimes called the 'Viceroy or King of Benin' and also because both men were attacked and sent into exile by the British. (Jacob Egharevba, *A Short History of Benin*, Ibadan University Press, 1968, pp.48–59; and Sir Harry Johnston, *The Story of My Life*, London, 1923, pp.212–3).
4. Findlay's memory of this event is also inaccurate. Nine Europeans together with two hundred and forty natives set out for Benin City on the 1st of January, 1897. Five government officials, including James Philipps (the Acting Consul-General) and two traders were killed in an ambush. The two Europeans who escaped were Captain Boisragon and the Vice-Consul, Mr. R.F. Locke. Amongst the dead was the Mr. T. Gordon referred to by Findlay but there is no mention of anyone named 'Gardner' and it seems probably that Findlay was confusing the name with 'Gordon'. (James Egharevba, op.cit., p.49.) Photographs of members of the expedition are provided in James Pinnock, *Benin: The Surrounding Country, Inhabitants, Customs and Trade*, Published by the Journal of Commerce, Liverpool, 1897, pp.15–21).
5. Confirmation that in this instance Findlay really means Nana and not Ovonramwen is given in G.W. Neville's 'Nana. Oloma of Benin' (Journal of the African Society, Vol. 14, January 1915, pp. 162–7.) This shows that after his defeat Nana was attacked by his enemies so made his way to Lagos. Neville helped him with clothes and money and then Nana surrendered to the British authorities. He was detained at Old Calabar and then sent to Accra in the Gold Coast. He was allowed to return in 1906 and established a new town at what is now KoKo in Nigeria. Ovonramwen was exiled to Calabar. He died in January 1914, and was buried at Old Calabar. (James Egharevba, op.cit., pp.60–61.)
6. P. Ratcliffe and Company, Limited, was not acquired by Lever Brothers until 1912. (Charles Wilson, op.cit., Vol.1, p. 181, and *U.A.C. Hist.*, p. 58.)
7. John Walkden began trading to West Africa in 1865. At first he operated from his home in Manchester using the mail order system made possible by the advent of regular steam ship services. The business prospered and with the assistance of his four sons he established an office in Manchester and several trading stations in West Africa. The Company became 'Limited' in 1900 and, after several years of close co-operation, was purchased by Lever Brothers in 1917. (*U.A.C. Hist.*, p. 57.)
8. The Bathurst Trading Company, Limited, was purchased by Lever Brothers in 1918. (*U.A.C. Hist.*, p. 58.)
9. Findlay's home was at Barncailzie Hall, Castle Douglas, Kirkcudbrightshire.
10. Lever Brothers established the Bromport Steamship Company in 1916 at a time when the West African shipping conference was not operating because of the First World War. Only part of Lever's cargoes could be carried in their own ships (the balance was carried by Elder Dempster) but the operation was a great success while tonnage was in short supply. By 1923 condi-

tions were very different and the vessels of the Bromport Steamship Company were sold to the Royal Mail Group of which Elder Dempster was a prominent member. (*Trade Makers*, pp.200–2, 211, 215, 220–1, & 224; M.J. Merriweather, 'The Bromport Steamship Company,' Unpublished MS. by the then Manager of Palm Line's Liverpool Office, 1963, and R. Kohn, *Palm Line: The Coming of Age, 1949–1970*, Published by the Company, London, 1970.)

11. Lever's found that the transport of palm oil from West Africa was an expensive business and attempted to reduce costs by chartering a tank steamship in 1913. Elder Dempster refused to permit this and with the aid of the deferred rebate system were able to have the project ended. Thereafter Lever Brothers waited for a suitable opportunity to enter the shipping trade themselves – hence the establishment of the Bromport Steamship Company in 1916. (*Trade Makers*, pp.178–81).
12. Lever was out of England for most of 1919 and left his directors to buy the Niger Company. This was a task entirely outside their previous experience for Lever normally gave them little opportunity to exercise their authority, but even so they ought not to have proceeded without '. . .instructing the Company's Auditors to make a full investigation of the Niger Company's books before completing the deal.' (C. Wilson, op.cit., Vol.1, pp.252–9, and *Trade Makers*, pp.210–12).
13. The African and Eastern Trade Corporation was formed in 1919 by the amalgamation of the African Association with the two 'Miller' firms and Swanzys. Until 1928 it made moderate profits but a deficit then caused a loss of confidence amongst the financial institutions which normally provided its working capital. A full examination of the Corporation's position then showed that only a merger with the Niger Company could save it from liquidation, and an agreement was reached in March, 1929. The result was the establishment of a new trading firm, the United Africa Company, in which the Niger Company and the African & Eastern held equal shares. (*U.A.C. Hist.*, pp.110–16 and *Trade Makers*, pp.235–37.) *The Lion and the Unicorn in Africa*, by Frederick Pedler (Heinemann, London, 1974) provides a complete history of the origins of the United Africa Company from 1787 including an account of the amalgamation of the Niger Company and the African and Eastern Trade Corporation.
14. Lever's erected kernel-crushing mills at Opobo and Apapa (Nigeria) and at Adjuiah (Gold Coast) in 1910. A further mill was constructed at Yonnibannal in Sierra Leone in 1912. (C. Wilson, op.cit., Vol.1, p. 181.)
15. Unilever's history was written by Charles Wilson, op.cit. Note that a third volume was published in 1968.

4. D.D. AFRICANUS COKER

INTRODUCTION

Little is known for certain about D.D. Africanus Coker except that he was born in Sierra Leone. Coker is, in fact, a common name in that country – most families of Cokers originating in Hastings, near Freetown, taking their surname from a black American pastor who was the village manager in the 1820s. In his definitive *History of Sierra Leone*, Christopher Fyfe mentions the death of an old lady in Hastings in 1909 and records that she had one son working in the Cameroons and another in the Congo. The *Sierra Leone Weekly News* dated the 27th of February, 1909, states that the death was of Mrs. Fanny Coker, mother of J.J. Coker (working at Matadi) and of S.W. Coker (working at Duala). If 'J.J.' is a misprint for 'D.D.' then this could be the employee of John Holt and Company whose erudite letter is reproduced below.

Throughout the nineteenth century the Creole inhabitants of Sierra Leone regarded the pursuit of education as a particularly useful method of raising their financial and social status. To some extent their aspirations were encouraged by successive governments and the more able amongst them achieved responsible positions in the medical services, in the armed forces, in public offices, in the church and in education itself. Many of the growing number of literate Africans could not be found suitable employment within the confines of Sierra Leone so they spread into numerous occupations over the length and breadth of West Africa.

The Victorian era's view of education as a kind of panacea for many of the evils which beset the average Sierra Leonian then gave way to an Edwardian denial of aroused expectations, for the more rewarding employment was progressively reserved for European expatriates. Thus Africanus Horton and his contemporaries in the mid-nineteenth century felt 'the same kind of basic loyalty to the British crown that Englishmen felt in England'. The changing situation in respect of the employment of educated Africans meant that by 1910, although '. . .Still staunchly grateful for the benefits received from Britain in the past, they felt wounded and let down at the change in their former friends and benefactors.'

Coker's letter to John Holt and Company personifies the dilemma of many Sierra Leonians at this time. Clearly trying to give objective advice at the end of his career he found it difficult to conceal the bitterness he felt about the unjust treatment of African employees. Yet he seems anxious to believe that if only the true state of affairs could be revealed to those in authority the damage could be repaired to the mutual advantage of all.

Coker's regard for James Deemin is obviously sincere – the fact that Deemin did little more than demonstrate compassion, fairness and a degree of humanity shows, perhaps, the very low standards of his colleagues. But it may be that they should not be blamed too much for their views and actions. They were, after all, in very good company for even such an eminent author as Albert Schweitzer revealed much insensitive contempt for the educated African in his writing.

Sources:

Christopher Fyfe, *History of Sierra Leone*, Oxford University Press, London, 1962.

Christopher Fyfe, *Sierra Leone Inheritance*, Oxford University Press, London, 1964.

Christopher Fyfe, *Africanus Horton*, Oxford University Press, New York, 1972.

Sierra Leone Weekly News.

Albert Schweitzer, *On the Edge of the Primeval Forest*, A. & C. Black, London, 1922.

Albert Schweitzer, *More from the Primeval Forest*, A. & C. Black, London, 1931.

LETTER FROM D.D. AFRICANUS COKER

Messrs. John Holt & Co. Ltd., Royal Liver Building, Liverpool.	Imo River 28th March 1921

Dear Sirs,

In accordance with instructions received we here record our observations of the conditions of trade at Imo Station. It is difficult for me to give you at the present time something to aid you in your future management of your firms interest here, considering this station was opened during an abnormal state of things, which abnormal state we are still passing: however there are certain things that are almost the same in all conditions, with this idea we proceed with the hope our effort will be of some help to you.

The writer arrived here on the 2nd December 1919 with instructions to hurry the construction and get ready to start produce buying in January 1920. On the 14th January 1920 we started produce buying, and on the 17th March of the same year the shop was opened for cash sales.

Trade for 1920

Palm Oil	January to December	143308 gallons
	Average being	11942 gallons per month
Palm Kernels	Jan. to Dec.	16152 bushels
	Average being	1346 bushels per month
Cash Sales	March to Dec.	£1945:7:7
	Average being	£914:10:9 per month

We started buying @ 4/1½ per gallon oil and 11/6 per bushel Kernels; in about a month prices had gone up to 5/7½ per gallon oil and 14/3 per bushel Kernel. The highest paid here was £45:7:0: per cask oil by G.B. Ollivant and £45:5:0: by A & E T[1] & Miller Brothers. About the middle of March prices start falling and rising to the close of the year which left us paying £9:7:6 cask oil and 6/6 bushel Kernels.

Principal Traders & Markets who feed Imo with trade

Traders Akwete, Okrika, Opobo, Bonny, Oframbele, and New Calabar. These bring their produce by canoe, and some small traders who bring

Kernels by rail, and two who bring Kernels and oil by rail for W.B. McIver[2] and A & E T. Corp. Some women and few men from surrounding towns are also contributing their share however small, these bring their produce on their heads.
Markets Obibo, Asa, Akwete, Owerenta*, Ntamini, Omomah, Ipe, Okpoala, Amokpo, Oburutu, Owaza, etc. etc.

Festivals

The Seasons observed by the people here are New Year feast and Christmas. In short, the things that touch the trade here are those which have to do with farming; Viz:– Brushing, Planting & reaping. The last named is the only one observed as a feast, the other two are just the opposite of feasting. Christmas is observed by all as a time for merry making even by those who are not Christians.
Months Brushing starts in some parts in December and in others January. Planting in March; reaping in some parts starts in July and in others September. Trade is generally dull during these Seasons.

Labour

Expenses on labour seems abnormal when compared with up line stations, on the ground that each factory has to transport to its beach all produce by rail. After bargaining with a trader, he asks for boys to bring the produce; Yes rathèr in most cases you have to tell him that your boys are ready to bring the produce; if you are not ready with boys, others will easily knock your hand off and take the produce. I understand it was not so at the start, this state of things was brought about by the firms in trying to out do one another till it has become the general rule.

When traders prefer goods to càsh and vice versa

When prices are lower than what they are paying at the market, traders prefer goods to cash, although they have to sell the goods to cash or manilas before they could buy produce, the reason for this is that these firms when prices are low, in order to get their share or more of the produce give out goods at cost and I believe in most cases less than cost. Not wishing to take you to the remote past, let me here give you as an instance an incident from the immediate past. On Wed. 23rd November last, a trader by name Fred George of Okrika brought three casks of Oil for sale; he, being our customer came to us first, finding prices very low he resolved to take three things, each for a cask, Viz.

* McIver's, Millers, & Associations are said to be buying these.

Tobacco, Kerosene and Soap instead of cash. The agreed price between the firms here at the time was £12. per cask oil. We accordingly offered him 330 heads tobacco, 4 cases each 56, 2 lb bars popular pale soap, and 8 cases Kerosene for the three sacks. Not satisfied he went to our next door neighbour W.B. MacIver, there they offered him 410 heads tobacco, 13½ cases each 20, 2 lb bars pale soap and 10½ cases Kerosene for the three casks oil. According to our cost the 13½ cases Kerosene £14:14:0 and the 410 heads tobacco £13:13:0 under such conditions one can only fold his hands and let others take the produce.

During brushing time traders prefer cash to goods, on the grounds that most of those who generally buy their goods are busy brushing, it will take them as much longer time to make a turnover with goods than the usual.

Important Goods for Produce Trade

Tobacco, Salt, Soap, Kerosene, Stock fish, Low Madrass, Fine imitation Madrass, R.J. Madrass, Trade Pork, Matchets, Trade Spirits etc., etc. The first 5 (five) named are the most important in produce trade. November to April one should be well stocked with Salt, although they buy Salt all the year round, yet, never so much as during the above mentioned time; One should have large and small bags; large or 90 lb. bags for traders by canoe, and small 40 or 50 lb. bags for traders on foot who are mostly women and carry theirs on their heads. It is also necessary to have soap in 10, 20, 40 and 56 bar cases and not all in 56 bar cases as at present, for it is sometimes stiff to make some of these traders believe that 4 cases each 56 bars contains more soap than 10 cases of each 20 bars; in fact, with some of these traders it is useless trying to explain as they will never believe.

Trade Spirit

The writer is of the opinion that you can hold your own in West Africa without selling this article. This I assure You Sirs, is not an hasty conclusion. Although I was not an alcohol drinker when I entered your service in 1902, and thankful to be able to say I am not an alcohol drinker up to this time when I am about leaving you for good, yet I used to argue, if a man wants it, let him have it, every man knew or ought to know what is good for him, and as man was made with a free will, no man has the right to require another to do or refrain from doing anything without his free will, if any does, he simply deprives another of his God given right. After seeing what alcohol has done and is doing, I am now from experience of a contrary opinion. I have found out that most of us Africans are like babes, in that we do not in all cases know what is for, from what is against our betterment. Some of us are still of the opinion that whatever comes from the whiteman's country is the essence of purity and therefore good for our moral, physical, and financial progress without taking the trouble to ask the why and wherefore about it, we let the whiteman do our thinking and take whatever he tells us as Gospel truth. I now argue this:- A razor is useful in the hand of a man, but dangerous in that of a child, (baby) whosoever places his razor at the reach of a baby is solely responsible for the consequence; therefore the blame for the moral, physical, and financial ruin of millions of Africa's Sons is at the door of the whiteman. First, the Government who permits it to be sent out, and then the Merchants who sent it and are sending it out to ruin the bodies and souls of our people who are like babes. Some of the villages in the Ogowe & Ngomo rivers in the French Congo are the most wretched I have seen in my life, looking at the miserableness of the inhabitants, one is driven to ask himself whether those people were made out of the dregs of humanity. Trying to find out the fact of their conditions: I found that they were brought to such a low state of existence by trade spirit. The men will spend weeks and months in the bush cutting mahogany and other logs for the European trade; after selling these logs, they will buy barrels, Kegs, and jars of rum, gin, aniseed, Kumel etc. (trade spirits) and take them to their villages and will do nothing more until they have finished the whole by drinking themselves drunk, dead drunk; when they become sober, they found that they have been working for nothing, or rather solely for the benefit of the whiteman, for the whiteman has the logs which they had cut and also the money which were paid to them for the logs whilst they were left morally, physically and financially poorer than they started, so much so that they are not able to do the necessary repairs of their villages; they become a burden to themselves and their surroundings. This station was opened only last year, today we have more than three hundred cases of trade spirit in stock, but not a bag of salt; now Sirs, the two, which is the more beneficial? there is no comparison. If things were to go on like this, in ten years hence, the people here would have been made as wretched, miserable and almost worthless as the Akebo, Asekians and some of the Galoas of Ogame and Nkomo rivers if not worse. Now Sirs, I, a negro of Africa, is telling you in simple English that you are in no way contributing to the betterment of the African by sending trade spirit into their land, on the contrary, you are truly helping to degenerate them, in short you are trying to create a sort of sub humanity in Africa.

You may ask, why then am I selling trade spirit for you? In Nigeria,

Imo River is the only place I have had the degrading job of selling trade spirit: Although I am dead against it now, yet as long as I have not informed you of my mind towards this stuff, I have no moral right to obstruct your trade; with this idea, when I was instructed last year to give a good note to those who would ask for trade spirit, I did so accordingly without hindering the progress of your trade by any means. It was in January this year that I was informed that licence had been given for the sale of trade spirit at this station. There were two courses open to me, to ask for a transfer to a place where I shall have nothing to do with spirit selling, and failing to obtain this, to send in my resignation. If a loyal person asks for a transfer, he will surely give the authorities up to three months to get some one to replace him before taking the other course. According to my agreement I am to give three months notice before leaving, considering I had at the time six months to complete my term, I drew the conclusion that the game will not be worth the candle therefore the best thing for me to do is to abide my time. I have now made up my mind that after Imo River, I shall, and will, under no circumstances, and for no earthly reason, be employed in selling trade spirits.

England Expects Every Man to do His Duty

I am not an Englishman but a Sierra Leonean, whatever that may mean, however since I know myself up to this moment (time of writing) I look upon myself as a member of the British Empire and therefore my duty to seek the peace and prosperity of the Empire. I do not think there is a single person in the world who does not want to better his standing in life. The human family as one man is after something which I may be permitted to call contentment or satisfaction. 999 out of every 1000 of the human family think money is the chiefest among the things that lead to the obtaining of satisfaction. Although we have seen that money does not give satisfaction, as there are men in the world today who have more than enough money to last them a thousand years twice fold had they such length of time to live, who are still not satisfied, but are trying to get more money by any means foul or fair, yet for the purpose of our discourse, we take money as the chief means to obtain satisfaction.

We see men to better their financial standing have formed companies to carry on business. We are of the opinion that the sole mover of each individual member of a company is self interest, we are sure that the best way for a member of a company to seek and secure his personal interest, is as it were for him to forsake and forget self and to put all his pounds to seek his firms interest, for in the prosperity of his firm lies his own interest. We are of the opinion that each firm is to treat the interest of the state in which it exists as a member of a company a right to treat the interest of his company by putting the interest of the state first before that of the firm and not allow any commercial reasons to turn him from this motive, for the peace and safety of the state is indispensable to the success of the firm. We also believe that the Government of a state ought to put the interest of truth and justice before that of the state, and not to allow any political reason to turn them from this rule. For in the unbending carrying on of truth and justice lies the solidity and stability of the state. We believe the peace of a state does not rest solely with those in government employ, but with every individual member of that state. In an Empire like ours which is composed of the Black, Brown, Red, White, Yellow varieties of the human family, (you will note I used the term varieties instead of races, on the ground that I acknowledge but one race among men, and that is the human race. Although we have more lives among the cat kind than among man kind, yet we call the cat kind the feline race, we do not say races; it is rather funny we can acknowledge this fact among the cat kind but not among mankind).

It is very essential that every sound minded true lover of the Empire to put the interest of the Empire first before that of the variety or hue to which he belongs, this can only be done by every member treating any other member regardless of the variety to which he belongs as he himself would like to be treated by any other member. I assert without fear of contradiction that 9/10 of the unrest which have caused what is called punitive expeditions to be sent into one part or other of the Empire were caused and are being caused by the high handed treatment which some of a delusive idea or antipathy or both inflicted on others who are not of their hue. The trouble which caused a punitive expedition to be sent to the interior of the upper Ngoonia during the years of 1906/7 amongst the Ashogoh and Ashira people in the French Congo was really caused or brought about by the actions of some whiteman of a delusive idea who thought the blackman is nothing but their football. Yea rather some less in value than their football, in that they are not only free to kick them about as much as they like, but can kill them as much as they like with impunity. At first, it was a mystery to the people, thinking of the good old Europeans with whom they had come in contact in trade at Sette Camma. Men like good old Frank Williamson and others of long ago. The mystery turned to mild protest, and from mild protest to last resort in self defence. I believe a fabricated cooked something was sent to Europe as the cause of the trouble. We have however two things to console ourselves viz: He that is highest regardeth; and there is a judgement. As prevention is better than cure, it is therefore best for us to try to the best of our ability to prevent such a thing from taking place any more in any part of our Empire. I am telling you that naturally some of the men you are sending out from Europe are inflicting mortal wounds on the feelings of some of the black employees of yours and many of those who are not in your employ. There are some black men who refused to be made as footballs by any and so receive the animosity of those who think themselves superior beings because they are white to such an extent as to make them forget or ignore their duty to their firm and their Empire. Let us leave out the Empire as the majority of them do not know their duty to their Empire, but take the firm that sent them out. If you have at the head of your business one who is of the new or Georgian School of thought and under him are stations occupied by blacks and whites, if one visits the station he will see the difference; stations occupied by whites will be well stocked, all facilities given for the success of the trade, and everything will be done for the Europeans personal comfort; on the other hand at stations where blacks are in charge, you will see a poorly stocked shop, facilities not one tenth of that given to the European; personal comforts, sometimes not even a bed, a chair, or a table. Among the blacks the station will show three different appearances, at a factory where the black man in charge is one of those who think the whiteman a small god and ready to tremble at his presence and cry 'Zaki or Zerhah'[3] his factory will give a better look than the average, on the other hand if a black man among them is outspoken, his station will show the worst appearance and therefore the worst return; he will as it were be tied hand and foot, and then ask to walk or swim; his position will be intolerable, the white overlord will set trap for his black underdog in order to get him into a mess, as a certain white employee of yours once said to me, 'I would not mind telling a few lies to get that so and so into trouble'. I believed him because I knew a good bit of his natural tendency. I have seen a black-man in spite of all restrictions in all things tried his best to overcome, his trying insures more hatred from the head of the business. How could an educated person, a European, and an English man at that, be so blind to the fact that the interest of all stations belonging to a firm are really one – regardless of the person in charge, and that whatever he does to hinder the success of any, he is really doing it to the detriment of the firms interest and not the individual in charge, is beyond my comprehension. If truly love is blind, I believe prejudice is surely more blind. It is possible for you in Liverpool to detect this sort of thing, when you have at the head of affairs one who puts the interest of the firm before colour and prejudice, you will note that almost all stations under his control is doing well regardless of the person in charge, as he (the head) will do his best to enable all to do their best so much so that the returns of each station according to the conditions of things in it will give or rather show something pleasing. We Africans know and do feel that we are not receiving what is called fairplay or square deal, with this idea in our mind to be receiving pin pricking indignities in the bargain is heart rending to the utmost, if it continues it will lead us sooner or later to the breaking point, for many of us are so pressed that we are crying, who shall deliver us from the body of this death, the whiteman's burden, which is prejudice and injustice.

I am very glad to be able to say that I have met up with some in your firm who are worthy the name of Englishmen. Among these men James Deemin[4] stands first; to me he belonged to the old or Victorian School of thought, therefore he is by far superior to these of the new or Georgian School of thought. About the end of 1903 or beginning of 1904, we were then in Gaboon, Mr. Deemin was then what is known now as Divisional Agent. One day Mr. W.G. Platford who was then our beach master was doing some work with the boys, wanting them to move quicker, he picked an empty bottle and threw it as it were at them, knowing what I did of Mr. Platford I was quite sure it was not with the intention of hitting any of them, unfortunately the bottle strucked something and break a piece flew and gave one of the boys a cut just above the heel on the calf muscle; in about a week in spite of the boy receiving treatment from the hospital, the foot grew from bad to worse, at this stage Mr. Deemin took upon himself the office of a dresser by washing and dressing that black labourers sore foot until it was cured. I tell you Sirs, by that deed Mr. Deemin erected an imperishable monument in my mind; I shall not only keep this monument during my stay in this terrestrial region but will take it with me when the time of my translation comes to the celestial. Mr. Deemin did not know that I took note of the act, but I did, not on paper, but in my mind. I believe he Mr. Deemin has forgotten the incident, but I have not, it is as fresh to me today as the time it took place. Men like Mr. Deemin are the real knights though man may not acknowledge them as such. My own brother cannot plot against men of like qualities as Mr. Deemin to my knowledge, I will surely take his part as long as I have my wits and vitality about me. In Gaboon when he (J.D.) is at the factory, he rises first in the morning before any, opens the shop before the clerk in charge of the shop is ready, he does almost every work that any other man at the agency does, he uses hammer and driver as good as any, he enters sales, attends to buyers, arranges goods on the shelves, opens cases, our Carpenter used to tell us how Mr. Deemin used to work with them when at their work place. He was very strict, in fact so strict that the whites used to grumble. He never used to smoke in the shop and allowed none, from the District Agent, Mr. Thomas, downwards to smoke in the shop. The rule not to smoke in the shop or store was very laudable to me. I believe that some of the great fires that have taken place in one part or the other of the world have their origin from cigar or cigarette ends and matchsticks thrown by some careless smoker, and according to the nature of the article, on which it fell, people awoke at night perhaps three or four days after to find their store burning without being able to trace the origin of the fire. I cannot tell you all the fine qualities I know of Mr. Deemin, let it suffice for me to repeat that Mr. Deemin is truly a member of the old or Victorian School of thought, he is therefore an Empire builder of the first rank. I am of the opinion that such a disciplinarian as he should have been a far greater blessing to the Empire had he entered the teaching profession, to mould the minds of the young for better citizenship. Although coast and commercial life had already touched him before I met him, yet he still takes the first place in the things that count amongst those I have met with in commercial circles.

Grievance and Suggestion for Redress

One of the irritating things in Nigeria and which helps to hinder the progress of trade at a station occupied by a blackman is the tendency on the part of some of the authorities to give more credence to what a European of another firm tells them to that of a blackman working for them. Take a station at which white and black are in charge of the factories and there be an agreed rule between the firms as to prices and dashes in nine cases out of ten, the European will break the rule in order to get more than his share of the produce, if your blackman were to report or do the same in order to get for you your full share of the trade, no credence will be given to his report, and he will be told stop; As a wire was once sent to a certain black man, 'Stop buying produce with soap dashes else I remove you from charge'. In very truth the white man who reported him was giving out 10 times more soap and tobacco dashes. I being at another station heard the report of the tricks that European was playing in order to get all the trade; the black chap did not know that I have received all the facts from different sources, in spite of all the whiteman was doing, he had the audacity to report the poor blackman as a breaker of the rules, for which he the blackman received such a wire. This sort of thing dear sir, is pin pricking to a sensitive mind.

Remedy It will be better to place in charge of stations one you know well and therefore can trust well. In order to have such a person train them, you can let them pass through every department and then appoint them as assistants from one department to another and then as locum tenens to those going on leave or on sick list; by the time an individual has gone through all these you will be able to know his worth and what credit to give to his words and how to treat reports sent against him. One of the advantages derivable from having your staff well trained in all departments is that you can remove one man from one work to another with confidence, there will be no need for you to seek for one to take the place of another who is going away or sick because you have them. You can take a probationer for head quarters and send to out stations the well trained in whom you have perfect confidence, this will all tend to benefit your trade.

Comforts for Native Staff. I have said that in some cases where you will see the European with all things necessary for his comforts you will see the Africans without even a chair, a table or a bed although both are working for the same firm and are both perfect strangers in the place. When I was sent to relieve Mr. Van Hers from our shipping station Lowinbassi during the agency of the late Mr. Watson, I was told Mr. Van Hers was to retain the key of the house until he removed his personal belongings. Under that circumstance I was obliged to sleep on the damp unfinished pavement of the shop until I took a severe cold in the stomach, not a chair, table or bed was supplied to me, I had to manage the best way possible to relieve the situation. When Mr. A.W. Jones was sent to relieve me from the same place he went up with his supply of chairs, tables, bed, cooking utensils etc., etc. to make him comfortable, I stayed with him for some time till he was quite familiar with his surroundings before I put in my resignation; Mr. Foster who was sent from Lagos to relieve Mr. Watson said to me he thought I had gone to N'Bila Gonu, I said no, as I had received no written instruction about N'Bila Gonu and to make it short I will not go. At the death of Monsieur Montvalon, instruction was sent from Liverpool that I be sent to take his place, Messrs. Watson and Foster called me and gave me the information but I refused for various reasons best known to myself. I presumed a cooked something was sent you at this time as the purport of my refusing to go and of my resignation but none of these things moved me.

Mr. Romaine through instruction received from Mr. Harrington the then agent at Lambarene wrote me two letters and sent a wire for me to go to Lambarene; according to African custom I ought to have obeyed his first letter, although I did not obey even his second till I received his wire before I went. When I got to Lambarene I was sent as an assistant at Cape Lopez, where I was placed in charge of the shop. On my arrival there I had to lodge in the office of the new house which was then under construction, without a bed, table or chair; when the new house was completed the European removed into it and the old one was pulled down and sent to Ngonga for re-erection, I was then given as a dwelling a bamboo hut-something built on the ground without a window, a small door-way without a door, one had to hang a cloth in place of a door. For one to sleep on the ground which is all sand and full of fleas as that of Cape Lopez and where the wind is almost always strong can be better imagined than described. I did my best to relieve the situation, until all the other works were completed, the new shop was completed and we had removed into it and the old one was changed into a shop store, other stores for goods and produce were all quite completed before I asked for a house; my request was so self evident that it was sanctioned immediately. Materials were sent for the house and same was started; but my good friend the European whose assistant I was, who prided himself to be a negro hater, though I knew and do know that he and all his like do not really hate the negro, for I am sure if they have the power to change at will the negro into carpets they would have them spreaded about their houses night and day, or into a horse they would ride them almost every moment of their lives; what they really hate is the betterment of the negro. To have a negro who feels that he is a man, made of the same stuff as all other men, and by the same God who made all other men, and fears no man but God his creator, and requires to be treated equally as all other men, aha! these are the men they think they hate: He tried to take a step with me which I objected, I made him to know that what he thinks of himself is what I think of myself, in short, I simply taught him manners. Not finding any way to revenge, he took the building of the house as the best way to do me. He would let the carpenter work on the house two or three days then find some unnecessary work for them to do simply to retard the building; he went so far as to lend to Mr. Tardison of the Belgian factory, some of the materials specially sent for the house, and then the carpenters are to be doing some less necessary work with the plea, they are waiting for another supply of the very materials he lent to others. During all this, I did not say a word, but made as if I was not seeing, whilst in very truth I was enjoying him, experiencing a little more of the so called superiority of the whiteman over the blackman. I tell you sirs, this condition of things went on until I left Cape Lopez for Gaboon. On my departure, my good friend spoke to me in very fine words of the entire satisfaction I gave and how the trade had increased; the part I enjoyed most was his apology for the delay of the house. I thanked him because he gave me the chance of knowing the whiteman better. I am glad to say that in spite of all this, that gentleman did not forget his duty to the firm that sent him out, he did all he could for the success of the trade, he gave me all the help he could, so that with our combined efforts we break all previous records and break and re-break our own records; I sincerely hope by this time he is enlightened enough not only to know and do his duty to his firm, but also those of his Empire and of justice.

When I went to Duala in December 1915, I met a different state of things to what I left in Lambarene. There I was sent into the main shop to receive cash and enter sales. Two things compelled me to make up my mind to leave at the end of my term which was then wanting of two months to be completed. The more important of the two things was that there were two selling prices in the shop, one for black and one for white, the black man pays higher for an article and the white man less; I thought with myself how came this about? Here are two classes of men, the least among the one class is having six times more salary than the highest among the other class, and yet the less paid class is required to pay more for an article than the high paid class, how came this to be so? Could it be that the so called inferiority of the black man inferiorates the coin coming from his hand though he does not mint coins; and vice versa with that coming from the white? I then called to mind a certain whiteman who went to our shop at Lambarene in 1912, I was then in charge of the shop at Ogency, that gentleman asked for an article, he was told the price; he asked whether we are going to give him a whiteman the same price we give the blacks, I told him, we really ought to charge him a whiteman more for an article because he was earning by far more salary than the blackman, therefore he is capable of paying more, in spite of this fact we are asking him to pay exactly the same as the poorest blackman. My good friend had nothing more to say, but went out and there the matter ends.

Duala was therefore to me quite another place from Lambarene, according to my nature I could not stay in such a place, the mere thought was tormenting, I was really doing my work absentmindedly. Mr. Deemin was there at the time, when I told him I was going to leave at the end of my term he tried to persuade me otherwise but I refused, he told me that I was foolish in taking the step I was about to take, he is the only whiteman that has used that expression to me, but as it is said, faithful are the words of a friend, I saw his good intentions, the expression was therefore no insult to me but the manifestation of his good wishes. I was in my heart very grateful to him, as I saw clearly he does not know my feelings and could not feel with me. The minor thing was where we used to take our breakfast at the factory. I had nothing to complain about the house that was given us at Akma Town, the house having been built for Europeans had tables, beds, chairs, and cupboards, as there was no more necessity for keeping Europeans at Akma town, blacks were allowed to occupy the house. Our works place was at Bell Town, a good distance from our dwelling we had therefore to take our breakfast at the factory. Not having a better place, we had to go into the small verandah of the engineers store which was then being used as carpenters shed. Think a little, a carpenter sawing on one end and another using his plane on the other and some men squeezing themselves in the centre taking their breakfast. Can you imagine the quantity of sawdust and microbes that we took daily with our food? I saw the same thing at Port Harcourt; I have seen your Chief Clerk Mr. Bruce not once nor twice taking his breakfast in the carpenters shed, two carpenters working, one on either side of him and he on a box or piece of timber on the ground taking his breakfast. The quantity of particles one is bound to take in such an unsanitary place with every mouthful is beyond imagination. Looking at the shop at Port Harcourt I said to myself, if these Europeans have a real interest in their African staffs they could easily make a hut at the back of this building similar to the one in front, have it walled, give it a door and few windows, two or three tables, some chairs, a filter or two for water, and as a finishing touch, few good books. What a blessing this would be to the tired body. Considering the distance segregation has placed them, many of them would not take the trouble of going home at midday, but arrange for their food to be sent them, the time spent in going and coming could be used in reading and resting. I mentally built the hut, walled it, gave it windows and a door, arranged the tables and chairs, placed two filters and a book shelf with some good books; then stood and watch them at mid-day, how instead of going home they turned into the resting place prepared for them, their food having been sent against the time of closing they simply sat at meal, during which they drank from the filters pure cool and sparkling water; after their meals they chose each a book and spread themselves in their deck chairs and started reading until they were lulled into sleep and quick rest. I then said what a boon, what a boon. I was entranced to see my people as it were in paradise; then I came to myself and said alas! it is simply a castle in the air. It is therefore plain that if they do not sometimes give not even a bed, table, or chair, things like kitchen and table utensils would not be thought of. Can you imagine then how much I have spent since I entered your service in supplying myself with these necessaries? Considering the consequences of moving from one place to another; how there are some articles one cannot carry, one is sure to forget some, and those that will be broken in transit, so that in every new station one has to buy new articles to replace others.

Remedy: In all places where staffs are living far from the factory it is necessary for you to give them a place of rest similar to the description given above, and in all your out stations to supply them with places worth living, furnished with beds, tables, chairs, and cooking and table utensils and last but by no means least, a book shelf with some good books like 'Sunday at home' etc., etc. I need not venture to say something about the value of good books considering you know better than the writer; I am therefore advocating books for both white and black staffs. I believe all book lovers amongst both classes will appreciate such a consideration. Again, you know that your staff are not pensionable, if you want them to feel that you take or have an interest in their future, specially the black who in nine cases out of ten, yea rather in 999 cases out of 1000 are not going to receive a bonus, it will be good if you make it possible for any of them to invest in your business whatever savings he may be able to make every year, you can give him at least 5% interest per year; this will make them feel that you have a very good wishes for their comfort during their old age; I am sure they will take more interest in the firm or rather in the success of the firm, they will say, seeking the firms interest is seeking their own present and future interest. I believe in the matter of salary there is a great deal of injustice going on, there being no rule or system, it is as it were topsy turvy, this state of things needs rectifying. There should be an arranged rule for grading from the probationer to the chief clerk. If it is possible for you to grade European staff, surely it ought to be possible for you to do the same for your African staff. It will be very good if all Europeans are lectured as to their treatment of the blackman in Africa before sending them out, you can get some good old Europeans in England to write out what may be termed instructions and advice to Europeans as to their treatment of the blackman in Africa. We believe the personality of the Englishman throughout the world goes a great way to the safety of the British Empire.

Conclusion

At the end of June this year I am expecting to leave you for good. I have therefore nothing to gain or lose by these suggestions. I am however of the firm belief that if these suggestions are heeded, it will tend in the long run to the benefit of your firm and the good of the Empire. It was in 1902 when I came in contact with the great injustice that was and is being inflicted on my people by the whiteman that I started thinking seriously and to find out by experience the truth of the so called superiority of the whiteman over the blackman. I have found out that there is not the slightest, the same faults that I have seen in the one I have seen in the other, in many cases the blackman was by far superior in morals and justice. When the great war started in 1914, I was then in the Abanga river; in my letter to Ogency I wrote something to the effect that it was and is a shame and disgrace to Europeans that after or upwards to two thousand years of civilization, they have not been able to devise ways whereby international disputes may be settled without resorting to the use of arms, which course ought to be seen only amongst savages but never amongst civilized beings, considering the many promising lives to be sent to untimely graves, the many women to be made widows, the many children to orphans, the numberless to be incapacitated for life, and the miseries that will fall on humanity at large. I was driven to ask myself, what has civilization done for its people? Particularly it has so far made them experts in the invention of instrument of destruction.[5] I said to myself, I would rather be an illiterate person than an inventor of anything to destroy human life and happiness and increase his misery and sorrow. Can you say in truth, the whiteman is superior to the blackman? In very truth, the whiteman on account of his superior culture and advantages ought to show superior character, I ought to hear that in London, the greatest city the world has seen, and the most civilized in the world today, there is no need for a watchman as the inhabitants are all superior beings, and therefore perfect, the shops have no need for anyone to be looking after them, the goods are all arranged and labelled in readiness for the superior people, of London, who have been accustomed to enter shops and select exactly what they want, look at the label for the price, go to the draw themselves and put the value of the article or articles they have selected, take their change if they are entitled to any and go out without doing the slightest injustice. Then I shall be able to say Europeans are nearing perfection. There are places in Africa today where people do not keep their firms products in houses but in the open with none to take care of them without fear of thieves. I have found out that the pure negro is by far more trustworthy than those who have come in contact with Europeans. I have now come to the conclusion that the most perfect civilization will be developed in Africa. Because I had and do have the English language as vernacular, and the treatment I received from the members of the old or Victorian school of thought,

I had been thinking and calling myself an Englishman; but thanks to the members of the new or Georgian school of thought who have expressed it in plain English that a blackman is not to think himself the equal of a whiteman and therefore not entitled to just and equal treatment, they have so put this idea into practice that today I feel and do assert that I am not an Englishman. I believe this idea and treatment of the blackman has become a sort of second nature to the whiteman, therefore, one day, sometimes, sooner or later, oppression will wake us up to the realization of our capabilities, and our relation to our surroundings. We shall then have the necessary illumination to know that we can get just and equal treatment from the whiteman only by convincing him that we too are men as any other men, by doing whatever any other men have done and are doing, by the same methods they have and are using viz: Unitedly, organizationally and industrially, and when this does come I am perfectly sure as I am sure that it is I myself who is penning these lines, the whiteman shall have no legs to stand on in Africa. But may I ask, why will you allow this state of things to take place? Why not cast away all morbid introspection and face the whole actual truth manfully, leaving the unsafe and choosing the safe path for the good of the British Empire? Why not endeavour to give just and right treatment to all regardless of their hue, why not endeavour as it were to go out of your way to give satisfaction to the millions under the British flag who are not Englishmen? Consult past and present historians about great Empires who forsook truth and justice and thought they were Almighty and see the fate that will surely befall all Empires that will refuse to give just and equal treatment to all.

I have done my duty, think and decide.

Your obedient servant,

D.D. Africanus Coker

Notes

1. The African and Eastern Trade Corporation. See above, p. 150 and footnote 13 on p. 154.
2. See above, pp. 137–9.
3. God!
4. See above, pp. 93–4.
5. Albert Schweitzer's views on this topic are given in *On the Edge of the Primeval Forest*, op.cit., p. 138. Schweitzer's home and hospital in Africa were at Lambarene, mentioned in the text.

5. PETER STUART

INTRODUCTION

Peter Stuart (senior) settled in Liverpool after serving in the Royal Navy at the Battle of Trafalgar. He then established himself as a very successful master carpenter and built up a large and prosperous business. His second son, Peter, was born in 1814 and was apprenticed to the cooperage trade. Peter (junior) followed his calling so energetically that by the age of 26 he was, himself, the owner of a thriving cooperage business. Many of his casks were destined for West African merchants, so because of this association he gradually became interested in the trade itself. In fact, before he was thirty he had already imported palm oil from the Coast in several vessels and had laid the foundation of what was to become one of the more substantial firms engaged in the commerce of West Africa.

In 1843 Stuart was joined by Peter Douglas and two years later the firm of Stuart and Douglas established a branch of the Brass River. Thereafter the West African side of the business steadily expanded, the partnership utilising a large number of hulks for this purpose including: *Victoria*, *Dayspring*, *Ben-My-Chree*, *England's Queen*, *Earl Derby*, *Erin-Go-Bragh*, *Athelstan* and *Hannah Salkeld*. The extract from Finigan's *Life of Peter Stuart* which follows provides an outline of the firm's business activities on the Coast. It is particularly valuable because of the insight it gives into the profitability of the trade when properly organised.

Peter Douglas died in 1883 and his share in the Company was then purchased by Peter Stuart and the firm continued under the old name of Stuart and Douglas. In September 1888, Peter Stuart also died and the following year the African side of the business was merged into the African Association. The cooperage, however, remained a profitable and independent concern and as late as 1923 it was being claimed that its works covered four acres and was 'the largest and most up-to-date machine cooperage in Europe'.

Sources: L. Finigan, *The Life of Peter Stuart*, Books Ltd., London, 1921.
Elder Dempster Magazine, September 1923, p. x.
Wharton MSS.
Interview with Francis Ronald Stuart, grandson of Peter Stuart, 20 September 1965.

PETER STUART

As a business man the career of Peter Stuart[1] is an example of what straightforward dealing supported by foresight and courage can accomplish. Had he not an entirely sound belief in his views of the future of West African trade, there is little doubt that the heavy financial outlay he found necessary, from time to time, would have deterred him from following that trade. He was, however, as the reader will have gathered, a man of strong character, and once having considered a problem and reached certain conclusions he seldom departed from his decision.

In these days the African trade needs no introduction, as the Imperial Government have been made fully aware of how great an asset the produce from our West African market is in the chain of British and Colonial trade expansion. The credit of seeing all that we now so well recognise is due to the early pioneers of our oversea trade, amongst whom Peter Stuart stands out distinctly. It was partly through the knowledge of the purpose for which the large casks were required that Peter Stuart first recognised the commercial possibilities and decided to enter the West African business. He took pains to acquire from every available source the trading position and prospects of that oversea market, and, having done so, entered into one or two shipping transactions which gave some practical insight into the trade.

In the course of his dealings he made friends with Peter Douglas, who had an extensive first-hand knowledge of the West African Coast trade, and the result of that meeting was that the two Peters joined forces. They quickly settled their plan of campaign, and in 1845 established the firm of Stuart & Douglas. In 1854 they conducted their business from No. 2 Paul Street, Vauxhall Road, under the title already mentioned, and which has remained in the commercial annals of Liverpool for the better part of a century.

It is interesting to mention that his partner, Peter Douglas, was a medical man by training, and some time previous to joining Peter Stuart had been a super-cargo agent with the old-established Liverpool house of Messrs. W.A. and G. Maxwell and Co., of King Street.

In the year under review the barque 'Adriana'[2] was despatched to the Brass River, and though only 282 tons register, she made a successful voyage. She was followed by the 'Woodpecker',[3] which was unfortunately lost on her homeward journey. In all undertakings of a commercial character the success depends not alone on the principals but upon those who are associated with them, and when the Brass River trade was opened up by Stuart & Douglas it was firmly established by the active assistance of Mr. C.J.S. Jackson, who was engaged as their principal agent.

Mr. Jackson was a man of undoubted ability, and he looked after the firm's interest at Brass for over three years. It gives one some idea of the money that could be made in the early days of West African trading to recall the fact that in three years' time Mr. Jackson's commission amounted to £10,000. To the regret of those who found his services so satisfactory Mr. Jackson retired from business at an early date and bought an estate in the South of England, where he settled down.[4]

In 1848 the firm sent the 'Jemima',[5] of 816 tons, to Old Calabar, and a few months afterwards followed that venture with the 'Rothschild',[6] a vessel of 647 tons, to Bonny. By this time their West African trade was in full swing, and every effort was made to establish it on a secure basis. To do that was more difficult than now appears, as in 1848 there were no land factories or such constructions, and business was carried through on a stretch of land obtained from the natives and cleared of the greater portion of its growth. The actual trade barter was done on board the ship, which was housed over with bamboo and matting; the top-masts and fore-masts being struck and re-fitted when the vessel was ready to return home.

It was the custom for agents at Bonny to have a vessel also at New Calabar, and to work both Bonny and New Calabar through the services of an assistant agent at one or other of the Rivers. The custom may have been convenient to the agent, but in practice it had several disadvantages, and accordingly Mr. Stuart decided to make New Calabar an independent station. It was characteristic of the man, once having seen the disadvantage of a double river custom he lost no time in taking action. Accordingly in 1851 the 'Heroine,'[7] a vessel of 387 tons, was sent to New Calabar and arrangements made to work that port as a separate agency.

About four years after New Calabar had been working separately the firm bought a new iron vessel of 1,388 tons, which they christened the 'Ellen Stuart'. She was promptly sent to Old Calabar, where she created something of a sensation on the Coast, being the largest vessel that had ever visited the River, up to that time. The 'Ellen Stuart'[8] was a fine oil vessel, and her hold was said, even in the hot West African climate, to be beautifully cool, no doubt due to the fact that all vessels belonging to the firm were painted white. She was found, however, too large for the

West African services and removed from that trade and placed on other routes, including the Australian.

An extension of the policy of Stuart & Douglas was carried out by opening trade with Opobo, and they were the first British firm to establish a commercial service between the Opobo River and Liverpool.

Money has only recently become recognised by the natives in West Africa, and in Peter Stuart's time one of the mediums of commerce was the manilla – a metal token made somewhat in the shape of a small horseshoe. Great store was set by the natives on obtaining a bronze manilla known as the L.N.T. which the firm of Stuart & Douglas for many years had manufactured exclusively for them by a Birmingham maker named Thomas Horne, who supplied the bronze manillas to an agent named Forsberry from whom Stuart & Douglas obtained and used them in their West African business. The natives used to bury these bronze manillas and after being in the ground for quite a long time they would quickly burnish up again. The natives were so expert in detecting the genuine L.N.T. bronze manilla that they could tell the closest copy simply by handling it, whereas a European would be unable to distinguish between them even on the closest investigation. Peter Stuart recognised that, to some extent, his trading goodwill in West Africa lay in the use of the manilla made by Horne, and he acquired control of Horne's output by an arrangement which was carried on until Horne's death.

The firm, of course, had their difficulties to contend with like every other trading concern, but the worst perhaps were the feuds carried on between two West African Chiefs, and who were well known in West African trade circles in England. These two dusky warriors were Oko-Jumbo and Ja-Ja,[9] and they frequently quarrelled over matters connected with land and labour problems at Bonny.

En passant, it is not without interest to mention that leaders of native thought were not far removed from some of our own English labour leaders who, in the present year of grace, apparently find it no easy matter to induce agreement amongst their followers.

The end of the disturbances between the native chiefs was that Ja-Ja left the Bonny River and set up a new establishment at Opobo. That action was a nasty blow to Oko-Jumbo, because fully three-fourths of the palm oil trade of the district took its rise from the Opobo River and was sent, by creek, to Bonny.

Peter Stuart caused enquiries to be made regarding the trouble which had arisen between Ja-Ja and Oko-Jumbo, and the result of those enquiries was that the firm decided to support Ja-Ja, whom Peter Stuart believed had good cause for the steps he took when he removed to Opobo.

The hulk 'Earl Derby'[10] was towed from the Bonny to Opobo, and arrangements made to handle the trade, which was indirectly under the offices of Ja-Ja. Extensive depots were erected at considerable cost on a large clearing of land close to the river bank, and Ja-Ja was so pleased with the support that Stuart & Douglas gave his new venture that his friendly interest was aroused, and the result was noticeable in the increased trade which the firm was able to carry on from Opobo.

The success of Stuart & Douglas' move was followed by other firms, who erected factories and shore buildings to cope with the business, and which has ever since been of a very important character.

For a short time they carried on trade at the River Cameroons, but the returns were small and the difficulties with the natives and other problems persuaded them to discontinue that particular branch.

One draws attention to that fact merely as illustrating the pioneer efforts of the firm, and to show how they endeavoured in every way possible to open up the West African trade in a manner worthy of the country's resources.

It is difficult, after the lapse of so many years, to appreciate the work which Peter Stuart, and those who were associated with him, carried out in the early days of West African trade. The present generation has reaped of the seed which he, and others, planted so successfully.

A further opening was later made at Lagos, but that also was finally abandoned, principally owing to business complications having arisen through the incompetency of the firm's Lagos agent. The time had now arrived when a number of traders had established themselves on the West African Rivers, and at the instigation of Peter Stuart four other merchant houses joined forces with Stuart & Douglas in order to extend the interior markets. Factories of an up-to-date character were built, and valuable plant installed, as well as steam launches sent out fully equipped for the growing trade.

A schooner was constructed at Liverpool, the 'Belzoni',[11] with which the Benin trade of the firm was founded. The venture was not the first of its kind undertaken by Mr. Stuart, for just previous to his joining partnership with Mr. Douglas he had sent a vessel to trade at Benin. With that single-handed undertaking Mr. Stuart was not quite pleased, because Benin proved itself to be an infected plague spot. On the second occasion, however, when the 'Belzoni' made the trip, the district was much more healthy and the prospects of success correspondingly greater. The reason in sending out the 'Belzoni' was part of the new policy of opening up the interior trade of the country. The district was found thickly covered with mangrove trees, but they were cut down, and a clearing made, on which a large factory was built. Sand was brought from outside banks and used for making firm ground and outlining road approaches. Eventually a special type of factory was erected, and as the dwelling rooms were on the top floor it was regarded as a fairly healthy one.

A few years previous to the opening of the Benin trade a Liverpool firm had established regular monthly sailings of mail steamers to the West Coast, and that may be said to have settled the fate of the schooner trade. The firm of Stuart & Douglas had in commission no less than eighteen vessels, some of which were built to Mr. Stuart's special design.

Although the trade with West Africa was the principal part of the business of Stuart & Douglas, the firm were interested in other shipping directions, such as the East Indian and Australian routes.

A propos of Australia; in the early days Peter Stuart was asked to accept, in settlement of a bad debt, a stretch of land in Australia upon which the greater part of the city of Melbourne now stands, and he refused it.

As an illustration of Peter Stuart's business dealing, the following enables one to appreciate how he held, and merited, the respect of all those with whom he did business. A firm of Mersey shipbuilders had just completed a vessel for Peter Stuart, and he had been shown over by the builder, who remarked that he had lost £700 on the contract price of the ship. The vessel was beautifully finished and quite satisfied Mr. Stuart, and he invited the builder to accompany him to the firm's Liverpool office, where he, somewhat to the astonishment of the builder, handed that gentleman a cheque for £700, with the remark that he wished no one to be at loss in business dealings with him; added to which he was thoroughly pleased with the build and construction of the vessel.

Reverting to their West African business, one is pleased to record that it continued to prosper, and in 1885, through the death of Mr. Peter Douglas in 1883, an arrangement was made under which Peter Stuart purchased Mr. Douglas's interest and carried on the firm himself, though still retaining the title Stuart & Douglas. In 1889 the African portion of their business was acquired by the African Association, Limited, now known as the African & Eastern Trade Corporation, Limited, in which Messrs. Stuart & Douglas are largely interested.[12]

Letter from Peter Stuart to Peter Douglas.

London, 30th December, 1876.

I would much prefer that you would place Hartz on an equal footing with ourselves in the Old Calabar River, that is, by giving him 33% of the net profits. It was on these terms that I put Jackson when he went to Brass, and on these terms Jackson's share of the profits amounted to £10,000 in 18 months. Now, I think if Hartz does the same amount of trade for us and himself as he has done for Thomas Harrison,[13] his share would be at least £7,000 a year. Harrison's cannot offer him such terms as these, for there are three of them already in their firm – four, if Mr. Hartz agrees to this offer.

Let him bind himself legally to go out for us next season and we will bind ourselves to him. This is necessary, for we shall have to go to great expense in getting a splendid hulk ready for him to go out in the season. He will never have such an offer repeated. Indeed, nothing could be more liberal, and the reason why I make this offer is, that when a man feels he is working for himself he will soon repay those who employ him, and relieve us of much anxiety when we have, as it were, a partner in the River to look after our interests.

Notes

1. L. Finigan, *The Life of Peter Stuart*, Books Ltd., London, 1921.
2. *Adriana* was a barque of 282 tons. She had been built at Yarmouth in 1833. (*Lloyds Register*, 1848, A.122.)
3. *Woodpecker*. The only vessel of this name was a snow of 216 tons built at Sunderland in 1842. In 1848 her owner is given as 'Williams' and her home port as Bristol. (*Lloyds Register*, 1848, W.373.)
4. See pp. 178–9.
5. *Jemima* was a ship of 816 tons. She had been built in Quebec in 1847. (*Lloyds Register*, 1848, J.282.)
6. *Rothschild* was a ship of 648 tons. She had been built at St. Andrews in 1835. (*Lloyds Register*, 1848, R.423.)
7. *Heroine* was a ship of 387 tons. She had been built at Dundee in 1831. (*Lloyds Register*, 1848, H.345.)
8. *Ellen Stuart* was a ship of 1373 tons. She had been built of iron at Liverpool in 1854. (*Lloyds Register*, 1857, E.520.)
9. See above, pp. 59–60 and footnote 35 on p. 90.
10. *Earl Derby* was a barque of 500 tons, measuring 147 x 25 x 16 feet. She had been built at New Brunswick in 1852 and was hulked at Opobo in 1880. (*Lloyds Register*, 1880, E.32.)
11. There is no vessel of this name listed in *Lloyds Register* in the relevant years. This may be because she was very small.
12. See above, p. 150 and footnote 13 on p. 154.
13. Thomas Harrison and Company traded with West Africa for many years. The firm operated a fleet of sailing vessels to carry its cargoes and continued with this practice until they were absorbed into the African Association in 1889. (*U.A.C. Hist.*, pp.73–4.)

6. ALFRED LEWIS JONES

INTRODUCTION

Alfred Jones was born in Carmarthen in 1845 of respectable middle-class Welsh parents. When he was three years old his father decided to move to Merseyside and from then on his home was to be Liverpool. At the age of fourteen Jones decided to strike out for himself and succeeded in obtaining a job as a cabin boy with the African Steam Ship Company. He was only to make one journey to West Africa for on his return he was recommended to the Company's Liverpool agents and obtained a position as junior clerk with them.

The office of W. & H. Laird (later Fletcher and Parr) was a small one but the staff contained several members who were destined to make important contributions to the development of West Africa. These included Alexander Elder who acted as superintendent engineer, John Dempster who was then the chief clerk and John Holt at that time an apprentice to the coal side of the business.

Alfred Jones remained with the Liverpool Agents until 1877, gradually increasing his status and earning capacity. The following year he established the firm of Alfred L. Jones and Company and this proved to be highly successful in the fields of shipping and insurance broking. The Company also chartered a number of small sailing vessels to carry goods to West Africa and in 1879 it chartered a steamer for the same purpose. This had immediate repercussions and Jones eventually accepted a Junior Partnership with Elder Dempster (his former colleagues) who by then were managing agents of the British and African Steam Navigation Company. Within five years Jones was the senior partner and both Elder and Dempster had left the Company they had founded. Thereafter Jones spent the remainder of his life in strengthening the position of Elder Dempster in relation to the two British lines serving the Coast and in ensuring that these British lines retained a preponderant share of West African cargoes.

Jones's two main problems were the maintenance of friendly relations with and between the two established British lines – the African Steam Ship Company and the British and African Steam Navigation Company – and the elimination of interlopers. Individually these were quite substantial difficulties but fortunately for Jones they tended to cancel one another out. Thus by keeping on the closest terms the two regular lines were able to put up a solid barrier against any outside interest and Jones made it clear to them not only how much could be gained by co-operation but also how disastrous rivalry would be.

The success of Jones's policies in this respect then enabled him to enhance Elder Dempster's position in the trade. By 1890 Elder Dempster were managing agents of both British shipping firms so he was able to really control and integrate their two fleets. He gradually eliminated all other competition on the British West African route and made an agreement with the Woerman Line of Hamburg whereby the Continental/West Africa route was shared. Their understanding was formalised by the setting up of the West African Lines shipping conference in 1895.

After this date Alfred Jones was in a position to control the external communications of British West Africa and he used this authority to expand and diversify his interests in many ways. Jones acquired the boating companies in West Africa, he instituted a branch line service, he provided tugs, lighters and river craft – all to supplement and support the external communication system. Other of his subsidiary companies provided hotels, cold-storage and victualling facilities and, in time, he created a complete network of integrated concerns that helped to channel the produce of West Africa to his mainline ships. Jones also established the Bank of British West Africa to help ease financial transactions; he assisted in the establishment of the cotton growing industry; he invested in the exploration for mineral wealth and he purchased two collieries in South Wales to provide fuel for his growing fleets and coaling stations.

Following the establishment of a coaling company at Las Palmas, Jones built up a substantial interest in the Canary Islands and was instrumental in developing the banana industry and selling the fruit to Britain. At the invitation of Joseph Chamberlain, Jones then attempted (in conjunction with Fyffes) to assist the growth of the banana industry in the West Indies. He also operated his ships on a number of routes which were not concerned with West Africa – the most important of these being the Gulf trade, the Canadian trade and the Canadian/South Africa trade.

The result of all these activities was that Jones enjoyed great, but not absolute, power. He could not afford to upset the merchants in case they combined against him and he could not fix freight rates at too high a level in case he encouraged an interloper to enter the trade. The need to keep the tacit approval of the British and Colonial governments meant that he had to act in a reasonable manner at all times, and make sure that he did not alienate public opinion.

Jones's success in promoting Elder Dempster's interests led almost inevitably to an enhancement of his own personal situation and ultimately to a knighthood. He invested heavily in the African Steam Ship Company and at the time of his death in 1909 owned 75% of its issued capital. He also possessed a controlling interest in the British and African Steam Navigation Company after it was reorganised in 1900. These and other assets were valued at £583,461 when his estate was settled in 1910.

Sources:

Trade Makers, op.cit., pp.52-6, pp.73-91, 114-65.

P.N. Davies, 'Sir Alfred Jones and the Development of West African Trade', Unpublished M.A. Thesis, University of Liverpool, 1964.

A.H. Milne, *Sir Alfred Lewis Jones, K.C.M.G.*, Henry Young & Sons, Liverpool, 1914.

SIR ALFRED LEWIS JONES

Although I do not consider that my autobiography can be of very much general interest; I feel that it would be discourteous to say 'no' to the request made to me on the subject, and so without further preamble, I shall set to work on a task which, I must admit, has all the charm of novelty.

I was born in 1845 at Carmarthen, South Wales, my father being the only son of Alderman Charles Jones, who was a well known resident of that town, while my mother was the eldest daughter of the Rev. Henry Williams, Rector of Llanedi.[1] I was only three years old when we permanently left Carmarthen for Liverpool, and possibly the fact of spending my most impressionable years in an atmosphere – so to say – of business in a place where there is little room for idlers or the half-hearted worker was not without its influence in shaping what I have seen alluded to as my 'successful career' for, let me here say to youthful readers who may be at the beginning of a commercial life, there is no royal road to success in business, and it is only by unceasing toil and undivided attention that one ascends the ladder.

I was one of a large family, and my life as a child was happy and uneventful. I cannot recall any amusing escapades or stirring adventures, but I vividly remember the time when I was sent to school, and do not think I ever had the slightest objection to being instructed; indeed I was regarded as a rather studious boy, was always particularly fond of arithmetic, and had a good head for figures generally.

In this branch of my education there was no difficulty in being near the top of the class, and perhaps it is well to acknowledge that I had a good deal of ambition and was eager to succeed in life. Having a strong constitution, I have never been handicapped by ill-health, and consequently, both in youth and manhood could get through an unlimited amount of work.

At fifteen I entered the office of Messrs. Laird, Fletcher and Co., who managed the African Steamship Company trading between Liverpool and the West Coast of Africa thus from the start I was connected with a country which has always possessed an intense interest for me. Small pay and plenty of work were my lot but I continued my studies in the evenings at the Liverpool College, where I remained a student for a considerable time.

Looking back on my boyhood, it seems to me that I really preferred work to play, for I was not particularly keen on games, though I was extremely fond of swimming, and rather prided myself on my staying powers in the water. I also enjoyed sailing, and I had, and still retain, a genuine affection for dogs.

There is nothing particular to chronicle about the years immediately following. Suffice it to say I was appointed manager to the firm, which subsequently became Fletcher and Parr[2] (Mr. Laird having retired) and when these gentlemen gave up their African steamship management, I determined to strike out for myself.

I took an office in Liverpool and started as a shipping and insurance broker, came in early, stayed late, and took few holidays, but had the satisfaction of gradually extending my circle of clients and making my business pay. Any anxiety experienced at the start was more than compensated for by the independence of my new position, and the knowledge that success depended on my own exertions.

It was in 1879 that I joined the firm of Elder, Dempster and Co. as junior partner. This house, as most people know, has long been associated with the African shipping trade; its fleet, when I threw in my lot with it, comprising twenty ships, the largest of which was of 2,000 tons burden.

Until one has made himself practically acquainted with every detail of the business which he is called upon to direct, it is impossible to gauge its possibilities or properly carry out the duties of a director: therefore my first object was to become thoroughly acquainted with each branch of the work the firm was engaged in, a thing not to be done in a moment. However, in a year or two it was clear to me that our business could be greatly extended, while my old desire to develop the resources of the British West African Colonies appeared at last to be within the bounds of possibility.

'All things', say the French, 'come to him who knows how to wait,' and be this as it may my opportunity came soon after, when on the retirement of Mr. Elder and Mr. Dempster, I rose to be senior partner of Elder Dempster and Co. Subsequently we opened new branches of our house in England, on the Continent, and in various places abroad, including Montreal, New Orleans, Grand Canary, and Teneriffe; and banks at Lagos, Sierra Leone, Accra, Secondi and Cape Coast Castle.

I have often been asked what made me undertake the resuscitation of the Canaries, a question to which I reply: 'The poverty of the natives, and the fertility of the soil.' During my first visit to those islands (which was really to see whether it was advisable to establish a coaling station there for our African Line) the sad state of the Spanish population greatly struck me. Their chief source of income had been derived from the production of cochineal which sold readily at 10/- per lb. The advent of the aniline dyes, however, made cochineal a drug in the market and the unfortunate Spaniards were paralysed by the loss of their chief means of subsistence.

It was really touching to see how overwhelmed they were by their misfortunes, not one ray of hope illuminating the darkness of the future, though, had they but known it, the soil – then uncultivated – was rich enough to yield them a golden harvest. Recognising its suitability for fruit growing I bought a large piece of land and grew bananas for the English market. Besides this, I visited many of the residents, and pointed out how by fruit growing they could regain their old prosperity.

Finding that they were willing to follow my suggestions, I promised to buy whatever quantity they could bring our manager, and in several instances where these poor people were almost penniless, I gladly advanced the money required to start them in their new enterprise. I have been well repaid for any little outlay or trouble by seeing how quickly the inhabitants have recovered themselves financially.

Indeed, they are better off than formerly, for the Canaries soon sprang into fashion as a health resort, and besides bananas, the islands yield an immense annual crop of tomatoes, onions and potatoes.

Bye-the-bye, my original motive in going to the Canaries was not lost sight of, and Elder Dempster and Co. established the Grand Canary Coaling Co., of which the Admiralty, and hundreds of streamers, sailing to all parts of the world, avail themselves, the island being regarded as a 'halfway house' by the different lines running between Europe and the 'Dark Continent.'[3]

But West Africa offers a wider scope for one's energies than the picturesque islands of the Canary group, and its natives are far better types of humanity than dwellers at home imagine. The Kroomen, who are largely employed in the factories, are a fine race, and if fairly treated will conscientiously serve their white employers. After all, there are traits common to all of us, whether our skin be black or white, for so far as my experience goes, Africans are by no means insensible to justice and kindness, nor are they wanting in intelligence. The youths who come to the Congo Training Institute at Colwyn Bay, pick up knowledge readily and become skilled tradesmen before returning to their own country.

It would be well, however, if greater facilities for technical education could be given to the natives in their own districts, and it seems to me that such instruction would be a valuable addition to the civilizing efforts of missionaries of every denomination.

It may, perhaps, be interesting to say, that the introduction of a currency instead of barter at Lagos, Accra, and other places on the West Coast, has been fully appreciated by the natives, and has certainly helped to break down the tribal exclusiveness which too often led to raids and civil war.

Regarding the gold fields of West Africa, I have, from the first, held the most sanguine views. Long ago, when the generality of Englishmen regarded the country as a valueless fever-stricken place, I was egotistical enough to differ from them; and although West Africa has proved itself well worth the attention of the commercial community, there are still sceptics about its gold fields.

That more gold will be found there than in the Transvaal is an opinion that I have long entertained, and to which I cling tenaciously. I became a large shareholder in some of the first companies formed, and have since taken a considerable interest in numerous other concerns which have commended themselves to me, with the object of assisting in the development of the gold mining industry. I am now, however, by no means alone in my optimistic ideals, one mining company alone having five millionaires amongst its subscribers, although a decade ago the genus millionaire carefully avoided West African mines.

From time to time I have received interesting visits from noted Africans coming to England whom it has been my privilege to entertain at my house near Liverpool, and I may specially name Mrs. Martha Hicks, who was my guest when she came over on her famous mission to see our late Queen.

Travelling and meeting people of various nationalities has been one of the most congenial parts of my business; for although I have been in many places, my journeys here, as a rule, had an object other than mere recreation.

The days of my youth were long past before my pet scheme took shape, but as the Liverpool School of Tropical Medicine[4] is the outcome of a long-cherished idea, I shall mention it before concluding. That West Africa suffers severely from malarial fever must be freely admitted; but it occurred to me that medical science could find a sure weapon to fight this dread disease if special facilities were given for the purpose, and if investigations as to the cause of the fever were made on the spot by medical men skilled in such work.

The Liverpool School is, so far, justifying my hopes, and before the new century is many years older I firmly believe that West Africa will have lost its reputation as the hot-bed of malarial fevers. That they will ever be completely stamped out is generally doubted, but I have throughout my life objected to 'give in' when there was the slightest chance of accomplishing a worthy object on which I had set my mind. Therefore – laugh at it as you may – I cherish the hope that medical science will one day transform Western Africa into a country where there is little more danger of disease than is to be met with in any of the great cities at home.

ALFRED LEWIS JONES

A biographical note by his sister, Mrs. Mary Isabel Pinnock.

Oaklands,
Aigburth, Liverpool.

Alfred Lewis Jones – Born Feb. 24th 1845 – Died Dec. 13th 1909.

No history of his life could be complete without a reference to his boyhood which in the very earliest days showed such promise, born of a good old Welsh family, he had the most beautiful reverence for his mother whose sweet character influenced him all through life. His mother was the eldest daughter of the Revd. Henry Williams Rector of Llanedi South Wales. His father the only son of Alderman Charles Jones, Carmarthen, S. Wales – His parents came to Liverpool with a family of ten children seven of whom died early. Alfred had many friends and his honest and earnest energy won all hearts. Mr. Parr[5] of the firm Fletcher & Parr with whom he spent many years of his life was exceedingly kind to him and gave him many good gifts to help him on also paid his fees at the Liverpool Institute for some years and constantly invited the boy to his home – in those days Alfred had to walk some four miles to his work at the Dock starting very early and taking his lunch with him which consisted mostly of bread and butter and coffee and to mention a little incident of those days may help us to understand how he overcame many difficulties and by his perseverance gained so much. On his way home he had to pass a Broker's shop in the Brunswick Rd. and one day seeing in the window an old China Teapot fixed his heart upon it – inside was a kind but cute old gentleman and when Alfred asked the price – he said not your price my lad. Oh, said Alfred, but a few days later he called again and said what about that teapot. The old gentleman again said much the same and looking into the boy's beautiful honest eyes seemed sorry to see him go; a week elapsed and Alfred called again and said, 'Look here I want that teapot for my Mother, what will you take?' 'and the old man met him and Alfred carried home the teapot in triumph to his Mother and it now stands in his beautiful home at Aigburth where Dresden & Crown Derby can never lessen the value of this, his first treasure. Those who knew Sir Alfred will recognise this trait in his character all through. Never to be dismayed by a first refusal – when quite a boy he made a voyage to the Coast and the sad state of things so impressed him, he determined no effort on his part should be wanting to better the condition of the natives and a little wicker basket worked by a native years ago bears inside the touching words 'Alfred Jones The negroes friend.' It was his rule until quite the last year of his life to interview each captain on his return and often take him out to his home at Aigburth and eagerly listen to every detail of his trip. There was never any man from the highest Governor or any man who had any interest in Africa whom Sir Alfred did not interview or entertain. Sir Alfred's breakdown may be dated from the awful earthquake at Jamaica. The failure of all his hopes for Kingston just when he saw it on the verge of the prosperity he had toiled to gain then the death of his much esteemed friend and partner, Mr. W.J. Davey[6] and his faithful friend Mr. A.F. Warr (of Messrs. Warr & Bateson).[7] Although as he often said he had many able men, still the vast concern of which he was the leader laid heavily upon his sensitive and anxious nature. Many of the great and good men who accompanied Sir Alfred on the unfortunate trip to Jamaica bore testimony to his noble unselfishness and expressed their great admiration of their Princely Host as they justly termed him – and now to dwell upon a few of his marvellous and prosperous undertakings – his great and untiring work for the Empire – by one who knew and worked with him for years – When Sir Alfred Jones left Fairfield where he had resided for many years he lived in Cressington Park and was Vicar's Warden at St. Mary's Church for some 3 years. He had a good deal to do with building the parish room there and instituted evening entertainment for the people which was much appreciated, Madam Clara Butt and her company being one of the first and in due time Lecturers such as Sir Robert Ball and others also Max Okell (Corney Grain) and the people of Grassendale much appreciated his generous interest in the neighbourhood.

IN THE GREAT DAYS OF "A.L.J."

Liverpool–West African Sidelights[8]

The other day, taking the apparently calm office of Elder Dempster Lines in Colonial House as a pivot, my thoughts went back to the office that used to throb with life at 14, Castle Street.

My introduction to the West African trade took place in the middle '90's when, as a youth, I was sent by my father to see Mr. Alfred Jones, as he was then, to ask for a job. I had heard a lot of Mr. Jones; of what he was and did in the days of Fletcher & Parr, and I had pictured him as a sort of hero in fiction. When I met him, I became infected with his altertness, reality and strength.

Our interview was brief. "You are no use to me if you can't write shorthand."

I taught myself shorthand, and called again, and I got: "I'll let you know if I want you."

I was afraid that that was the end, and got a job elsewhere. Three months later, he wrote and asked me to call. I had been coached to keep calm and not to be nervous if he scowled – it would be a test, and I must get into the office.

His dark eyes shot a challenge. His moustache seemed to bristle, but I tried to look confident. Briefly, I told him who I was working for and what they paid me, and his expression changed and became almost simple, as though he was surprised. Then, suddenly, he was the keen business man, and offered me 10/- a week!

Becoming infected with his keenness, I countered: "I'm sure, Mr. Jones, with my experience, I would be worth 15/- to you."

There was a half-amused look in his face as he snapped: "No, you wouldn't. But when you can write shorthand you shall have it."

"I can write shorthand now, sir," I gave back, determined to get that extra 5/-.

Instantly, he tore a slip of paper from a bundle that hung by a string from a nail, threw a pencil across, and began to dictate: "My dear Bond, – Your letter of," and so on.

Then he snatched the slip from me and handed it across to Mr. Davy (an expert shorthand writer), who twirled his moustache, and with a non-committal expression in his face scanned the paper. In my heart, I prayed that he would not be too critical. Then in a calm, judicial manner, he said: "It's all right, Mr. Jones."

"I'll give you 12/6d. to start!" rapped out the great man. "That all right?"

Realising that further argument might be fatal, I grasped the offer.

"Start on Monday at nine sharp. And I hope you'll be with us a long time."

"But I must give a week's notice, Mr. Jones."

"Very well, following Monday. How's your father?"

"Quite well, thank you, sir."

The Day's Round

My duties began, actually, at 8-30, when I had to open all letters (other than private) and sort them into baskets. Those for our department were entered in a book by my assistant. Even now I can feel the drive – opening a letter, scanning its contents, dumping it into a basket.

We sat in Mr. Davy's office, and every now and then Sloan, of the forwarding department, came in and took what letters were for him, at the same time making remarks that sometimes made my hair almost stand on end. If there was a particularly heavy mail we might not be finishing at 9-10 a.m., when we would hear the click of the swinging door and the quick footsteps.

Even the air seemed to tell us that Mr. Jones had arrived, and then Mr. Davy walked in sedately. We had to rush to be in our places under our respective bells, which would soon be ringing energetically.

The only man who could quell Mr. Jones was Pirrie,[9] of Harland & Wolff. He combined the characteristics of Jones and Davy, as alert as the one, as steady as the other.

The partnership of Jones and Davy was not without certain elements of that between Don Quixote and Sancho. Jones the active one, always hurrying, taunting, driving, Davy the follower, watchful, staid, ready with tactful advice:

"Eh, Davy? That right?" given out like gun-fire. And Davy's slow and calm: "Yes, Mr. Jones," or "I think so, Mr. Jones," etc.

Mr. Jones could be playful, and on a certain occasion offered me the pursership on the maiden voyage of what was then their finest ship. "Ask your father about it!" he replied to my eyes, that had opened wider. Father said: "Take no notice of him – he's making fun of you. You're too young." And that was the end of it.

Mr. Jones was proud of his power to dictate rapidly and sometimes "showed off" before another business man, and it was impossible to take his words verbatim. All we poor shorthand writers could do was to grasp the purport and put down a base. Sometimes we only got two words on a line, then to our seats as quickly as possible, to fill in from memory.

Once I heard a word that I had never written before, and failed to fix it. I remembered what I thought he had meant and wrote "nonsense". Before he signed the letter, he called me in and snapped out: "What I said was 'bunkum'." That was all.

Sometimes, at night, before we had finished our letters, we would hear his roll-top desk being shut, and the next moment he would rush into the department area and say: 'Where shall I sign?' Often before we had time to look at our note books and tell him, he would have signed a blank sheet, and we had to spread out or squeeze in the matter we had.

The Lighter Side

As a contrast to the strain and bustle, there was a lighter side when clerks worked late, and pipes were smoked.

Before the two companies were housed under one roof, the book-keeping department was at the far end of the office, and partitioned off. A certain wag would come back from tea, and stand at Jones's desk and imitate him dictating letters: 'Say er ... Say er ... Say er,' and give his actions to the life.

Once someone applied for a berth, and enclosed a highly finished cabinet photo. He requested that it should be returned as it was the only one the applicant had. But somehow it was passed round the office, and when returned to us it had a grotesque pipe and twirls of smoke added in red ink to the man's mouth and the bowl. There was nothing to do but return it as it was, and we expected a strong complaint, but none was made.

Sometimes jokes went a little too far.

A boy was sent by Mr. Sinclair[10] to his house for what was a new yellow leather Gladstone bag. The boy put it under the counter. Somebody found it and, thinking it belonged to one of the staff, filled it full of coal. When it reached Sinclair he was furious, and threatened instant dismissal to the culprit. Inquiries went on for days, but those who knew, never divulged. This episode, however, sobered practical jokers for a time.

SIR ALFRED LEWIS JONES, K.C.M.G.

By Rudolph de Cordova[11]

Whenever men go down to the sea in ships, wherever a vessel proudly carries the British flag, and even in countries which have not the privilege of counting themselves maritime, the name of Elder Dempster and Co. is a household word. That famous firm, however, represents to all intents and purposes the activities of one man, Sir Alfred Lewis Jones, who, in recognition of the services he has rendered to our great West African possessions and of the herculean task he has set himself in endeavouring to rehabilitate the fortunes of Jamaica, last year received the honour of knighthood.

Many men – perhaps most men – could with the aid of wealth and opportunity win a success by developing a business along its line of least resistance, but by no means a large percentage even of these could control interests whose ramifications extend throughout the whole civilised globe. Sir Alfred Jones, however, started with none of these advantages. To say that he began on the bottom rung of the ladder is to speak the truth in its simplest form. He has been the maker of his own career, the arbiter of his own destiny, and it only needs one glance at his strong leonine head and face for the least observant to mark him as a man of more than ordinary ability, who does not need to have his opportunity made for him.

I have said that he began at the bottom rung of the ladder. I will prove it. When he was only twelve, in 1857, he was apprenticed by his father to Messrs. Laird Fletcher and Co., of Liverpool, a shipping firm, whose vessels traded between Liverpool and the West Coast of Africa. As an apprentice, the boy Alfred Jones had to do whatever he was bidden, but part of his regular duties consisted in getting the office ready in the morning, copying the letters and taking them to the post, duties which scarcely suggested that in the not too distant future he would become the manager of the firm. Yet it was so. For five long years he was bound by his indentures, and during the whole of that period his wages amounted to one hundred pounds in all. Money was not then, however, his first thought. His ambition was to prove his worth, and he did it to such good purpose that he speedily went from one department to another until, when he was only five and twenty, he became manager.

For some few years he remained in this position. Then he determined to start for himself. The money which he had saved was, however, hardly enough to equip the little fleet of sailing ships with which he intended to start, so he borrowed what he needed, getting it with the greatest ease, for his reputation for probity had preceded him. It did not take him long to see that steam ships were making great advances in favour, and, as he always determined to be in the van of progress, he sold his sailing vessels and invested in steamers. Indeed, on one occasion Sir Alfred Jones let me into one of the secrets of his success by the statement 'I never keep anything after it has served its purpose, if I can possibly get anything better.'

It is significant of Sir Alfred's energy that so earnestly did he work in his first year that he made more money than he had done during all the years he had been with his employers. Naturally, everybody in Liverpool began talking of the success of the wonderful young man. The eyes of the shipbuilding world were turned upon him with something like wonder, and Messrs. Elder Dempster and Co. suggested that he should enter their firm. The young business man saw his chance and took it. The one condition he made was that he should be allowed to buy the shares of the company. By the time the senior partners wished to retire, Sir Alfred Jones had acquired practically all the shares; so that, although for trading purposes the name is still retained, Elder Dempster and Co. are really – or were at that time – Alfred Lewis Jones and Alfred Lewis Jones alone.[1 2]

The first of the great economic feats with which Sir Alfred's name is associated – for it is indeed an economic feat to take a bankrupt country and transform it into a highly prosperous community – is with the Canary Islands. In obedience to his plan of examining everything with his own eyes and coming to conclusions with his own brains, he determined to go to the Canaries to see whether it would not be possible to arrange a coaling station for his African trading steamers on one of the islands. By that time the cochineal industry, by which the people of the Canaries practically lived had been ruined by the wonderful series of discoveries which resulted in transforming the refuse of coal tar into aniline dyes. In looking over the soil Sir Alfred saw the extraordinary fertility of the soil, and that it only needed energy and determination, backed by sufficient capital, to transform the ill cultivated areas into fruitful gardens capable of supplying England's needs – through the medium of steamers of Elder Dempster Line.

He accordingly bought a lot of land and began to grow bananas. That, however, did not yield enough to satisfy him, so he sent agents all over the Islands offering to buy at a given price, whatever fruit people could grow, and even made them advances to enable them to extend their cultivations or to start them. From bananas the people developed the growing of tomatoes and other produce, and now the annual export of fruit and vegetables is considerably over a million sterling, though this does not represent anything like the full fruit producing capacity of the Islands, for the value of the exports increase every year.

It was Sir Alfred too, who saw the opportunity of developing the climatic conditions of Las Palmas to make the Island the health resort it has become. This he did by forming a company to build an hotel,[13] after which he was instrumental in establishing great engineering works at which all sorts of repairs can be done to the shipping which throngs the harbour – shipping which he has developed to such an extent that while less than twenty years ago a single steamer used to call at Las Palmas every week, the present time there are something like a hundred.

In Western Africa he has far larger interests than in the Canaries. Already indeed his interests are greater than any one else, and he sees in that part of the world a wide opening for trade through the education of the negro, in whom he has a great belief, but whose work he also believes, must be controlled for the present, at all events, by white men.

The work which Sir Alfred is doing in Jamaica is much like that he has done in the Canaries, for he is developing the fruit trade, and every fortnight the specially built steamers of his line bring some 20,000 to 25,000 bunches of bananas, which find a ready sale both in London and the provinces, and the industry is to be developed as far as possible.

No description of his career, however, would be complete without touching on the way in which he has helped to develop the resources of Canada, from which, every week, his ships bring some 30,000 tons of produce – butter, cheese, bacon and timber – which is distributed for the most part in the cities of London, Liverpool and Bristol.

It would, however, be impossible to tabulate in their entirety the various interests of Sir Alfred, but it may be mentioned that Sir Alfred is associated with Elder Dempster Shipping Co. Ltd., The African Steamship Co., the Beaver Line, The British and African Steam Navigation Co. Ltd., The Inter Insular Steamship Co., The Compagnie Belge Maritime du Congo, The Imperial Direct West India Mail Service and the Ocean Transport Co. He also owns over a hundred steamers, four coaling companies and a bank with many branches in many parts of the world. A man who has thus made his own name – it need hardly be said, he is a rich man – is eminately calculated to speak on so important a subject as the gospel of wealth.

It is, however, no easy matter to see Sir Alfred long enough to settle down into a leisurely conversation, although he is kindness itself. He is inundated with applications for appointments both in Liverpool and in

London, between which cities he practically divides his time. Still Sir Alfred did find time for me one busy day, and when I asked him what his views were as to the obligations of wealth and whether he thought that a man should give ten per cent of his earnings in charity, he replied unhesitatingly, 'I think a man should give all he can spare, and I certainly think it should be more than ten per cent. Still I am well aware of the fact that there are conditions under which men may not be able to spare even ten per cent at a given time, and you must remember in considering this question that the charity of a business man must always be of a fluctuating character. You must also remember the great maxim "Judge not." before you make harsh remarks, for a man may make a million pounds one year and nothing, or relatively nothing the next; and if in this year of plenty he gave his tithe, he might in his leaner year still give his tithe, and the smallness of the amount would be misunderstood and misinterpreted.'

' "Do I believe that the majority of wealthy men follow the old Jewish custom of giving a tenth of their possessions in charity?" No I don't, but I should think that few people have ever used that rule as a basis of their giving. Now don't misunderstand what I am going to say, but interpret, in the broadest spirit possible, my statement that I don't believe in charity, as it is commonly understood. The best charity to my mind is to teach men to be useful to themselves. By work a man not only ennobles himself but he becomes a valuable asset in the world. That is the charity which needs money.'

'To give a man a good dinner, or to feed the hungry is a very admirable proceeding, but it is better both for the community and the man himself that he should be made to work first and earn his food, for by that means you save his self respect; and I am bound to say at the risk of my opinion being traversed, that I believe there is always work for a man to do if he will only do it. True there are times when work is slack, but every man ought to keep the possibility of those times in view, and should practice thrift, so that when the rainy day comes he may not be without a place of shelter. Indeed, in my opinion people should be taught to be thrifty as part of their education. At the present time we are far too much inclined to be indulgent to ourselves. England, from the highest to the lowest in the land seems lost in her pleasures. Though I should be the last to decry out door amusements, still they cannot help being detrimental when men become slaves to them.'

'Nothing is more distressing to me than to go through certain neighbourhoods in London and Liverpool, and see men sleeping on the grass in the parks or on the benches in the public places. Yet I realise that merely to give those men a good meal is not to solve the problem of existence for them, for they will be hungry again in a few hours. You have to make these men work if you really want to serve them.'

'That is one of the great problems we have to solve in Africa. Again I wish you would rightly understand what I am going to say. It is no use to send out a missionary with the Gospel alone. It is no use saying to a negro "Believe in the teachings of that Book, and ten, twenty, forty, fifty years hence, when you die your soul will go to Paradise." You have to save that man's body during those ten, twenty, forty, fifty years while he lives on earth. You cannot, in my opinion separate God's work from man's work while men live on earth. The two must go hand in hand, and if you send your missionary with the Bible in one hand let him take a pick axe or a hatchet in the other, and let him teach the native how he may preserve his body alive at the same time as he teaches him how to save his soul. That is the reason why civilisation in Africa is so backward at the present time. It is because men have forgotten the needs of man and have not taught the native that greatest of all lessons of the gospel of wealth – to be useful to himself.'

Sir Alfred has a great belief in young men of brain and brawn who, instead of devoting all their strength and intelligence to games and athletics, are ready to go to the ends of the earth for the furtherance of the industrial supremacy of their country. He is a patriot of the old English type, although he is a Welshman born in the Principality, and he believes in the civilising mission of Britain through her trade as well as through her missionaries. If a visitor were to drop in upon him at his London office in Northumberland Street, Strand, he would probably find his room full of men – mostly young, virile, enthusiastic – more than one of whom would probably have arrived that very day from some far outpost of the Empire – British Columbia, Western Australia, or perchance, Ceylon. The conversation would proceed merrily for Sir Alfred seems capable of doing half a dozen different things at one and the same time. These young men come to him to report progress. One has been growing coffee, another has been prospecting, another is a young engineer with ideas about shipbuilding. They find Sir Alfred a guide, philosopher and friend, who is always busy but never impatient or bored. Such a man is a great asset to the nation.

The article that appeared in the October number of the Sunday Strand on Industrial Missions would appeal particularly to a man of Sir Alfred's temperament. He believes in making the best of both worlds in the best sense, and although he is essentially a man of commerce who thinks in terms of trade, yet he is by no means blind to those things which are greater than the real civilising and uplifting agencies which have made the great western nations the arbiters of the world's destiny.

I left Sir Alfred with the thought uppermost in my mind that here was a man whose Christianity was truly practical. In doing the best for himself he has never forgotten to take his fellow man along with him. He might be called an Imperial philanthropist, and it is a title of which any man might be proud.

'SIR ALFRED JONES–AN APPRECIATION'[14]

To the non-commercial man half an hour spent in the company of Sir Alfred Jones was a revelation. It mattered little to him whether you met him in his office, in a big hotel, on a train, or on shipboard, you could not fail to learn the secret of his success, and in learning it marvel how one man could accomplish so much and control so many enterprises.

And what was the secret of his success? Boundless energy, sagacity, the wisdom never to take in hand any work which he could not personally direct, and the power to gather round him men he could mould to his various purposes with the ease and rapidity with which a potter moulds a rough lump of clay. No master of shipping ever attempted to carry on so many services at one and the same time. It seemed that as soon as one line was fairly established he developed fresh energy, which he expended in the building up of another.

Thus it came about that the great businesses which he concentrated under the style of Elder, Dempster & Co. stretched out their arms to nearly every part of the globe. Liverpool to Canada, New Orleans, the Continent, the Grand Canaries, and scores of ports on the West African Coast; Avonmouth to the United States, Canada and the West Indies; and London to a multitude of foreign lands, are embraced in the schemes operated by this colossal firm.

To spend half an hour in his company was, as I have said, a revelation to a non-commercial man, and I may add to a commercial man as well. It was my fortune to spend many hours in his company. Before our first meeting he had been described to me as a hustler. Now a hustler, as a rule, is not a very attractive person. Nobody likes to be driven, least of all by an individual who drives solely for his own profit, irrespective of the feelings of those who are driven. Sir Alfred Jones did not come within this definition. Like all big men, he was intolerant to opposition. Red tape he abhorred. If he wanted a thing done he would accomplish his purpose by travelling along the most direct road. Put unnecessary obstacles in his way and he chafed. Some people would be inclined to walk round or over them, but he preferred to push them on one side. Of course, he did not always succeed, and then there was trouble. It was the way he dealt with obstacles – unnecessary obstacles – which led those whose acquaintance with him was merely superficial to describe him as a hustler. Still the appellation stood me in good stead. Our first interview of any length took place on board the *Port Kingston* three days out of Avonmouth. It was on his last trip to the West Indies – a trip rendered memorable for all time by the terrible earthquake which devastated Jamaica while he and his party were on the island. He was anxious to stimulate trade between Bristol and the West Indies: to revive a commercial connection between the two places which in earlier days had brought wealth and prosperity to both. It was at a round table conference that we met; so ideas were freely exchanged. It was not till we were on the eve of dispersing that the powers of Sir Alfred were displayed to their full extent.

Then, in a few terse sentences, he summarised the whole of the discussion, focussed our attention upon the salient points, and dismissed us with a clear picture in our minds of what we were striving for, and how best our end could be attained.

Conferences on this and kindred subjects were of daily occurrence. It was at one of them that arrangements were made with the Earl of Dudley for part of his estates to be converted into a cotton plantation. The earthquake rendered abortive most of the other plans considered, but the fact that they were put before us in so concise and workable a form afforded abundant evidence of the real practical character of this commercial king. At the time he was in indifferent health, but that in no way damped his enthusiasm. Relieved of the daily, nay hourly cares which harassed him at home, he spent his leisure in trying to increase the prosperity of the bantling amongst his many commercial enterprises – the Imperial Direct West India Mail Services Company – instead of putting on one side all business difficulties and worries.

Numbered in the party were several of his young assistants, and he insisted upon the presence of these at all the meetings he arranged. They had no direct interest in some of the subjects debated, but, as he said on one occasion, 'Young men should never miss an opportunity of broadening their experience and developing their knowledge.' He acted upon this principle at all the interviews I had with him after our return.

The last time I met him was at breakfast at the Royal Hotel in College Green. He fixed the hour at eight o'clock, although it was two before he retired overnight. Yet when I arrived punctually he apologised for the meal being half over on the ground that he had a busy day before him. He never travelled without a shorthand clerk in close attendance, and directly breakfast was finished the business of the day commenced.

A huge packet of letters awaited his attention; incidentally, I may mention that half-a-dozen telegrams reached him before we left the table. While these were being dealt with, by the aid of his secretary, he kept up a vigorous conversation with me on matters connected with the welfare of our docks. He was not in full harmony with our dock policy, which he regarded as too narrow and unambitious to be successful. The last letter I received from him contained this sentence: 'Make Avonmouth a cheap port, attract trade, and keep what you have got.'

Callers of all sorts soon began to be introduced. One, the representative of a London merchant, complained of the delay which had taken place in the discharge of a cargo at that port, and Sir Alfred's answer clearly showed that, though he objected to some Bristol methods, he realised that we are in front of our rivals in this all-important matter. He said, 'We must send some of those people down to Avonmouth to learn how to handle a cargo quickly. They ought to come the next time a banana boat arrives.' It has been said that his method of dismissing a visitor was not always courteous, but on this occasion he adopted the very simple plan of turning to his correspondence when he thought an interview had lasted long enough.

Up to the time of his last and fatal illness he was, at the age of 64, as active as many men of 40. At the first glance you would have judged him to be a man whom the world of commerce had treated merely with ordinary generosity. It was only when you looked at his keen eyes, shining beneath dark, bushy brows, noted the quick grasp of every subject with which he dealt, or listened to one of his aphorisms that it occurred to you that the man was out of the ordinary. His grey hair, side whiskers and little tuft on his chin suggested that he cared very little for fashion. The sallow-complexioned face had at times a rather weary expression, but it was that of a man who was always as fearless and daring as he was generous. The thoughtless no doubt characterised Sir Alfred Jones as nothing more or less than a mere money-grabber – a man whose appetite for work arose from the love of gold. A greater injustice could not have been done him. He was too keen, too deeply interested in everything he took in hand to patiently endure loss. And it was his dislike of failure which made some regard him as hard and relentless. Some of the schemes he embarked upon, particularly those which may fairly be regarded as Empire work, gave small promise of profit at the outset. If they eventually led to his garnering gold, he was hardly to be blamed for exercising his rights with regard to it. He certainly tried to dispose of it quickly in costly trade experiments and in philanthropy.

The full magnitude of his philanthropy has never been revealed. There were times when he would not hide his light under a bushel because by giving himself he sought to make others give as well. But there were occasions when he did good in secret. He took what honours were bestowed upon him, not as by right, but in the way of recognition of the motives which were the mainspring of his life. To better his fellow-men, he had first of all to succeed himself. Many are inclined to wait for the opportunity of doing this, but he invariably made the opportunity. As he once said:— 'The man who never makes an opportunity does not get on in this life.'

H.E.R.

Notes

1. See details of family tree on p. 202.
2. Fletcher and Parr were the Liverpool Agents of the African Steam Ship Company. They were the successors to W. & H. Laird – brothers of MacGregor Laird – who had taken the agency in the early 1850s. (*Trade Makers*, pp. 52–6.)
3. For further details of Jones' activities in the Canary Islands see *Trade Makers*, pp. 126–7.
4. Liverpool School of Tropical Medicine, *Historical Record, 1898–1920*, Liverpool University Press, 1920, pp. 5–8. See also B.G. Maegraith, op. cit., and R. Ross, op. cit.
5. Mr. Lawrence Hodson Parr lived at 'Beach-Lawn', Waterloo, near Liverpool. He died on 6 November 1885. (Obituary is in *Liverpool Courier*, 9 November 1885.)
6. See above, p. 79 and footnote 53 on pp. 91–2.
7. Mr. Augustus Frederick Warr was Jones' solicitor.
8. *West Africa*, 26 March 1938.
9. Details of Lord Pirrie's career are given in the *Elder Dempster Magazine*, Vol. 1, No. 2, June 1922. See also *Trade Makers*, pp. 171–2.
10. Alexander Sinclair was the Manager of the African Steam Ship Company's Liverpool Office from 1875 to 1890. He became a partner in Elder Dempster and Company in 1890 when the management of the African Steam Ship Company was transferred to their care. (*Trade Makers*, pp. 80, 82, 89.)
11. *Sunday Strand*, November 1903, The New Gospel of Wealth (IV).
12. It is unlikely that the two Senior Partners retired as suggested here. Both were comparatively young men – Elder being fifty and Dempster forty-seven – and both were to remain actively in business in Liverpool for another sixteen years. For a discussion of the considerations which led to Jones obtaining the authority he wanted see *Trade Makers*, pp. 83–6.
13. This was the Hotel Metropole (*Ocean Highways*, op. cit., p. 36.)
14. *Bristol Times*, 15 December 1909.

FAMILY TREE OF SIR ALFRED LEWIS JONES

c. 1800 John Lewis m. Mary and kept the Half Moon Hotel in Carmarthen

- Margaret Lewis m. David Evans
  - William Evans, Vicar of Rhayader
    - J. Bagnall Evans. Barrister at Law, of Nantyregewys, Llanbosdy
  - John Evans, Archdeacon of C. m. Elizabeth – half sister of the Lord Bishop of Llandaff
- Thomas Lewis, Vicar of Llanstephen
  - Dr. Fred Lewis, of Cross Hands
- Mary Lewis m. David Brigstock
  - Son
    - T.E. Brigstock. Wine Merchant, of Carmarthen
- Elizabeth Lewis m. Charles Jones – an Alderman of Carmarthen
  - Son
    - Rev. Isaac Hughes Jones
      - Picton Hughes Jones 1880 – 1951 m. Eleanor Mary Edith.
        - Rosemary Hughes Jones
        - Peggy Hughes Jones
      - Lawrence Jones 1874 – 1930
        - David Lawrence Jones
  - Daniel Jones m. Mary Jean Williams. (Daughter of Henry Williams, Rector of Llanedi, & Jane d.1867) — Daniel Jones d. 1869; Mary Jean Williams 1809–1877
    - ALFRED LEWIS JONES 1845 – 1909
    - 7 other children died very young
    - Mary Isabel m. John Pinnock — 1847 – 1914; 1846 – 1878
      - Owen Harrison Williams m. Florence Mary Pinnock — d. 1934; 1871 – 1946
        - Florence Norah Williams. m. John Sydney Manning Mocatta d. 1959
          - Joan Mocatta m. Edward Francis Tetlow. 1953
          - Peter Charles Manning Mocatta. d.1959 m. Helen Elfreda Kerr 1956
          - Geoffrey Donald Mocatta. m. Georgina Ellen Dorsey May 1962.
        - Alfred Hugh Harrison Williams d.1912
        - Frances Mary Williams. d. 1922 m. Edward Richmond Paton. d.1951
          - Mavis Richmond Paton
          - John Michael Richmond Paton. m. 1939 Xenia Winnifred Leslie Melville
          - Frances Mary Richmond Paton
      - Blanche Elizabeth Pinnock 1873 – 1921

INDEX

For Product Safety Concerns and Information please contact our EU representative GPSR@taylorandfrancis.com
Taylor & Francis Verlag GmbH, Kaufingerstraße 24, 80331 München, Germany

www.ingramcontent.com/pod-product-compliance
Lightning Source LLC
LaVergne TN
LVHW010628300926
849162LV00001B/96

* 9 7 8 1 0 4 1 2 9 5 8 0 8 *